TEILHARD DE CHARDIN
ON THE GOSPELS

D1520750

Teilhard de Chardin on the Gospels

The Message of Jesus for an Evolutionary World

Louis M. Savary
Foreword by Richard Rohr

Paulist Press
New York / Mahwah, NJ

Cover image by Denis Tabler / Shutterstock.com
Cover and book design by Lynn Else

Library of Congress Cataloging-in-Publication Data
Names: Savary, Louis M., author.
Title: Teilhard de Chardin on the Gospels : the message of Jesus for an evolutionary world / Louis M Savary ; foreword by Richard Rohr.
Description: New York : Paulist Press, 2019. | Includes bibliographical references.
Identifiers: LCCN 2018060662 (print) | LCCN 2019020359 (ebook) | ISBN 9781587688416 (ebook) | ISBN 9780809154494 (pbk. : alk. paper)
Subjects: LCSH: Teilhard de Chardin, Pierre. | Bible. Gospels—Criticism, interpretation, etc.
Classification: LCC BX4705.T39 (ebook) | LCC BX4705.T39 S29 2019 (print) | DDC 226/.06092—dc23
LC record available at https://lccn.loc.gov/2018060662

ISBN 978-0-8091-5449-4 (paperback)
ISBN 978-1-58768-841-6 (e-book)

Published by Paulist Press
997 Macarthur Boulevard
Mahwah, New Jersey 07430
www.paulistpress.com

Printed and bound in the
United States of America

I believe that the universe is an evolution.
I believe that evolution proceeds toward spirit.
I believe that in man spirit is fully realized in personhood.
I believe that the supremely personal is the universal Christ.

—Pierre Teilhard de Chardin, "How I Believe"

Contents

Contents

Foreword

IN THIS IMPORTANT and ready-for-prime-time book, Louis Savary leads us on a journey with one of the greatest human minds and largest Christian hearts of recent centuries, so great in fact that many of us are just beginning to recognize the truly alternative worldview that Teilhard de Chardin offers those of us with smaller minds and less capable hearts. The same pattern history had with Jesus, one might say.

Savary rightly begins by recognizing the dead-end effects of the rather complete mistranslation of Jesus's inaugural words of the original Greek word *metanoia* (Mark 1:15; Matt 3:2). Peter uses the same word in his first sermon after Pentecost (Acts 2:38) and continuing elsewhere, but it is invariably presented as the prerequisite for *earning* forgiveness of sins (Acts 3:20), or what many of us call *transactional religion*, as opposed to a *transformation of consciousness* that allows us to enjoy that we are all swimming in a complete sea of forgiveness, often referred to as a worldview of abundance instead of scarcity.

This transformation might best be described as a movement from a *quid pro quo* worldview (where most people start) to the *quid pro nihilo* (something for nothing) world inside of which an infinite God with an infinite love fully operates. This is the only real and much-needed change of mind. A finite human mind is largely incapable of this by itself. I am told by neuroscientists that the human brain cannot actually *think* infinity or eternity.

So "change your mind" seems to be the first words out of Jesus's mouth in at least two Gospels, and yet we have lost centuries of collective development by continuing the early and very unfortunate Vulgate translation of "do penance" (grief over your sinfulness) instead of what the word clearly means in the original Greek, which is "go beyond your mind" or "change your mind"—implying growth, change, and actual newness. This sends us toward a positive worldview of continual improvement and development, and a much larger seeing than mere rational thinking. "Go beyond your limited mind and believe some really good news" (Mark 1:15), Jesus says (in my translation). How did we succeed in making this great Gospel bad news for so many of God's people and for the Earth itself?

Maybe because we largely stayed in the dominant cultural world of "tit for tat" or retributive justice and never learned to swim in the much broader sea of healing or what many are now calling *restorative justice*? This is very similar to what Charles Eisenstein calls a "gift economy" instead of the prevailing and capitalistic worldview of profit and loss, reward and punishment, win or lose, counting and weighing faults and rewards. It creates small people and makes the great cosmos into a zero-sum game.

Jesus's parables and teaching are clearly not about maintaining the status quo, shoring up the rich and powerful, or "believing" in the persistent war and greed economy that has characterized most human cultures to this day. We must all try to let go of our politics and egoic economics and admit that this is almost entirely true. Only the universe itself (and by implication God) seems to operate inside of an infinite gift economy. In fact, the universe is still expanding—and at an ever-faster pace. This is anything but zero-sum.

Jesus gave us something truly new in religion that was supposed to send us on a positive path of appreciate change and expected growth (ironically, through letting go and loss), a religion of future hope and larger goals (which we called resurrection). It was quite different from the preservationist society, cultural imprisonment, and museum curation that most of Christianity clearly became in our first two thousand years—and which it still largely is. Whatever virtues you want to ascribe to God, patience and humility must be at the very top of the list!

Savary rightly refers to Kuhn's famous "paradigm shift" as a very accurate description of what this change of mind looks and feels like. Until such an underlying, radical shift happens, most of Jesus's teachings (and Teilhard's too) will always be misunderstood and crammed into a merely religious frame. Both knew that God's work was much bigger than the typical structures of religion would by themselves allow. We need full-reality contact (cross and resurrection) in Jesus's paradigmatic change and in Teilhard's understanding that included the confirming and helpful lens of science in its many forms.

I believe Teilhard, and Savary's study of Teilhard, send us on a

Foreword

very concrete understanding of how that paradigm shift looks and feels. I will not develop these themes, but if you read this book, I suspect much of this will fall in place for you:

1. Any authentic experience of the Divine Absolute leads you into a gift economy on all levels (kingdom of God). Evolved religion changes your economics and your politics, and not just your mental attitudes.
2. Your notion of justice changes from one of retribution to one of restoration. God "justifies" things by restoring them to their primal and better state, not by punishing them, as every good parent learns. Note the primacy of healing in the daily ministry of Jesus. He punishes nobody.
3. Such grace moves you to a win-win worldview and away from a win-lose worldview, or what became the small frame of rewards and punishments that characterizes almost all early-stage thinking and early-stage religion. Win-lose is sports; win-win is salvation.
4. The surprising but very real effect of this is to give one *a very positive and hopeful anthropology of the human person and a very dignified view of all creation*, which in my experience most evolved people acquire. And why? Because God's "growth hormone" is seen to be inherently planted inside of all living things—from the beginning (see Eph 1:4, 9–11; Rom 1:20).

Believers call it grace or the Indwelling Spirit, scientists call it instinct or evolution, and the ordinary person on the street calls it hope or vision. Without these, Christianity is hardly good news at all, and surely not a "joy for *all* the people" (Luke 2:10) as the angels sang at our second creation story. We did not get the message of implanted goodness from the first creation story (Gen 1:10–31); we later worshiped it in the person of Jesus, but the "second coming of Christ" in an evolving humanity is still in the making.

Richard Rohr, OFM
Center for Action and Contemplation
Albuquerque, New Mexico

Preface

JESUIT PRIEST Pierre Teilhard de Chardin (1881–1955) was the first to integrate the discoveries of modern science and the theory of evolution with Christian theology. He presented his insights to the church for publication, but they were not welcomed by the Holy Office in Rome. In fact, he was forbidden to lecture or publish on any theological topic. As a result, many of his religious insights that he wanted to develop went unexplored. For example, he could not shape a moral theology that integrated the findings of science and evolution. Nor did the church permit him to lecture on the Gospel writings from his evolutionary vantage point, though he recognized the value of doing so. As he wrote in *The Divine Milieu*, his book on spirituality,

> The mystical Christ, the universal Christ of St. Paul, has neither meaning nor value in our eyes except as an explanation of the Christ who was born of Mary and who died on the cross....However far we may be drawn into the divine spaces opened up to us by Christian mysticism, we never depart from the Jesus of the Gospels.[1]

Because of the Vatican interdict, Teilhard had little hope of publishing any religious writings. In an unpublished piece written in 1933, "Christology and Evolution,"[2] he reenvisioned the gospel message. Teilhard might have described Jesus's good news as *God's wish to share with us the fullness of life, beginning now and continuing forever.*[3] Many of Teilhard's contemporaries considered life on Earth to be a test for worthiness to enter heaven, and Earth to be a dangerous place full of sin and temptation. Teilhard's writings invite us to see Earth as our home. He saw our home as an unfinished divine project, brimming with opportunities for progress toward the fullness of life, and open to continual improvement. Teilhard saw Jesus's teaching as integral to a universe in continual evolution. He wrote, "If we are to remain faithful to the gospel, we have to adjust its spiritual code to the new shape of the universe." Science has discovered that evolution is a force that permeates everything in God's creation. For Christians, then, "the universe assumes an additional dimension for our experience....It has become the great work in progress."[4]

Teilhard sees evolution as central to understanding God's project. For him, evolution is the underlying force driving growth in the kingdom of God.

With the discovery of the universality of evolution, our moral responsibility in this divine project becomes clearer. For Teilhard, we are to become, "for God, the reinforcement of evolution."[5] For Teilhard, presenting the gospel as an evolutionary force is the only way "capable of justifying and maintaining in the world the [gospel's] fundamental zest for life." In this way, he reveals the gospel as "the very religion of evolution."[6]

In this book, we explore the four Gospels from this perspective, as Teilhard himself might do if he were alive today. Furthermore, the book responds to requests from people on retreat using *The New Spiritual Exercises in the Spirit of Teilhard de Chardin*. They are seeking an evolutionary perspective on specific events and teachings of Jesus found in the four Gospels. Since Teilhard never provided such commentaries, this work relies heavily on basic principles of his thought.

The four Gospels were written by men who were completely unaware of evolution. They held a view of the universe far different from the one science has revealed to us. Their universe was cyclical and static. There was "nothing new under the sun" (Eccl 1:9). God controlled and directed every event. They could never have grasped the ideas that their Earth was a spherical planet orbiting in deep space, connected to the sun only by the invisible force of gravity. They couldn't believe that almost every star they could see in the night sky had planets, like Earth, orbiting around them.

They assumed that human life began with Adam and Eve, an innocent pair who spent their days lounging in an impossibly beautiful garden. They believed that this couple's first act of disobedient curiosity gave birth to all our familiar evils of sin, strife, suffering, and death. The evangelists believed that this single act of our first parents infected humanity with pride, jealousy, greed, lust, deceit, and violence.

They couldn't imagine that our first parents evolved from higher mammals and lived in caves. They had no idea that sickness, death, greed, lust, anger, pride, laziness, and curiosity had been part of animal life for millions of years before the first humans emerged.

Most likely, the evangelists never truly understood Jesus's teaching about seeing the kingdom of God growing and evolving around them. They only knew his teachings were important and were from God. Thankfully, they recorded his teachings and stories as best they could, in his actual words. It was as if they were saying to us, "We don't completely understand what he said, but this is what he said."

Yet, the Holy Spirit, who inspired those evangelists, had been present at the first moment of creation and had guided the cosmos in its evolutionary progress over billions of years. This Divine Spirit must have inspired these first-century Gospel writers to document the words and deeds of Jesus of Nazareth in a way that could be relevant for believers, millennia later, who would live with an evolving world consciousness.

For Teilhard, the Gospel texts must be meaningful and useful to us today, since we are challenged to integrate into our religious beliefs and practices many facts that modern science has revealed. We are challenged to walk in faith each day aware that we live in a continually evolving universe. Teilhard says that we must learn to see Jesus of the Gospels as "the Christ of evolution."[7]

Teilhard believed that Matthew, Mark, Luke, and John were providing for us the elements of a path—Jesus's Way—that would remain relevant even for our modern world. For Teilhard, Jesus's Way provides a guide that can successfully bring the fullness of life to each generation of believers, from the first century to the twenty-first and beyond. His Way provides a manner of living and loving that leads us toward our evolutionary future.

Teilhard knew that the four Gospels hold special relevance for us who live in a culture that is thoroughly evolution-conscious. Hopefully, this book will be helpful to those interested in exploring Teilhard's ideas in relation to the Gospel teachings of Jesus. As my editor suggested when we discussed writing the book, "Just do what Teilhard never had a chance to do. Christians living in an evolutionary world need to know how to read their faith's most important writings in a new way." Thus, my goal is to explain how these four Gospel texts show that (1) God has plans for an unfinished universe; (2) Jesus had a sense of these plans; and (3) the Holy Spirit allowed the evangelists, without their awareness, to present their message with relevance to a world that they could never imagine.

Teilhard was thoroughly familiar with the four Gospels. He had studied them academically in his Jesuit theological coursework and contemplated scenes from Jesus's life in daily meditations throughout his life. Teilhard made an annual retreat, as all Jesuits do, based on *The Spiritual Exercises of St. Ignatius*. Many of its contemplative exercises focus on the life and teachings of Jesus of Nazareth.

Therefore, praying over Jesus's teachings as if I were Teilhard living today, I asked myself, "How would Teilhard reenvision the sayings of Jesus to make them relevant today? How would he reinterpret the parables? How would he reflect on events that happened to Jesus? What insights would he glean from his perspective on the Gospels? What would these texts reveal to him about the nature of God, the divine purpose in creating the universe, the roles of love, faith, suffering, sin, morality, and the purpose of human life?"

Presumably, Teilhard would begin reenvisioning the Gospels by using all the contemporary scriptural resources of his day. Each of the New Testament books was originally written in Greek. The first official translation from Greek into Latin was completed early in the fifth century by St. Jerome.

In Teilhard's youth, for example, French translations from St. Jerome's Latin Vulgate—and the Latin version itself—were the principal Gospel texts at his disposal. During his theological studies, the New Testament on his desk was St. Jerome's Latin Vulgate. When he cites Scripture, he usually quotes the Vulgate. Since the 1960s (Teilhard died in 1955), we have access to more accurate English biblical translations based on the earliest Greek and Hebrew texts.

Significantly, Teilhard would also want to discover what Jesus really said, the actual words he spoke. We know that when Jesus addressed the crowds and his disciples, he did not speak in Hebrew, Greek, or Latin, but in Aramaic. Only in the last quarter century have scholars been looking at the subtle changes of meaning of Jesus's sayings that might be revealed in his Aramaic words.

Perspective

My exploration of the Gospels assumes that religious beliefs and humanity's understanding of God are, and have always been, on an evolutionary journey. Our loving God continues to nurture religious development among all human communities in order to bring the fullness of life to the human family. Mosaic Law and Jewish religious teachings are, in themselves, an evolutionary leap forward in the history of religion, our understanding of God, and moral principles.

The Gospels make another evolutionary leap forward in the human journey beyond the Mosaic Law. In Jesus's teachings, he gives us the revelation of God as the loving Father of all. Jesus's parables describe the dynamics of the kingdom of God. They reveal that God has a grand divine project underway. And we are called to participate in that project.

This short study of the Gospels from Teilhard's perspective has two distinct purposes. The first is to demonstrate how *Jesus's gospel message initiated an evolutionary advance beyond the Hebrew Scriptures*, as these holy books were interpreted by the Jewish people of that time. Jesus's evolutionary advance impacts not only religion but also what it means to be human. This advance also allows for and welcomes future continual evolutionary advances.

The second is to show that Teilhard recognized *how the gospel message also welcomes the new knowledge of creation that modern science continues to discover*. This includes emerging information about creation's beginnings and its evolutionary story on Earth. In his writings, Teilhard shows how scientific discoveries enrich our theology. They have already enlarged our understanding of God, our grasp of God's grand project for creation, and our growing awareness of what humans are being called to do in their lifetime on Earth.[8]

Looking ahead at the trajectory of evolution, Teilhard recognized a forward step in the unification of humanity's mind and heart emerging in our time. Some of the elements in this "next step" have been outlined in my other books on Teilhard.[9] For Teilhard, many of these forward steps are grounded in Jesus's teachings within the four Gospels. Exploring these scriptural texts is where Teilhard suggests we begin.

Most of us read the Gospels to discover the meaning of life. This is what thinking people do in a fixed universe. Their search for meaning becomes primarily an intellectual pursuit. Teilhard discovered that Jesus is teaching us that *the purpose of life is constantly evolving*. In other words, life's purpose is not to find more meaning, but *to find more life*—to keep deepening and expanding the experience of life. As Jesus stated clearly, "I came that they may have life, and have it abundantly" (John 10:10). By keeping that purpose of ever more life in mind, we begin to approach the Gospel texts with Teilhard's "new eyes." In his language, the purpose of life is the continual deepening and expanding of consciousness. To open one's consciousness is to be open to more life.

Acknowledgments

I OWE SPECIAL THANKS to several professional friends for their patience and kindness in reviewing my manuscript and for their insightful comments. All of them share a fondness for Teilhard's ideas. I received continuous encouragement from Sr. Kathleen Duffy, SND, physics professor at Chestnut Hill University in Philadelphia and editor of the scholarly journal *Teilhard Studies*. Thanks for a gentle but needed push from Edward Vacek, SJ, theology professor at Loyola University, New Orleans. Special gratitude to Roger Haight, SJ, professor at Columbia University and former president of the Catholic Theological Society of America, who suggested an accessible structure for this book and guided me around some hermeneutic pitfalls into which I could easily have stumbled. I am deeply indebted to Neil Douglas-Klotz for the unexpected blessing of his books and scholarly research into Jesus's Aramaic words.[10]

Blessings on Susie Timchak for doing a painstaking review of the manuscript's every sentence and offering hundreds of helpful suggestions for making the text more grammatically accurate and easily readable. Thanks to lifelong friend Peter Esseff for explaining the deeper roots of Hebrew religious teachings. Boundless love to my faithful wife, who keeps me on task and reminds me that, as long as I am breathing, I have work to do for God.

Deep gratitude to Paul McMahon, my very supportive editor at Paulist Press, and to the editorial team who believe that books on Teilhard, accessible to the ordinary reader, deserve to be published and kept in print for future generations.

PART I

HERMENEUTICS, EVOLUTION, AND *METANOIA*

1

Hermeneutics

THEOLOGIAN Fr. Roger Haight, SJ, pointed out to me that the purpose of this book is not a deeply complicated problem, but a straightforward task. It is to do what biblical scholars call the familiar work of *hermeneutics*:[1] *how to take documents from another period or culture and find in them relevance for us and for our culture.*

People from every historical era who read the Gospels were faced with this hermeneutic issue. As they pondered a passage, they asked, "How does this Scripture passage apply to me and to the people of my time?"

Today, many want to live the Christian life more fully—twenty-one centuries after Jesus spoke his words. They still ask the same question: "How do Jesus's words apply to me and to people today?"

In this book, we revisit the Gospels from the unique perspective of Pierre Teilhard de Chardin. The hermeneutic question he faced when reading these New Testament texts was, *How do the Gospels address and make sense to a culture that is being shaped by science, technology, and a growing awareness of the universality of evolution?*

The answer to this question is twofold.

First, we must recognize that *the Gospels are evolutionary documents.* That is, they tell the story of the origins of Christianity, an evolutionary movement in religious history. Each of these four narratives begins with a good-news announcement about the transformative nature of the kingdom of God.

To truly recognize the newness of the gospel's message, people need to undergo a *metanoia*. A *metanoia* describes a change in one's way of thinking about and perception of reality. This mindset shift that Jesus required to understand his teachings could be called a *first-*

century metanoia. It required that his listeners change the way they thought about God and the kingdom of God. For them, this *metanoia* was an eye-opening, mind-opening event. Many Christians today have never made this first-century *metanoia*.

Second, Teilhard proposes an additional *metanoia* that recognizes that *Jesus's Way of living allows for—and even promotes—the continual evolution of humanity*. Integrating into theology and spirituality such a flow of future evolutionary advances requires a further eye-opening, mind-opening process. Teilhard's *metanoia* involves a continual deepening and expansion of life and consciousness. It allows us to interpret the gospel message "with the full moral depth that new horizons enable us to see in them."[2] It integrates the gospel message with the present and future findings of modern science and enriches contemporary theology, spirituality, and ethics.

Our hermeneutic challenge is to validate both stages.

Bringing Teilhard Forward

Like many educated people of Teilhard's day, including church officials, many believers today compartmentalize religion. As believers, they continue to live in a fixed universe. As educated people, they accept new scientific facts as true. In effect, they separate the findings of science and evolution from their spiritual lives and the teachings of Jesus. They treat science and religion as two unrelated worlds that do not intersect.[3]

Teilhard cannot, in conscience, maintain that separation. He is both a dedicated scientist and a priest. He loves both Earth and God passionately. He is especially grateful for the wonderful revelations about God's creation that new scientific tools are making known. He believes that the loving Creator is delighted that humans have finally learned to create technology that can uncover amazing facts about our universe, facts that past generations never knew. Many of these discoveries, like the vastness of space or the inner workings of each living cell, are realities that earlier scientists never imagined could be observed or filmed. Other discoveries, like dinosaurs and earlier hominid species, are realities that scientists in earlier centuries never suspected were buried in the earth—waiting to be found.

The theory of evolution emerged as a major scientific break-through. The evidence for evolution surprised most biologists. Charles Darwin's 1859 book *On the Origin of Species* formed the basis of a new way of thinking.

For Teilhard, the discovery of evolution has much wider implications. For him, the fact of evolution becomes a major divine revelation. Evolution provides an entirely new way of looking at God's creation. However, it also poses a challenge for traditional theologians.[4]

For Teilhard, scientists didn't invent the evolutionary process. God did. Scientists merely recognized, verified, and named it. Neither did the universe eventually generate the evolutionary process on its own. Evolutionary forces were effectively operating from the beginning.[5] Evolution was integral to the divine creative process from the first moment of space-time.[6] The Creator had to have lovingly implanted the law of evolution in each of the countless subatomic particles and photons of light that first exploded into physical existence at the big bang.

Without this built-in evolutionary drive to unite and form new connections and develop new capabilities, the original subatomic particles would have merely floated around endlessly in empty space. They would never have connected and united with other particles. Without the inner drive to connect, elemental atoms—helium, hydrogen, oxygen, carbon—would never have formed, each with its unique variety of chemical properties. Without its built-in tendency to unite into larger and larger wholes, our universe would never have given birth to its stunning variety of nebulae, stars, planets, and galaxies.

Teilhard, the God-loving, Earth-loving scientist, developed evolutionary eyes. For him, the law of evolution—the drive to connect, unite, and interact—permeated every part of matter from the first moment of creation. His opened mind could see that the same evolutionary drive—to connect, unite, and interact—continues to drive humanity today in all fields of human endeavor. Teilhard's consciousness was open to new experiences of life—new awareness, new insights. His mind was making new connections. Instead of separating religion and science, he united them.

Teilhard explains the implications of evolution for the theology of divine providence. "Properly speaking, God *does not make: He makes things that make themselves.*"[7] Earth is full of living things—from bacteria and plants to fish and birds to animals and humans. All these

5

species make themselves. They reproduce. They spread their kind. They adapt and change. They learn, they create, and they interact with each other. They form new connections. This is the kingdom of God quietly at work all around us.

That is why God does not need to break into creation in order to change or transform it. According to Teilhard, God continually transforms the universe *from within, undetectably*. God is lovingly acting simultaneously on all the elements of the entire body of creation. That divine action makes itself felt "at the core of each element of the world *individually*."

God created the universe from its first moment as an "assembly of *individually vitalized* beings."[8] Consequently, there is no discontinuity between God's operation and the laws of physics, chemistry, or biology. God's creative action is undetectable by science because the divine action is simultaneous and "co-extensive with the whole duration of the universe."[9]

Evolution taking place in the biological domain does not captivate Teilhard as much as transformations happening in the minds and hearts of human beings. For him, God is continually transforming humanity—individually and as a whole—*from within, undetectably*. God has made us so that we could make and remake ourselves, individually and as the human family. God has made us so that we can continue to open ourselves more and more to the experience of life. "I came that they may have life, and have it abundantly" (John 10:10).

For example, Teilhard notices that people all over the planet are changing the ways they think, communicate, and interact. Discoveries and events that transform humanity continue in fields such as physics, aeronautics, astronomy, psychology, genetics, government, communication, transportation, energy, and even religious beliefs.

Evolution works by making new connections. It drives even apparently disparate fields of study to connect and unite, such as astrophysics, paleobiology, astrophotography, genetic psychology, psychopharmacology, ecoenergy, and so on.

During the Time of Jesus

Teilhard may have asked, as we are asking on his behalf, "Can we identify any signs of evolution occurring in the minds and hearts of people during Jesus's lifetime?"

Teilhard knows that, even if evolutionary things happened at that time, people would not have named them as evolutionary events. They had no word for evolution. However, because the *concept* of evolution wasn't in their vocabulary does not mean that evolution wasn't happening.

For example, Teilhard would note that in the Sermon on the Mount Jesus was talking "evolutely" when he said he had not come to reject the Mosaic Law but to "fulfill" it (see Matt 5:17). His purpose was to help the Mosaic Law become what it was meant to be, to take it to its next stage of development. That's evolution.

Teilhard learned how to recognize and identify an evolutionary event. Unlike most of us, Teilhard developed the ability to see evolution at work all around. He saw things as evolutionary that the rest of us do not see. Jesus had a similar experience. He often said of the crowds, "They look, but they cannot see."

A good analogy of being able to "see," like Teilhard and Jesus, is to take the word *eye* printed on a piece of paper. If you show the paper to an infant, the child sees the word *eye* as only squiggles on a piece of paper. But as an adult you no longer see the letters as squiggles. You see the very intelligible word, *eye*. In fact, you cannot unsee it. Similarly, Teilhard was able to see intelligibility in things happening all around that most of us could not see. While we, like the infant, see only "squiggles" in certain events that occur, Teilhard could see evolutionary meaning and purpose, to the point that he couldn't *unsee* them.

Similarly, when Jesus uses the expression *the kingdom of God* or *the kingdom of heaven* (for him, both expressions describe the same reality),[10] Jesus is seeing what his hearers cannot see. Jesus sees God's meaning and purpose revealed in the events occurring around him. He recognizes divine processes actively at work. He identifies and marks steps in the progress of the divine kingdom. He can "see" the dynamics and thrust of God's project and can envision how creation is meant to unfold.

This is one reason why we look to Teilhard with his special vision. He is perhaps the first to recognize how to integrate science, evolution, and theology. He has eyes to see the unity of these three domains. While we are still unseeing, he helps to open our eyes.

What would Teilhard—with *his* eyes—see in scriptural texts that most of us might never notice? And what theological and moral insights does he grasp that we can begin to integrate into our understanding of the Gospel writings?

Recall our twofold purpose. The first is the hermeneutic challenge to demonstrate that *the Gospels are evolutionary documents*. To do this, we show that the teachings of Jesus initiate a transformative movement beyond the religion of his day.

The second, a more contemporary hermeneutic challenge, is to show that *the way of living that Jesus proposed also allows for—and even promotes—the continual evolution of humanity*. Here, the challenge is to demonstrate that Jesus's teachings can make practical sense to today's believers, that is, those living in a culture permeated by technological innovation, daily scientific discoveries, and a growing awareness of the universality of evolution.

The question arising from this second hermeneutic challenge is this: *How can Jesus's message make sense—be interpreted—in a culture that is thoroughly evolution-conscious?* Here, the task is to reveal the relevance of the Gospels for believers who are already consciously living evolutely in their daily lives.[11]

Using more academic language: *Can an appropriate proportion of major gospel themes be applied in an evolution-conscious culture as typified by Teilhard?* Even though the Gospel writings emerge from a nonevolutionary culture, does Teilhard offer an understanding of Jesus's life and teachings found in the Gospels that fits into an evolution-conscious culture? The answer is yes.

To demonstrate this, we must first learn to identify an evolutionary event (chapter 2) and recognize the significance of *metanoia* for a full understanding of Jesus's life and teachings (chapter 3). We can then explore each of the four Gospel texts.

2

Evolution

Detecting Evolution

CHARLES DARWIN was among the first to recognize evolutionary changes in the physical and biological makeup of plants and animals. He had the unique opportunity to observe such changes during a long exploratory voyage to strange lands and unusual settings. He realized that creatures making these mutations enabled them to adapt to their surroundings.

For example, he noticed how a specific species of birds developed differently in form and appearance when it migrated to different island environments. Over generations, in places where the nuts were harder to crack, birds developed much stronger beaks. On other islands, where these same species of birds were forced to get nutrition from the nectar of flowers, they developed longer, more pointy beaks that could reach more deeply into the nourishing blossoms. Other species adapted by changing feather color and size for safety and survival.

Following Darwin's lead, evolutionary biologists now observe and record changes in appearance, form, structure, function, purpose, and process in an organism under observation.[1] To recognize an evolutionary purpose of observed changes or mutations in an organism, researchers look for emerging abilities or new capacities that prove to be advantageous to it.

Darwin also noted that plants and animals seem to have an inner drive that enables them to find ways to adapt to changing environments and circumstances. He noticed that species tend to mutate in ways that make them more useful and adaptable to their different environments. He called this adaptation process "evolution."

It appears that, in creating the universe, God not only made creatures that could make themselves, God also made them so that they could adapt, mutate, and evolve by themselves.

Until recently, evolution's pace has been typically slow. It took a long, long time for *Homo sapiens* to evolve biologically. Today's humans have increased the pace of evolution. We now employ technology to speed up the evolutionary process, even biologically. For example, in just this past century, because of improvements in health care and nutrition, humans have increased, on average, more than an inch in stature and doubled their life expectancy. Much of this can be attributed to basic improvements such as pasteurization, reduction of pollutants, clean water, sanitization, and healthier diets.

Evolution in the Noosphere

When we hear the word *evolution*, most of us automatically think of physical evolution. We picture biologists tracing the phylum of mammals from early vertebrates upward through the great apes to hominids and to humans. Exploring physical and biological forms of evolution are not of primary interest to Teilhard. He is focused on emerging qualities and capacities in a domain of mental life that he calls the "noosphere."[2]

For Teilhard, the noosphere (from the Greek *nous* for "mind") describes the layer of mind and heart that today encircles Earth. Just as there are ancient layers of land, water, air, and organic life that cover the planet, he noticed another, more recent developing layer that covers our world—*the layer of mind or thought*. Just as Earth is surrounded and enclosed by an atmosphere, a hydrosphere and a biosphere, it is now also enveloped by a noosphere—a mind sphere. It is a new layer that only humans could have created, and to which only humans have access.

The noosphere is an immense body of knowledge created by humanity over the ages. It is a magnificent, evolving collective mind to which countless individuals have contributed. The noosphere is the layer where evolution is happening most evidently today. It is also the domain of mind and heart to which the teachings of Jesus contributed. In Teilhard's language, he would say that promoting evolution in the noosphere is central to Jesus's teachings on the kingdom of God.[3]

The noosphere's content contains all personal and collective recorded information. It includes scientific knowledge, spiritual wisdom, art, music, literature, biographies, as well as the feelings, desires, dreams, loves, and passions by which we connect with one another as brothers and sisters on Earth. The noosphere also encapsulates the beliefs, attitudes, and values we hold. It incorporates and makes accessible to everyone the scientific and mathematical formulas that we use in technology to transform the many dimensions of contemporary life—communication, transportation, information storage, as well as information dissemination. The ever-growing noosphere makes available to each of us—and to subsequent generations—not only traditional wisdom but also newly acquired knowledge, skills, and abilities. The noosphere is a source of "more life" and "more consciousness." It has become a planetized mind that thinks and feels on behalf of Earth. The noosphere continues to evolve. It is a Mind of minds that is shaping the union of all humans.[4]

Supporting its intangible nature, the noosphere has an essential physical dimension. Its contents are developed and stored in human brains, books, journals, digital records, videos, films, computer hard drives, cell phones, flash drives, discs, software programs, apps, robots, and the vast memory banks of social media companies.

The noosphere grows more complex each year. For Teilhard, the noosphere provides for each successive generation a *social inheritance, produced by the synthetic recording of human experience.*[5] He notes, "Only by reaching to the heart of the noosphere can we hope, and indeed be sure, of finding—all of us together and each of us separately—the fullness of our humanity."[6] Teilhard describes the noosphere as an evolving collective brain, "a Brain of brains."[7]

How to Recognize an Evolutionary Stage

In this book, our interest centers on the evolution of religion. We are looking for significant advances in the appearance, form, structure, function, purpose, and practice of theology, spirituality, and morals.

As we examine the Gospel texts, we are looking for those transformational changes that Jesus proposes to advance the Mosaic Law to its next evolutionary stage. Specifically, in the Gospels we hope to identify advances in the function, purpose, and practice of theology, spirituality, and morals.

Here is a simple evolutionary test:

An Evolutionary Test

As we read each section of the Gospel texts, we will be asking, Are the teachings of Jesus

- new and genuinely different from what went before?
- maintaining essential elements or functions of what went before?
- more complex than anything within their class?
- irreversible, such that, once presented and grasped, they cannot be denied?
- transformative, but not destructive of what went before?
- manifesting new emergent properties?

For example, using this test, it is easy to show that the Mosaic Law of the Hebrews marks an evolutionary advance over other codes of conduct in the ancient Near East, such as that of Hammurabi.[8] In the "Book of the Covenant" section of Exodus (20:22—23:33), many of the moral and social teachings given to Moses by Yahweh are radically new in that area of the world. For instance, Mosaic Law says that refugees and displaced persons have rights, that people in the lowest socioeconomic ranks ought to be cared for, and that money ought to be lent at no interest. These are Hebrew covenant ideas and they are new to the planet. A compassionate God tells Moses, in effect, that no person is "disposable."

In the Gospels, as we will observe, Jesus evolves the Mosaic Law to a higher stage.

Throughout the text, to clarify this higher stage, we compare the basic elements of Jesus's religious system to those same basic elements as proposed in the Jewish religious system into which Jesus was born. We look to see if new properties, abilities, capacities, and tools clearly emerge in human relations from Jesus's teachings. We also explore how these new capacities and tools might influence our current practice of theology, spirituality, and morals.

Even though the Gospel writers did not know how to recognize or identify an evolutionary event in Jesus's religious teachings, we can look at those teachings and their implications as they appear to us. To do this, we use two thousand years of hindsight and our heightened sensitivity to evolutionary processes. From this perspective, we will be able to recognize evolutionary dimensions in the gospel message.

The Second Challenge

As was stated in the previous chapter, the hermeneutic task for people of each period in history is to find some relevance for themselves in gospel teachings.

What is different for us, for the first time in history, is that we live in an age immersed in science, technology, continual improvement, breakthroughs in all fields, and evolutionary thinking. What relevant messages do the Gospels have for us in the digital age? Here are some ways that we might ask the perennial hermeneutic question today:[9]

- Is Jesus of Nazareth asking humanity to keep evolving into something genuinely new and different? Or do his teachings simply offer us a better way of keeping things as they are, but with clearer expressions of how to show love and acquire deeper peace?
- When Jesus asked and still asks us to follow him, is he speaking as someone who is already operating in a new and evolved state, one beyond our common experience of human life? Is he inviting us to grow and evolve into his higher mentality? Or is he simply teaching us a more effective and loving way to live in our present state of consciousness?
- Are the teachings of Jesus meant to show humanity the way to evolve into the next higher state of consciousness so that we can better help bring about the kingdom of God on Earth? Or is he just teaching individuals a surer way to get to heaven?

If Jesus's teachings are genuinely evolutionary, they must help bring about the further evolution of our species. They must help the entire human race to evolve to a level of union and love that is beyond anything people know today (except for a few). Those teachings must be able to define and bring about a collective *metanoia*, a shift to a higher mindset or way of thinking that does not yet characterize humankind.

In the noosphere, evolution happens most often through such a fundamental shift in thinking. That shift usually begins in individuals and spreads among the community.

The more contemporary term *paradigm shift* may help us understand a *metanoia* event.[10] Members of a scientific community—physicists or biologists, for example—share a fundamental perception of certain events. In other words, when scientists observe an event, they all "see" the same thing and understand it the same way. For example, before Einstein's theory of relativity, physicists saw space and time as fixed and unchangeable. And, before Darwin's evidence for biological evolution, biologists were content simply to categorize different species, not trace their evolutionary lineage.

Einstein and Darwin were observing the same phenomena and events, but they were seeing them in a new way that transformed their perception and understanding. Eventually, their insights called for and produced paradigm shifts, that is, profound changes in the fundamental perceptions of their respective sciences.

For Teilhard, Jesus introduced a paradigm shift into religious thinking. Jesus observed the same phenomena and events that others could see, but he saw them in a new way. His gospel was designed to introduce people to his *metanoia* by transforming their perception and understanding of who God is, what God is doing in the world, and our true role in God's work.

3

Metanoia

The Importance of Words

WORDS ARE IMPORTANT. Words in a biblical translation need to be carefully examined and compared to their original source. A translation may sometimes miss both the meaning and context of an important passage.

A mistranslation of a Gospel writer's original Greek word can lead to misunderstanding—even centuries of misunderstanding. A serious mistranslation can create distortions that permeate believers' spiritual practices, moral behavior, and theological thinking. The Greek word *metanoia* offers a clear case of such mistranslation and misunderstanding.

The word *metanoia* has special significance for us in this book, since it is key to the evolutionary potential of the Gospels. The word *metanoia* is prominent in the Greek text of three of the Gospels and the Acts of the Apostles. It refers to the process of changing one's mindset or way of thinking (*noia*) to a higher (*meta*) level. A higher way of thinking is one that incorporates a larger or more comprehensive perspective.

As used in the Gospels, *metanoia* calls for developing a whole new way of perceiving things, in this case, *seeing things God's way*. This *metanoia* provides access to fuller life because it is a new way of seeing, or as Teilhard likes to say, it's like having "new eyes."

Teilhard doesn't use *metanoia* in his writings, but the word accurately describes the way he is trying to help us acquire a new mindset. In both his major works, *The Divine Milieu* and *The Phenomenon of Man*, his intent is to teach readers to see with "new eyes," in order to

15

perceive things the way he does.[1] If you put on his new eyes, it will create a profound change in your fundamental perception of events happening in the Gospels and everywhere else.

An Unfortunate Translation

In the original Greek, the noun *metanoia* in the Gospels is typically translated into English as "repentance," and the verb in its imperative form, *metanoeite*, is typically translated as "repent." This inadequate translation—or mistranslation—appears in almost all English translations of the New Testament. Because *metanoia* represents a key process that is central to understanding the gospel's core message, it is important to present its meaning properly.

Several biblical scholars insist that the translation of the Greek *metanoia* into English as "repentance" is seriously misleading.[2] Such a mistranslation, they say, could skew the core meaning of the gospel message. Many other biblical scholars and commentators have trouble dealing with the inadequate English word *repentance* in the biblical text. One of them considers this mistranslation "a linguistic and theological tragedy."[3]

The *Oxford English Dictionary* says that to "repent" primarily means "to review one's actions and feel contrition or regret for something one has done or omitted to do." For example, repentance is the main purpose of the *Confetior* ("I confess") prayer recited by the worshiping community at the beginning of the Mass, where people acknowledge that they have sinned and promise not to sin anymore.

The *Merriam-Webster Dictionary* created a new English word, *metanoia*. It gives the definition as a "transformative change of heart; *especially* a spiritual conversion." This definition still misses the core meaning of the Greek *metanoia*, as a higher way of understanding, an opening of the mind, or a new way of seeing or perceiving reality.[4]

Pope Benedict XVI, a biblical scholar, agrees that the Greek term *metanoia* means more than mere repentance. He suggests that "conversion" and "reformation" may better approximate a connotation of *metanoia*. Either of those two provides a better one-word English translation of it than "repentance."[5] In fact, there is no adequate one-word English translation of *metanoia*.

Defining *Metanoia*

Metanoia denotes a significant change in one's mindset. It describes a revision or re-formation of one's way of thinking and perceiving. It is a mind-opening process that requires a change in one's state of consciousness so that one is no longer looking at the world and life in the same way but is seeing things from a totally new, deeper, and wider perspective and purpose.[6]

A *metanoia* can occur in almost any area of life, whenever it produces a new mental openness or offers a totally new perspective on events or experience. A *metanoia* happened among physicists with the discovery of relativity, among biologists with the discovery of evolution, and among mathematicians with the discovery of the calculus. *Metanoias* happen in all fields—music, dance, painting, filmmaking, and literature—even in one's personal life. Every loving parent that welcomes a newborn into this world experiences a *metanoia*.[7]

When people undergo a *metanoia* process, they experience it as an ongoing transformation of the mind. Whether the concept is applied to a specific area of knowledge, as in mathematics, or to life in general, as in parenting, there is no limit theoretically to the number of times one can experience a more comprehensive *metanoia*. In this sense, *metanoia* is open to continual evolution and helps produce it.[8]

Metanoias are the gateway to evolution in general. Teilhard would say that a *metanoia* qualifies as a personal evolutionary event.[9] The *metanoia* of the Gospels provides a gateway to understanding how God works in the world. The specific focus of gospel *metanoia* is to enable you to see, grasp, and comprehend creation, human events, and even your own life from God's perspective. When you experience the gospel *metanoia*, you begin to see things the way God sees them.[10]

Jesus effected a *metanoia* in the disciples before his ascension. "Then he opened their minds to understand the scriptures" (Luke 24:45). Jesus's primary concern is clearly to bring about a *metanoia* in his followers. He wants them to develop a new mindset to facilitate fuller understanding of his message. With this change of mental perspective—seeing things in a totally new way—comes a change in thinking, attitude, and behavior.[11]

17

Sources of Mistranslation

The misrepresentation of *metanoia's* meaning apparently began with the earliest translations of the Scriptures from Greek to Latin. According to David N. Wilkin, "The Latin Fathers translate the Greek *metanoia* into the Latin *paenitentia*, which in English comes to mean 'penance' or 'acts of penance.'"[12]

In the third century, Tertullian was quick to protest the unsuitable translation of the Greek *metanoeite* ("transform the way you think")[13] into the Latin *paenitentiam agite* ("do penance"). He argued, "In Greek, *metanoia* is not a confession of sins but a change of mind."[14] For Tertullian, *conversion* (from the Latin *conversiō*, "the act of turning one's life around") with its meaning, "change in character," provides a closer equivalent of *metanoia* than repentance.

You can be a deeply spiritual person and love God with all your heart, yet never enter a higher mindset, that is, never come to see the world the way Jesus saw it. Think of the rich young man who had kept all the commandments and loved God. He came to Jesus asking about a higher way. When Jesus told him the "price" required for him to make the necessary change of mind and behavior (*metanoia*) to be open to fuller and deeper life, the young man walked away sad (see Matt 19:16–22).

Importantly, this religious *metanoia* is *not* a requirement for baptism, for belief in Jesus, or for eternal salvation. However, entering Christ's way of thinking *consciously* is very valuable because it opens an "inward vision" that enables people to see what God is doing in the world. And the *metanoia* makes it easier for them to know how to cooperate actively in helping build the kingdom of God on Earth. "Thy will be done on Earth."

It should be noted that there are people all over the world who are living a life of loving service, even though they may have never heard of Jesus's Way. In their commitment to living in a spirit of compassionate love—even sacrificial love for others—they are essentially demonstrating his *metanoia*. One might say that they have unknowingly put on the mind of Christ.

Throughout Jesus's public life, he is amazed, frustrated, and angered that Jewish religious leaders, like Nicodemus, the scribes, and Pharisees, have themselves not undergone a *metanoia*. Of all people, those who know the Scriptures should have sought this inner transformation. It was described again and again in their prophetic books and the Psalms. Without this fundamental religious transformation, how could they as religious leaders possibly teach the people how to see the world as God sees it? If they had developed this *metanoia*, they would certainly have recognized Jesus, changed their minds about him, and believed in him.

Jesus was introducing *metanoia* to ordinary people, doing what the religious leaders had failed to do. "I did not come to call the righteous, but sinners, to *repentance* [the Greek text is *metanoia*]" (Mark 2:17 NKJV). "I came that they may have life, and have it abundantly" (John 10:10).

John the Baptist and *Metanoia*

The Greek term used to describe the purpose of John the Baptist's preaching is always *metanoia*:

> John the baptizer appeared in the wilderness, proclaiming a baptism of repentance [*metanoia*] for the forgiveness of sins. (Mark 1:4)

> He [John] went into all the region around the Jordan, proclaiming a baptism of repentance [*metanoia*] for the forgiveness of sins. (Luke 3:3)

> Repent [*metanoeite*], for the kingdom of heaven has come near. (Matt 3:2).

Clearly, John the Baptist is preaching the need for putting on a higher mindset in order to be ready to recognize the presence of the Messiah and to understand the meaning of what he teaches. In effect, the Baptist is telling his audience, "Unless you experience this inner transformation, you will fail to truly understand what the Messiah is really saying."

According to Mark and Luke, people — Jews and Gentiles alike — need John's baptism to open their minds to recognize *the Messiah as one who would deliver them from their slavery to sin.* In other words, John's *metanoia* would set their minds free from their preoccupation with sin, so that they could spend their energy doing good work for the kingdom of God.

For Matthew, people need John's baptism so that they can recognize the kingdom of God at work in their midst.

In the chapter following Jesus's baptism, Matthew reports Jesus's first and most basic message in his public ministry: "From that time Jesus began to proclaim, 'Repent [*metanoeite*], for the kingdom of heaven has come near'" (Matt 4:17). Interestingly, Jesus's words echo *the very words of the Baptist* (see Matt 3:2). Both the Baptist and Jesus require a *metanoia* as a starting point for understanding the messianic message. It's as if they were saying, "Open up your minds, so that you can see God's work going on all around you."

From the start, Jesus is affirming that the Baptist has it right. To truly grasp the dynamic presence of the "kingdom of God" requires undergoing a *metanoia*. It is a necessary first step if you want to enter the kingdom of God *consciously*.[15]

Later, in the Sermon on the Mount, Jesus spells out more fully what this change in mindset involves. Jesus sees his task not merely to describe to his audiences the nature of the kingdom; he must also lead people into this higher state of consciousness. It is the one way they can come to "see" the kingdom of God at work in their midst. It will enable them to understand how God wants to transform them and the world.

Jesus constantly remarks that when people don't make the necessary change of consciousness, his descriptions of the kingdom make little sense to them. "Do you have eyes, and fail to see? Do you have ears, and fail to hear?" (Mark 8:18; cf. Matt 13:13).

At the end of his time on Earth, and before his ascension, Jesus commands his disciples to preach *metanoia*. "And he said to them, 'Thus it is written, that the Messiah is to suffer and to rise from the dead on the third day, and that repentance [*metanoia*] and forgiveness of sins is to be proclaimed in his name to all nations, beginning from Jerusalem'" (Luke 24:46–47).

The apostles carry on Jesus's work by preaching *metanoia* as a basis for enriching their faith in Jesus and making it easier to contribute to God's work in the world. In his first public sermon on the day of Pentecost, Peter says to his audience, "Repent [*Metanoésate*] and be baptized every one of you in the name of Jesus Christ so that your sins may be forgiven; and you will receive the gift of the Holy Spirit" (Acts 2:38).[16] Baptism itself effects the forgiveness of sins.

A *metanoia* does not change what is happening in the world. Rather, it allows one to see and experience what is happening *in a new and very different way.* When you experience the gospel *metanoia*, you begin to see the world as Jesus sees it. A *metanoia* is not necessary for entrance into heaven, but it is certainly valuable during this lifetime because it provides you with new eyes.

Here are a few contemporary ways to better paraphrase the misleading common English translations of Jesus's statement in Matthew 4:17: "Repent, for the kingdom of heaven has come near."

- Put on a new mindset that will enable you to see how God is at work among us.
- Adopt a higher way of thinking about your life, otherwise you miss seeing that God is doing something big in your life and in the world right now.
- Transform the ways your mind is functioning, and you will be more prepared to recognize the great gift of fuller life that God has for you and for creation.
- Let go of the fearful ways you have been thinking about your life, so you can consciously adopt God's loving way of thinking and living.
- Open yourself to a higher way of thinking so you can put aside your preoccupation with sin and get consciously involved in what God is doing in the world.
- Elevate your thinking to a higher level so that your mind can recognize God's great plans unfolding for each of us here and now.
- Raise your consciousness so that you can look at reality in a new way. Realize that God is running the show.

The Challenge to Jesus's Disciples and to Us

Spirituality works best when "opening the mind" precedes "opening the heart." By opening the mind first, one sees and understands things more clearly. With clearer mental perspective, your heart not only opens, but you also recognize how, where, and when to show love most effectively. Once you can "see" the kingdom of God at work around you, you will more easily recognize where your love, your compassion, your courage, your creativity, and your ingenuity can make a positive difference.

As you enter this new mindset, you realize that the kingdom of God was and is an ongoing work project on Earth and involves each of us actively cooperating to help accomplish it.

Pope Francis says, "The future [of Earth] is in your hearts, in your minds, and in your hands. You are called to build a more beautiful Church *and a better world*."[17] For many believers, this is a new message.

Teilhard would say that undergoing a *metanoia* such as Jesus's disciples did would qualify as a personal evolution of consciousness. A *metanoia* happens, not in one's visible appearance, but in one's consciousness. Each personal *metanoia* has its cumulative effect in the noosphere, the mind and heart of humanity that circles the globe.

If enough people worldwide were to achieve a gospel *metanoia*, it would effect another evolutionary step in religion. It would also, in Teilhard's mind, mark an evolutionary step for humanity.[18]

The Four Gospels

Each of the four Gospels takes a different focus on Jesus's evolutionary message.

In exploring Matthew's text (part 2), we focus on Jesus's sermons, his parables of the kingdom, the active faith Jesus uses to heal people, and the power of faith he passes on to his disciples who are then able to do healings just as he does (see Matt 10:1).[19]

In Mark (part 3), we meet an active, on-the-move Jesus who wants to change the world. Since Mark spends much of his Gospel on the passion, we look closely at his presentation of Jesus's institution of the Eucharist during the Last Supper and the meaning of Jesus's suffering and death.

In Luke (part 4), we begin with the early life of Jesus as seen through the eyes of Mary. We end with his last days on Earth after his resurrection. We also analyze a few of the rather long parables that are unique to Luke's Gospel.

We could spend an entire book exploring John's Gospel (part 5) with the mindset of Teilhard. It will be enough to examine carefully John's Prologue and a few of Jesus's many teachings found uniquely in John's text. At your leisure, you might continue to delve more deeply into the rest of this Fourth Gospel.

Since most readers will be familiar with the gospel events, I do not provide a full scriptural text of each chapter. Any readers unfamiliar with the gospel text may keep a copy of the New Testament nearby.[20]

Instead of analyzing every passage in each chapter, we focus only on those passages where Teilhard would have found clear signs of *metanoia*. These texts present some action or teaching that is *different and genuinely new or novel from what went before* (i.e., the Mosaic Law) or meet other criteria for reperceiving it as "evolutionary."

PART II

THE GOSPEL OF MATTHEW

BIBLICAL SCHOLARS date the first appearance of the Gospel According to Matthew to about fifty years after Jesus's resurrection. During the early decades of the young Christian community, the body of believers matures. Matthew's mind and consciousness are being enriched by the reports of missionaries who are sharing the gospel message in foreign lands. He is also influenced by years of comparing his personal recollections of Jesus with the memories of other believers. During this time, he continues to participate in Christian worship (the various *ecclesia* bodies). He also has Mark's Gospel at hand.

Many believe that Matthew himself, the Jewish tax collector and apostle of Jesus, composed this Gospel text. Evidence in the document itself supports this claim. Certainly, the author was a Jew familiar with the Hebrew Scriptures.

Matthew's Gospel reflects a strong Jewish character and flavor and is directed to a Jewish audience: for example, Matthew's genealogy of Jesus (1:1–17). The story of Jesus's birth is from a Jewish male's perspective (1:18–23). The text explores Joseph's religious dilemma about divorcing Mary. Caring for the child Jesus's safety is presented as Joseph's responsibility (1:24–25). Finally, included in Matthew's infancy narrative are five Hebrew Scripture "fulfillment passages,"[1] which establish Jesus as the Messiah and show that his teachings grew out of Jewish tradition.

Matthew's Gospel emphasizes Jesus as coming to Earth primarily to bring his good news to the Jewish people.[2] Nevertheless, Matthew presents Jesus as a Messiah for *all* nations (see 2:1–12).

Stylistically, Matthew's Gospel is a well-written, well-organized document. He takes various sayings and teachings of Jesus and assembles them into five great speeches, the most important one being the Sermon on the Mount (chapters 5—7). He collects ten miracles and presents them in chapters 8 and 9. He gathers seven different parables of Jesus and groups them together in chapter 13. The other four chapters contain Jesus's missionary discourse (chapter 10), the parable discourse (chapter 13), the community discourse (chapter 18), and the eschatological discourse (chapters 24—25).

Teilhard's Perspective

Teilhard would be looking through the Gospel of Matthew for something very different from the academic and historical interests of biblical scholars. He would be searching for teachings and events that might qualify as "evolutionary." He would be looking at Jesus's teachings on theology, spirituality, and morality from an evolutionary perspective. As we read the text, Teilhard would be telling us to ask these questions: Are passages in this Gospel text

- different and genuinely new or novel compared to what went before?
- keeping essential elements or functions of what went before?
- more complex than anything within its class?
- irreversible, such that, once presented, it cannot be denied?
- transformative but not destructive of what went before?
- manifesting new emerging properties?

The above six questions provide "a simple evolutionary test" that can be applied to gospel events as well as to various teachings and parables of Jesus.

Although not every gospel event and sermon will pass the test and qualify as evolutionary, Teilhard would find many that do. There is enough evidence to confirm that the Gospels are introducing us to an evolutionary theology, spirituality, and morality—even though the Gospel writers are not "evolutionary thinkers."

As we read the text of each Gospel, Teilhard would want us to ask, "Does the material in this gospel passage qualify as evolutionary?" Teilhard's deeper question is, "Is Jesus Christ an Evolver?"[3]

Whenever you answer yes to the six questions of the evolutionary test, you can confidently affirm that the passage—the event or the teaching—is revealing something evolutionary.

The Task

We also continue the hermeneutic task. *We are examining documents from another period and culture, hoping to find in them relevance for us and for our culture.* Specifically, Teilhard sees the challenge as reinterpreting or reenvisioning the good news of Jesus—without distorting its meaning—and adapting "the gospel teaching to the modern world."[4]

From Teilhard's perspective, the hermeneutic question becomes more specific: *How are the Gospels relevant to a culture that is being shaped by science, technology, and a growing awareness of the universality of evolution?*

Since the issue of evolution is the most difficult to integrate into traditional Christian theology, Teilhard says that the first step is to show that Jesus himself thinks like an evolver, that he is living evolutely, and that his teachings are evolutionary.[5]

4

Preparing for the Messiah

Human and Divine (1:1–25)

IN HIS FIRST CHAPTER, Matthew's genealogy of Jesus affirms four facts about Jesus. He is (1) a true human being; (2) a "son of Abraham, and therefore a true Hebrew"; (3) the long-awaited Messiah; and (4) a descendant of King David, and therefore a possible legitimate heir to rule Israel (see 1:1–17).[1]

First, in the story of Joseph's dream to marry Mary (see 1:18–25), the angel clearly affirms Jesus as a genuine human being. In Mary's womb, the infant Jesus is gestating like all human fetuses. The baby growing in Mary's body is evident enough for Joseph to notice. If he isn't aware of it, more observant members of his family or his neighbors will bring it to his attention.

Second, the angel in Joseph's dream announces that this very human infant is also a very special divine being because his conception was brought about by the action of the Holy Spirit. "For the child conceived in her is from the Holy Spirit" (1:20). The angel of the dream also tells Joseph what the child's name should be: "She will bear a son, and you are to name him Jesus" (1:21).

Third, the angel tells Joseph in his dream that the divine child, the Messiah and Savior, will not grow up to become a military leader—sword in hand—to make Israel a world empire. Almost every Jew at the time was hoping for this. Rather, the child will be a Savior that will "save his people from their sins" (1:21).

Fourth, in the very first verse of his Gospel, Matthew affirms Jesus's Davidic descent. "An account of the genealogy of Jesus the Messiah, the son of David, the son of Abraham" (1:1).

At that time, if a Jewish man discovered he was engaged to be married to a pregnant woman and the child was not his, the Law of Moses gave him only two choices: either have her stoned to death or exile her from the community. The angel in the dream tells Joseph he has a third choice, not based on the Law but based on love. This third option establishes the Gospel's new hierarchy. It places love as a value above legal justice. This shift in values requires Joseph to enter a new way of thinking (*metanoia*) that puts compassion and care above the punitive rules that his Jewish religion prescribes in this situation.

EVOLUTIONARY IMPLICATIONS

In this story, an evolution emerges from within Judaism about the meaning and purpose of the Messiah's arrival. The Messiah's role, according to the angel in Joseph's dream, will be that of a moral leader, not a military one. He will be a teacher, not a soldier. To fulfill this purpose, the Savior will not be merely human, but also divine. Moreover, his reign will be based not on law, but on love.

Notice how the Gospel's understanding of the nature and purpose of the Messiah evolves from the traditional Jewish notion of the Messiah as a military conquering hero. Here, the six test questions have the following affirmative answers:

1. The Messiah as primarily a moral leader is genuinely new.
2. His moral leadership does not destroy the central element of what the Jewish people always thought their Messiah would do for his people; Jesus will still fulfill the role of their Savior—by doing it morally, not militarily.
3. People will also find it more complex to relate to a moral Messiah than to a purely military one.
4. The new moral and teaching role of the Messiah makes undeniable sense.
5. It requires a higher consciousness to grasp how living a love-centered moral life is more demanding than the Hebrew moral tradition of obedience to the Mosaic Law.

6. The Hebrews were looking for the Messiah to "save" and "set free" the Jewish people militarily. A moral Messiah will teach people to live their lives with a new kind of mutual love that can transform humanity. A loving Messiah offers a new freedom and gives new and fuller meaning to the word *save*.

The concept of "saving" or "salvation" has often been explained restrictively, as "saving from punishment due to sin." Christ's salvation does indeed set us free from such punishment. But beyond that, salvation has a much richer meaning in Jesus's teaching. His salvation brings us the fullness of life. "For freedom Christ has set us free" (Gal 5:1). It's as though we have been locked in a dungeon (of sin). Christ unlocks the dungeon and sets us free (from sin). But he doesn't walk away as soon as he unlocks our cell. He provides us with new ways to live in freedom, to spread love, and to enjoy the fullness of life (cf. John 10:10).

When the angel sets Joseph free to continue to love Mary, Joseph discovers another powerful evolutionary step: when a situation seems impossible, *love always provides another option*. This is a transformative insight.

Visitors from the East (2:1–12)

Matthew's second chapter begins with the story of the wise men from the East. Matthew wants to show us from the start that, Jesus's Way will attract people of every nation, especially spiritual seekers like the wise men. Jesus's Way is meant for the whole world. This marks another evolutionary step among religions. The stories in this chapter assure us that Jesus is presenting a *religion for all people*, not just for one tribe, one nation, or one empire.

Matthew also wants to tell us that God will find many ways to introduce Jesus to the world. God will use natural ways to provide an introduction or, more precisely, God will find ways that seem natural to each person and each kind of people. With Joseph, God sends dreams.[2] With the wise men from afar, God uses the appearance of a star (see 2:2). Although people today might not look for divine guidance from dreams or a star, the wise men, as astrologers, were accustomed to this kind of divine assistance. They expected God to provide them with heavenly signs in the stars and in their dreams (see 2:12).

Matthew is not telling us to become astronomers. Rather, he is indicating that, for all those with good hearts who want to find God, God will find a way to guide them. God's new call is not merely to Jews, the chosen people, but to all, like the wise men, who truly seek the divine.[3]

EVOLUTIONARY IMPLICATIONS

In the example of the wise men, Matthew is establishing new and evolutionary conditions for followers of Jesus. They personally need to (1) be searching for God and to discover God's purposes on Earth; (2) offer their talents and treasures to God's work; (3) offer themselves to him in person; and (4) learn to discern the different ways God might be guiding them in their day-to-day activities. These conditions call for a discernment-and-action-filled spirituality.

These four conditions for following Jesus transform the ways Jews traditionally followed the Torah and evoke yes answers to the questions in the evolutionary test.

"The Kingdom of Heaven Has Come Near" (3:2–12)

In the Hebrew Scriptures, the prophets promise that a Messiah will arrive when the time is ready. In every age, the Jewish people await his appearance. The Prophet Isaiah told his people to get the roads ready for his coming. Isaiah assured the Israelites that he, Isaiah, was not the Messiah. He was merely the voice of one crying out in the wilderness, "Prepare the way of the LORD, make straight in the desert a highway for our God" (Isa 40:3). John the Baptist, like Isaiah, is also a voice crying out in the wilderness.

In his version of John the Baptist's story, Matthew does not have this new prophet emphasize the arrival of Israel's Messiah. The Baptist announces a much larger event—the active presence of a much broader reality, the kingdom of heaven (God's kingdom).[4] "[Undergo *metanoia*], for the kingdom of heaven has come near" (3:2). In effect, the Baptist is saying, "In your old way of thinking, you expect the Messiah will usher in a Jewish kingdom, but, if you open your mind, you will see that the Messiah is focused on God's kingdom." Bringing about God's reign—not a Jewish empire—is central to the Baptist's preaching.

The ancient Jews had no higher or more powerful concepts than king and kingdom to talk about what their Messiah would accomplish. Jesus continues to use "kingdom" imagery in his stories, since it is a metaphor that he knew his listeners could grasp. People today who live in democratic nations may find images of royalty and empire antiquated, but we continue to use them liturgically. It is important to remember that they are *metaphoric* images, not to be taken literally. Jesus will tell us that God prefers to be addressed, not as King, but as Father. A Father is one who lovingly introduces us to the way of love.

Instead of encouraging an uprising or organizing a resistance movement, John reminds people of their selfishness and false self-righteousness as well as their need to be more caring of one another. His is not a call to arms but a call to consciousness. He wants his audiences to recognize that, while they keep expecting the Messiah to lead an overthrow of the Romans, their minds and hearts are not yet ready to greet their Messiah or to share his purpose for coming. To prepare, they need to undergo a *metanoia*, a change of perspective and behavior.

John is addressing his advice to anyone in his audience who will listen—pagans, soldiers, anyone. His call to change one's way of thinking is universal and not limited to Jews. God is no longer to be perceived simply as Israel's tribal god, Yahweh, but as a universal God. The Baptist is introducing his audiences to an evolutionary shift in religious thinking.

EVOLUTIONARY IMPLICATIONS

First, we learn that the kingdom of heaven, God's kingdom, is not something happening only among the people of Israel. Even during the time of Jesus, God's work is already active among the entire human family and all creation. It includes the Hebrew people but goes beyond them (see 3:9). God's project is a universal ongoing event. What God is doing in the world involves everyone on Earth.

Second, awareness of this vast "kingdom" as a divine evolutionary project is slowly surfacing among the early Christians for whom Matthew is writing. They are realizing that the divine realm that Jesus is portraying is not a geographical place but rather *a divine project in process on Earth.* This consciousness of the kingdom as an ongoing divine project is gradually being clarified at the time the Gospel writers are composing their texts. The need for our active involvement for the success of God's project becomes explicit in the Lord's Prayer (see chapter 9 below).

Third, followers of Jesus are realizing that God's plan operates primarily under the guidance of the Holy Spirit (3:11). The "fire" the Baptist speaks of refers to the Spirit's power (3:11–12). This "fire" image reflects a new urgency, eagerness, and enthusiasm felt by the followers of the Way.

Fourth, the Baptist also is clearly preparing his listeners for the only person that can show us the Way, the Messiah himself (see 3:11).

Fifth, as developed earlier, the Baptist clearly realizes that the kingdom of God will happen only when people not only acknowledge their sin but also put on a new mindset (a *metanoia*). John the Baptizer said, "[Put on a new way of thinking], for the kingdom of heaven has come near" (3:2).

In chapter 4, Matthew describes how Jesus begins his public ministry. It starts very simply. In fact, according to Matthew, Jesus preaches *the same* basic message as John: "[Undergo a *metanoia*], for the kingdom of God has come near" (4:17).[5]

In one sense, Jesus is inviting each of us to enter this *metanoia*, which allows each of us to think of oneself as a fisher of human beings (see 4:19). It is a role you can live out in whatever job or career you may have. Today, these "fisher-of-human-beings" roles include research scientist, engineer, doctor, nurse, teacher, writer, journalist, media specialist, actor, musician, artist, receptionist, financier, insurance agent, and so on.

Once you enter this new mindset, you can ask, "How can I help build the kingdom of God?" The answer is simply by following the Way. The loving example of your life is what will primarily attract others to join you in the pursuit of God's project.

The challenge is to discover, behaviorally, how to live in the new Way—the way of unconditional love—in whatever role in life you play, whether you are rich or poor, brilliant or mentally slow, healthy or sick, free or in prison.

Another major evolutionary aspect of the gospel message highlighted both by John the Baptist and Jesus is *the nearness of God to everyone*. Never—in any religion—has God been "nearby" and "available." In this new covenant, access to God's presence is not restricted to a certain few select people. God is accessible to everyone.

Nor were people ever invited to be involved with God's work on Earth—helping build the kingdom of God. Jesus's parables confirm God's nearness, activity, and the call for everyone to be involved in transforming the world. The divine presence and divine love become *immediately accessible to all believers for all times*.

Jesus Begins His Missionary Journey (4:23–24)

With his small team, he begins to move through various towns of Galilee, preaching and healing. He is preaching the good news, namely, that the presence of God's loving kingdom is already operating among them. His healings are clear examples of God's kingdom at work. Healings give more life.

Compassionate healing is a most natural response of Jesus to the suffering people that are being brought to him by others. Healing is one of Jesus's primary ways of "preaching" his message of good news. It is his personal way of affirming the active presence of the kingdom of God among us.

Someone who can perform healing miracles is good news. Such news spreads quickly. Crowds are already forming in villages where he is next expected to visit. Some who heard about Jesus are even traveling two or three days from Jerusalem to experience him (see 4:25).

EVOLUTIONARY IMPLICATIONS

People who are poor, sick, helpless, discouraged, and rejected seem most open to hearing the good news of God's loving and healing presence among us. Jesus does not begin teaching his theology the usual way by formal presentation to the wise and learned intellectuals. Rather, he shares it first with the poor. He does it personally by going from town to town and speaking directly to ordinary people.

Another important evolutionary lesson is that this new mindset—living Jesus's compassionate Way—works better when we act in teams. Jesus needs a team of apostles to work with him. He needs disciples. Even Jesus works more effectively within a team. God is inviting our cooperation in building the kingdom. God is enlisting us to join the divine team.

The Mindsets of Jesus and of His Audience

The Mindset of Jesus

JESUS IS CLEARLY operating from a mindset higher than that of anyone in the crowds that come to hear him. No one in Israel could have anticipated the evolutionary content that Jesus would present in his life and teachings.

In his humanity, Jesus must be an evolved human being. The following signs indicate that he operates with an evolved awareness of reality. It is a state of consciousness that none of his audience possesses—or can imagine.

Here are eleven points that Teilhard would have observed to identify the higher level of consciousness of the human Jesus:

1. Jesus knows that God is an unconditionally loving Father, whose very nature is love (see Matt 6:9; 1 John 4:8). No one else in the audience knows this (see Matt 13:11).
2. Jesus knows that everything in heaven and on Earth has been created in love and is imbued with love, since love for all people, even one's enemies, serves as the basis of his teaching (see John 6:16–17).
3. Jesus knows that love is the most powerful energy in the universe and nothing else can compare to—or compete with—the energy of compassionate, creative love (see John 15:13–14).

4. Jesus knows from his own experience of healing others that people at his level of consciousness can accomplish things they never thought possible (see John 14:11–13).
5. As Jesus stands in front of the crowd, he knows that God's kingdom is present among them at this very moment, fully alive and working (see Luke 17:20–22).
6. Jesus knows that everyone is destined to live and participate in his Father's kingdom and that everyone, no matter their state in life, is called to work to further this kingdom (see John 17:20–23).[1]
7. Jesus knows that establishing this kingdom on Earth is God's project and that this project has a long way to go before it will be fulfilled, completed, and perfect (see Matt 6:10; Luke 12:50)—when everyone will enjoy life in abundance (see John 10:10).
8. Jesus knows that making God's kingdom on Earth a reality will require everyone's cooperative effort.[2]
9. Jesus knows that the work of God's kingdom is urgent and demands total commitment, especially from anyone who aspires to be a disciple (see Matt 8:18–22; 18:15–22; 24:45–46; 25:14–30).
10. Jesus knows that the Father has lovingly blessed each person on the planet with unique talents and capacities to help move the divine project forward (see Matt 6:25–34; Luke 12:22–32). Jesus is there to tell people this (see Luke 4:14–30; Matt 18:10).
11. Jesus knows that the Father wants everyone to cooperate and lovingly conspire to accomplish the evolutionary process that the Father has put in motion (see Matt 8:12; Luke 5:32; Mark 2:17).

Jesus speaks to the people from within this all-embracing understanding of God and God's project. He is modeling the new *metanoia* in all its fullness.

Another point Teilhard might make is that Jesus is not talking to the people as God but as a fellow human being, albeit a human who knows more about God and what God is doing in the world than anyone in his audience.[3]

Jesus makes no claim to divinity at any time during his public life. According to Matthew, Jesus never directly claims that he is acting as God.[4] Again and again, he called himself "the Son of Man," never "the Son of God,"[5] except in the sense that we, like him, are all sons and daughters of the Father.

The Mindset of His Audience

For example, who made up Jesus's audience at the Sermon on the Mount? We can assume that most of the crowd is made up of people who come hoping to hear some good news. They are hoping to hear words of hope and courage. Many of those sprawling on the long, grassy slope are people on the margins of society. Among those listening to him, some are rebels and radicals, others are peacemakers, and others are being persecuted. In short, many among the crowd are the unsuccessful, the powerless, and the excluded.

We can also assume that not many rich people are there sitting in the hot sun on the bare ground. Richer folks are relaxing at home in their wealth and comfort. Most of the upper class that might wish to hear Jesus speak prefer to wait until he comes to their synagogue. There, they can sit in comfort and listen to him with interest, amusement, or contempt. Nor are busy businesspeople ready to spend hours listening to an itinerant preacher from the backward town of Nazareth.[6]

Therefore, his audience on this day form a motley crew. The people in the crowd are the focus of his address. Always keep in mind that he is speaking to them.

6

The Beatitudes

A Traditional Perspective Challenged (5:3–12)

CHURCHGOERS ARE so used to hearing Jesus's words from the Sermon on the Mount from Matthew's Gospel that they may miss the startling evolutionary nature of his teaching. As Matthew comments at the end of the sermon, the people in Jesus's audience were astounded for they had *never heard anything like what he is teaching* (see 7:28–29).

This first sermon will be his manifesto, revealing the true, loving nature of the kingdom of God. Father Richard Rohr calls the Sermon on the Mount Jesus's "inaugural address."[1] It is what he has been sent to Earth by God to announce. The opening verses of the sermon read like a psalm.[2]

Jesus "came to bring fire to the earth" (Luke 12:49). It is easy to minimize the importance of Jesus's first major sermon if it is treated as a discourse whose purpose is to improve the moral behavior of the Jewish people. Jesus has come, not to get people to behave better but to establish a new covenant with humanity.

The contents of Jesus's Sermon on the Mount are as revelatory to the world of his day as the tablets of the Law were to Moses and the Hebrew people in the desert. The Mosaic Law defined the former covenant God had with the Hebrew people. The Beatitudes and the rest of this great sermon define a new covenant, not merely with the Jews but with all humankind.

This sermon, as Matthew presents it, is an evolutionary document if ever there was one. Jesus's new covenant reveals the true loving nature of God and the working of God's kingdom. The eight beatitudes provide a most dramatic introduction to this new covenant.

Blessed

The pivotal first word in each beatitude is *blessed*. What does Jesus intend by using this paradoxical word? Arguably, one of the most difficult challenges in understanding the focus of the Beatitudes rests in the meaning and intent of that first word of each assertion, which we translate into English as "Blessed" or, in some versions, as "Happy."

In Greek, the first word of each beatitude is *makarioi*, which denotes people enjoying a deep state of blessedness, happiness, or inner joy. It is an experience of life at its best. This Greek word connotes a spiritual experience of some permanence, like the inner joy of parents of a newborn child, a joy that continues to grow deeper as the child grows. We must ask, What Aramaic word did Jesus use as the first word in each of the beatitudes and what did he mean by it?

It is important to study the original Aramaic, since reading "blessed" as "enriched" or "gladdened" does not quite fit with what comes afterward in each beatitude. Feeling enriched or gladdened is not the feeling normally associated with being, as the Beatitudes have it, spiritually poor, meek, lowly, sorrowful, suffering, persecuted, or rejected.

The contrast between the first and second half of each beatitude is paradoxical, to say the least. Surely, Jesus cannot be telling people to be happy with their lowly lot in life now because they'll eventually get their reward in heaven. That is not the "good news" of the gospel, which is, rather, that "I have come that they may have life and have it in abundance." Yet, for centuries, most Christians heard just such a confusing message in many sermons on the Beatitudes during their lifetimes.

Nor is this traditional understanding evolutionary.

We must remember that Jesus's Sermon on the Mount is his first great speech—his manifesto—announcing the presence of and evidence for the emerging and growing kingdom of God. The people in his audience that day were not likely the rich people of the world. They were mostly the poor, the sick, the grieving, servants and slaves, the downtrodden. Some were being oppressed and others were resisters looking for someone to lead them in throwing off the yoke of Roman authority. These were broken and exploited people looking for comfort and hope whom Jesus was calling "blessed."

THE ARAMAIC MEANING OF *BLESSED*

Possibly, none of the various English translations of the word *blessed* captures its full meaning as conveyed in Aramaic. That is the conclusion of Melkite Catholic Archbishop Abuna Chacour, a scholar of biblical Hebrew, New Testament Greek, and Aramaic.

Another professor, Vincent Ryan Ruggiero, hearing the archbishop's assertion, dug back into the Aramaic version of the Beatitudes. He found that the original Aramaic word that Jesus used did not have this passive quality of helpless acceptance of one's situation at all. Instead, the Aramaic word means "to put yourself on the right way for the right goal, to turn around, repent [*metanoia*]; to become straight or righteous."[3]

Archbishop Chacour believes that, in addressing the poor, meek, suffering, and persecuted folk, Jesus is not encouraging a passive acceptance of their current diminished condition in anticipation of a better life in the hereafter. Rather, Jesus is motivating these poor and disenfranchised to "wake up" to the challenge of being his followers. He is calling them to act and to work for a better society in this life — even though they are poor, lowly, suffering, and persecuted. At the same time, he is assuring them of his and God's support in their efforts. He is calling them to a *metanoia*!

Considering the active sense of the Aramaic word Jesus used in the Beatitudes, Archbishop Chacour offers more accurate renderings of two of them:

— *Get up, go ahead, and do something. Move, you who are hungry and thirsty for justice, for you shall be satisfied.*

Get up, go ahead, and move. Take action, you peacemakers, for you shall be called children of God.

The archbishop's point is that we need to revise our understanding of the Beatitudes and see them as a call for an active response. Jesus is doing something completely new. He is enlisting oppressed and demoralized people to join him in his work. He is inviting them to do something in their communities to make a difference, rather than to maintain a passive acceptance of their difficulties.[4]

Response to a Gift

We realize that sometimes a gift or a favor we receive implies a response of action. However, we don't usually think of poverty, grief, rejection, or persecution as gifts or favors. These are the human situations where people typically feel punished, helpless, and powerless to make a difference. Jesus is asking such people to turn their self-perceptions around (*metanoia*) and to *see their apparently diminished state as a position from which to make a positive difference.*

Even the underprivileged can contribute to what God is doing in the world. They can be agents of change. It is as if Jesus is saying, "If you feel you are living in a world where you don't fit in, start creating a new, more loving world. God and the kingdom of heaven are doing it with you. Act like you belong to God's kingdom. Do something beautiful for God."

Jesus possesses the rare human skill of looking at people and seeing both what is and what could be, current reality and future possibility. He can see both at the same time and he possesses the gift to show people the potential he can see in them.

Someone who is "blessed" can act with the power of God's Spirit. Jesus is telling his audience that they are all blessed in this way, whether they happen to be poor, sick, grieving, rejected, slaves, or anything else. He is telling them they are not helpless. Rather, they are all agents of God's work in the world. He is enlisting them as his disciples. They are to be part of his team.[5]

To paraphrase President John F. Kennedy, it seems Jesus was saying to this crowd, "Don't ask what the kingdom of God can do for you. Rather, ask what you can do for the kingdom of God." The poor, sorrowing, suffering rejected people are God's chosen agents of change. Jesus sees them as the best hope of transforming the world as it is meant to be. Why? Because the minds of the "insignificant" are not closed to a new viewpoint, while the minds of the "significant" resist Jesus's *metanoia*. Jesus's *metanoia* turns the values of the world upside down. "So the last will be first, and the first will be last" (20:16).

Evolutionary Implications

In evolutionary terms, Teilhard might say that Jesus is telling his ragtag audience that the success of God's loving plan for humanity is just as much in their hands as it is in the hands of the rich and powerful, the priests, the religious, or the wise and learned. They—the entire crowd—are being called to actively participate in what God wants to accomplish in the world. It is a message they have never heard before. No matter how weak and powerless society considers them, they are important to God. They can leave their imprint for God on the world.

Now that the weak, forgotten, and insignificant people have been made aware of their hitherto unsuspected power and potential, Jesus, throughout the rest of the sermon, tells them *how to act*. Once they realize they are blessed, they will be called upon to act in ways they have never heard before. Common sense is not necessarily God's sense.

Jesus is giving the least powerful people permission to use their power of love hidden in their weakness. He is asking them to turn it into action to help bring more life into the kingdom of God in their communities.

Teilhard would tell us that Jesus has come to Earth to present God's vision or dream for creation. The Beatitudes should inspire every human person to play his or her part in this transformation of the world, no matter what their situation. All these forgotten and mistreated people are clearly part of the divine vision of the kingdom. It is an evolutionary vision. Jesus is proposing a goal, a divine objective, toward which all are called to aim their lives and life purposes.

When God's own way of loving begins to emerge and be practiced by human beings, especially by the poor and the forgotten, we will have witnessed the truth of this powerful sermon. While we continue to interpret the Beatitudes in the traditional way, the forgotten ones will never hear Jesus's call to use their loving action to change the world.

What is also specifically evolutionary here is that, in the Hebrew tradition, Yahweh is basically a God watching over his tribe of chosen people, helping them win their tribal wars. For Jesus, God's vision for creation is very different. It is not one about Israel conquering its enemies. It is a vision of everyone involved in creating a planet filled with loving union.[6]

7

The Sermon on the Mount

Salt and Light (5:13–16)

JESUS CONTINUES addressing this motley crowd sitting on the hill. With the Beatitudes, he enlists them as his disciples—the poor and meek, sick and sorrowing, peacemakers and protesters. He is now about to give them their assignments. He begins by naming the two most important qualities they can bring to God's project on Earth. These qualities are symbolized by salt and light.

First, Jesus tells the crowd that, by their loving actions toward all those they meet, they can be the "salt" that gives the distinctive flavor to the emerging kingdom of God and to Jesus's work on Earth. Second, their loving actions can be the "light" that attracts others to join the divine work.

What an important job! What a privilege! Nobody has ever told the lowly and rejected people that they are important: important to God and to the success of God's work on Earth. Nobody has ever told them they are meant to be the salt of the Earth or a light to the world. But here is Jesus, spelling it out, "People will see what the kingdom is meant to be when they see how you live and show unconditional love."

Jesus is telling the poor, humble, and persecuted that they are the people who are to show the rest of the world the best way to live, the best way to love. They are ambassadors of light. Jesus tells them, "Let your light shine before others. Don't hide your ability to love."

In the rest of the Sermon on the Mount, Jesus tells these special people—the poor, the sorrowing, the forgotten—how to show a love that will stand out like a light on a lamp stand.

When Jesus tells them that they are the salt of the earth, he also warns them that if salt loses its ability to flavor food, it is treated as useless and thrown out. Jesus warns them that if they lose their ability to love or refuse to show it, this will happen to them.

How could they lose their saltiness? Easily, by just feeling sorry for themselves, by using their suffering or rejection as an excuse to be angry and resentful toward others, by seeking revenge and refusing to forgive, or by doing nothing but complaining and criticizing others. These are some of the ways they can lose their flavor as salt and ways they can hide their light under a bushel basket.

EVOLUTIONARY IMPLICATIONS

This sermon presents some new and startlingly evolutionary statements. First, Jesus is proposing a vision of God and God's project for creation that transcends any specific religion or any theological doctrine. It simply calls for the daily practice of love, starting with any healthy form of love, but leading up to the ability to show unconditional love for all.

Second, there is no membership requirement to become a disciple, except the commitment to grow in one's ability to become more all-embracing in one's expression of love.

Third, perhaps more evolutionarily, is that in spreading his vision Jesus gives primacy of place to the poor and meek, the sick and sorrowful, the oppressed and rebellious—not to the rich, the powerful, the most highly educated, or the religious leaders. The former are the first ones that Jesus enlists to be the salt for God's project and its light for the world.

Fourth, in his Sermon on the Mount Jesus is acting as a spiritual recruiter hoping to enroll people in God's grand project on Earth, namely, to establish the loving kingdom of God. His recruits will be expected to use the tools of true peace and unconditional ways of loving.

Fifth, to enlist in Jesus's loving team requires not only a "change of mindset" (*metanoia*) but also a "change of state" (*metamorphosis*). It's like changing from a caterpillar to a butterfly. Instead of continuing to see oneself as poor and powerless, one sees oneself as an active agent working on God's project.

The Commandments Reenvisioned (5:17–20)

After enlisting these followers in his project to help bring about the kingdom of God on Earth, Jesus then outlines the key points of his manifesto. He begins by telling them how they can live more fully the Ten Commandments, or as he calls them the "law and the prophets." Jesus begins, "Do not think that I have come to abolish the law or the prophets; I have come not to abolish but to fulfill" (5:17).

As Jesus points out, the way the Pharisees interpret the Ten Commandments, they miss each commandment's root meaning. According to Jesus, the Pharisees interpret the law and commandments legalistically. They view God as a strict Judge who treats the laws in an exact and legalistic sense. For example, the Pharisees take the commandment "Thou shall not kill" at face value. Provided you have not murdered anyone, they believe, you are fully observing this commandment.

EVOLUTIONARY IMPLICATIONS

Jesus does not approach the commandments legalistically. For Jesus, God, his Father, is not the traditionally portrayed harsh Judge to be feared, but an unconditionally loving Parent in whom to put complete trust. Jesus sees the kingdom of heaven governed not by strict justice but by compassionate love. Jesus views the commandments as God teaching us how to love each other the way God loves us. No one before Jesus had ever interpreted the Ten Commandments from the perspective of love. Jesus does not interpret them as obligations but rather as pathways to a deeper experience of life.

Unless we interpret the Ten Commandments in this new way— Jesus's way—we haven't grasped the nature of the kingdom of heaven. We haven't experienced a *metanoia*. In Jesus's mindset, heaven is a place where everyone's love is all-embracing, and those who are there continue to deepen their experience of life. For Teilhard, if we don't get it that love and "life in abundance" is the nature of God's world, we completely miss Jesus's message.[1] This new interpretation of the commandments is one more evolutionary dimension of Jesus's good news.

The Other Commandments (5:21–48)

In the rest of Matthew's chapter 5, Jesus considers other commandments and compares each one's traditional interpretation to the evolved interpretation he proposes, based on the perspective of unconditional love and openness to life. If we aren't looking at life from his *metanoia* perspective, we will miss Jesus's point again and again. He interprets each commandment as it is viewed in God's eyes.

He begins with the commandment concerning anger: "'You shall not murder'; and 'whoever murders shall be liable to judgment.' But I say to you that if you are angry with a brother or sister, you will be liable to judgment" (5:21–22).

In an atmosphere of unconditional love—in the divine milieu— there can be no room for name calling, insults, or anger toward each other. Forgiveness and reconciliation must be the order of the day. Don't even come to church if you harbor angry thoughts against anyone. First, go to that person and be reconciled, then come and stand before God in a holy place. If someone brings a lawsuit against you, don't fight it. Settle outside of court. Settle it in your accuser's favor. Clearly, Jesus does not expect his followers to settle for the minimum, that is, not killing anyone. They are expected to love all, even their enemies.

Jesus then takes up the commandment against adultery: "But I say to you that everyone who looks at a woman with lust has already committed adultery with her in his heart" (5:27–28).

The minimum level of fulfillment of this commandment is not to engage in the physical act of intercourse with a married person. Jesus takes this commandment much further. For him, just to lust for a married woman is equivalent to committing adultery. Women are not objects, but people sacred to God. In God's kingdom, every person and every relationship blessed by God is to be reverenced.

Next, Jesus turns to the commandment about swearing and using the Lord's name in vain: "But I say to you, Do not swear at all....Let your word be 'Yes, Yes' or 'No, No'; anything more than this comes from the evil one" (5:33–37).

In an atmosphere of love, there would be no need to swear oaths of any kind. Your word—or a simple handshake—is all that is needed to seal an agreement.[2]

Jesus goes even further in this area. Suppose someone, such as a family member or someone important to you, does something to harm you. How are you to respond? The Mosaic Law says that you can do to your enemy whatever he did to you or to your loved one—"an eye for an eye and a tooth for a tooth." Jesus's response is to be nonresistant, to "turn the other cheek" (see 5:38–42).

Jesus is coming from a mindset of unconditional love toward all, forgiveness for all. He invites us to show love and care beyond expectations, even to enemies. Many people today might say, "I can't accept that. If someone offended or harmed me, I would want justice."

You can begin to see how evolutionary Jesus is. There is nothing in traditional Jewish thinking that can accommodate this new approach. Jesus wants us to discover his new Way by looking at each commandment from the perspective of unconditional love.

From this perspective, there is no longer any person that can be called your enemy. "But I say to you, Love your enemies and pray for those who persecute you, so that you may be children of your Father in heaven" (5:44–45).

God's love is all-encompassing. No one is excluded from God's forgiveness or compassion. As much as we might like to exclude certain people from God's love, Jesus assures us that it can't happen. Everyone is Jesus's sister or brother.[3] That is another way of expressing the gospel's good news.

Jesus summarizes this list of commandments reinterpreted from a perspective of unconditional love by telling his hearers, "Be perfect, therefore, as your heavenly Father is perfect" (5:48). Love each other the way God loves you.

The Aramaic word Jesus uses that is translated as "perfect" might be better translated by another meaning, namely, "all-embracing."[4]

As we put on the loving mindset of Jesus, our first steps are likely to be far from "perfect." In fact, that word *perfect* might turn us off and make us give up without trying. After all, who can be as perfect as God is? But as we increase in our ability to love, we may begin to approach being more all-embracing of others, even of some others we currently find distasteful.

EVOLUTIONARY IMPLICATIONS

Jesus is not creating a religious revolution. He is not overthrowing the Mosaic Law and the Ten Commandments. He is reinterpreting them from the perspective of unconditional love. Instead of *not* doing something bad, love seeks to do something good. Instead of interpreting each commandment literally and restrictively, he looks at each commandment as an invitation to a new, all-embracing mindset. Hidden within each commandment is an invitation to a new way of loving each other, a new way of bringing more life to the community. He is showing us the way to look at everyone with new eyes, eyes that come with adopting his mind and heart.

8

The Lord's Prayer

ALTHOUGH MATTHEW places the Lord's Prayer (6:9–13) in the middle of a chapter on almsgiving, prayer, and fasting, it deserves special treatment as an evolutionary prayer.

The first line contains two very important words—"Our *Father* in *heaven.*"[1] It is important to know what images are in Jesus's Jewish mind when he uses the words *Father* (for God) and *heaven*, because Jesus's meanings may be quite different from what those words currently mean to us.

Our English word *God* comes from a Germanic root that means "good." When we say "God" in English, we picture someone who is totally good. And because we are either/or thinkers, we say that anything that is not good must not be God. We divide the world into good and bad. When we see evil or destruction around us, we say it cannot be of God. For us, God is pure goodness, the opposite of anything evil.

Jesus's idea of God is very different from either of those images. The Aramaic word Jesus uses for God in his prayer is *Alaha*. Its root means "sacred Oneness."[2] For Jesus, God is Oneness—a sacred Union or Unity. It is Oneness that embraces all that exists, all that can be seen and all that is unseen. *Alaha* embraces everyone and everything that exists—*exactly as it exists at any moment, including good and bad.*

That's why Jesus feels free to eat with sinners. He is completely at home with them. When Jesus says things about God and the kingdom of God, his words are based on this concept or understanding of God as *all-embracing Oneness* that loves everything that it embraces. In John's Gospel, Jesus makes explicit his understanding of God as sacred Oneness in his prayer to the Father at the Last Supper (see John 17:21–23).

The Lord's Prayer

Jesus pictures God as all-embracing Oneness or Union in Love. That is "God the Father" to whom Jesus prays. If we pray with this same picture of God, we will no longer feel the need to be overly concerned or obsessed with being bad, sinful, or unworthy. Rather, with this image of God as sacred Oneness we are set free to focus on God's love of us just the way we are right now. And we know for certain that no one can take that divine love from us.[3]

The opening line of the Lord's Prayer, "Our Father who art in heaven," presents a far richer meaning when we look at Jesus's Aramaic words. What Jesus said in Aramaic was *Abwoon d'bwashmaya*.

First, notice that Jesus did not use the formal title of Father, or Patriarch, when he gave us the prayer. For "Father," Jesus used the Aramaic expression *Abwoon*. Not *Abba*, or Daddy, but *Abwoon* — the Father whose love wants to gather everything into his Oneness. The Aramaic spiritual person might picture the divine Oneness — *Abwoon* — breathing out a flow of blessings, like a fragrant perfume drawing us toward him. This sacred Oneness is pure love. Love cannot keep from expressing itself outwardly. God's self-outpouring is like a continuous rainfall where the raindrops are made of love and grace. We all have felt this powerful force of love wanting to express itself outwardly to others — in words, hugs, kisses, gifts, blessings, and actions.

For Jesus and his Aramaic listeners, the word *bwashmaya* — the heavens — holds a much richer meaning than heaven as the place we go after we die. When Jesus uses the Aramaic word for "the heavens," he imagines not merely a collection of galaxies, stars, and planets in outer space. He is seeing *the outpouring of God's blessings on all of God's created reality*. For Jesus, heaven is a cosmic divine milieu pulsing with God's love.

By joining the two Aramaic words, *Abwoon* and *bwashmaya*, Jesus gives us the words by which one can recognize the divine Oneness — or God. The Divine Oneness dwells not in some distant, transcendent heavenly sphere, but is lovingly and actively present in and through everything that was, is, or will be. *Abwoon* is constantly breathing loving existence and blessing into everything that exists.

All that meaning *from the Aramaic* is packed into the opening sentence, "Our Father who art in heaven."

This is the kingdom of God that Jesus has come to announce. This is the "good news," the gospel message. *Abwoon d'bwashmaya* is one more way to express it. It is Oneness actively doing its divine loving unifying work among us right now. You can live in it fully aware, once you undergo the necessary *metanoia* that will open your eyes to see it.

To analyze each of the Aramaic words used in the Lord's Prayer is beyond the scope of this book;[4] however, a paraphrased interpretation of the Aramaic meaning of each line of the prayer is presented here:[5]

Our Father who art in heaven.
Abwoon d'bwashmaya.

O! Sacred Oneness, unconditionally loving parent, you continually reveal yourself by giving birth and ripeness to everyone and everything that has existed, exists now, as well as all that is still waiting to be revealed.

Hallowed be thy name.
Nethqadash shmakh.

May the experience of your holy oneness—the breath, the sound, the colors, the vibrations of your name and your creation—resound and reverberate in our hearts.

Thy kingdom come.
Teytey malkuthakh.

May we desire, as deeply as you desire, that your compassionate and caring guidance will permeate the world and give birth to the loving unity of all things, the oneness that you desire.

Thy will be done on earth as it is in heaven.
Nehwey tzevyanach aykanna d'bwashmaya aph b'arha.

May your heavenly heart's desire become the heart's desire of all of us during our lives on Earth, as we are supported by this planet you gave us for our home.

Give us this day our daily bread.
Hawvlan lachma d'sunquanan yaomana.

54

Please fill us with your daily blessings, especially the spiritual nutrition we need for our growth, both personally and for our life with others.

Forgive us our trespasses as we forgive those who trespass against us.
Washboqlan khaubayn aykanna daph khnan shbwoqan l'khayyabayn.

Wash us completely clean from what keeps us from truly loving ourselves, as we release others from what keeps us from loving them.

And lead us not into temptation
Wela tahlan l'nesyuna

Don't let us be seduced by the surface fascination of things that would divert or distract us from the true purpose of our lives.

But deliver us from evil.
Ela patzan min bisha.

Set us free from our immaturity, our self-absorption, our unripeness so that we may do for you what needs to get done. *Amen.*

The Two Parts

There are two halves to the Lord's Prayer. The first half sets up the foundation of the Gospel's message and the inner structure of the kingdom of God. We learn who *Abwoon* is and all that *bwashmaya* encompasses, which is everything visible and invisible, past, present, and future. We learn of *Abwoon*'s desire to have the divine project fulfilled. This project is for all things to become one loving unity or oneness in *bwashmaya* and specifically on Earth. Earth is just one part of *bwashmaya*. In reciting this first half, we express our desire for the fulfillment of *Abwoon*'s divine project, and we commit to actively participate in it.

The second half of the Lord's Prayer deals with our practical, day-to-day needs if we hope to participate in helping fulfill God's grand desire. Individually and collectively, we ask *Abwoon*'s help in fulfilling our part in this grand project. We express our need for four things each day. First, we ask to be nurtured and fed both in our inner and outer lives. Second, we need to have our slate clean, so that we are unburdened to do our work for God's project. Third, we ask to be freed from a state of inner vacillation, confusion, or agitation that we can easily slip into, and which can divert or distract us from the true purpose of our lives. Fourth, we ask not to become so inward and self-absorbed that we cannot be present to act simply and maturely toward others at the right moment.

Evolutionary Implications

The Lord's Prayer is evolutionary. First, it makes clear that God has a project ("Thy kingdom come!"). It is a project so big that it requires more of us than avoiding sin during our lifetimes. It is a project of loving unity that has not yet been fully realized.

Second, it affirms that we need to be consciously involved in helping complete this divine project ("Thy will be done on Earth…"). In the second half of the prayer, we ask for four things to carry out our personal involvement in this work successfully: (1) physical and spiritual nourishment; (2) souls unburdened and made clean through mutual forgiveness; (3) freedom from distractions and confusion; and (4) growth in emotional and spiritual maturity.

Third, mutual forgiveness is the only specific grace we ask for in the Lord's Prayer. The other three petitions are generic. Why is forgiveness so important to the success of the divine project, since God's forgiveness of us is so complete? Forgiveness among humans must accompany God's forgiveness since only in this way can true loving unity or Oneness be achieved. Without daily mutual forgiveness ("seven times seventy times"), God's project of total unity can never be complete.

An Example of *Metanoia*

When read in Matthew's original Greek text, the second half of the Lord's Prayer is a fine example of praying in the mindset of Jesus. It expresses, subtly but clearly, a shift in the person's attitude toward God. Jesus teaches us to pray to a God who is a loving, nurturing, forgiving, compassionate, and protective Father. We are to pray confidently.

People are used to saying these four petitions in English as they have been translated from the Latin. In Latin, "give us," "forgive us," "lead us not," and "deliver us" are in the *present imperative*. These imperatives imply that we are begging or demanding help from God. Matthew presents them differently. When Jesus says the prayer, these petitions are more an expression of polite gratitude and trust. The difference in emphasis lies in the verb choice.

Matthew's Greek verbs use the *aorist imperative* tense. In classical Greek in general, the aorist imperative is used to make a polite and gracious request ("May I please have…"), and it implies gratitude in response (an inferred "Thank you").

Further, the aorist tense implies that *a past action is continued without any limits or changes*. The aorist imperative implies, "You have been doing this for me all along and I am merely asking you to continue." It has the sense of ("Kindly keep providing [as you always have] our daily bread…"). It contrasts with the *indicative imperative*, which refers to a single immediate request ("Give me now…")[6] and can also sometimes, by tone of voice, be expressed as a demand. Here is a paraphrase of the four petitions according to Matthew's Greek text:

> *Kindly keep providing for us the full nourishment we need each day.* (Implied: You have always done it for us and we know you will keep doing it.)
> *Kindly keep forgiving us for our transgressions and we will keep forgiving those who transgress us.*
> *You are most gracious for not letting us be caught off guard when trials and temptations occur.* (Or: being tricked into temptation.)
> *And kindly keep coming to our rescue when we are being diminished* (e.g., by weakness, sickness, loss, disaster, the cruelty of others).

The Lord's Prayer is Jesus's own prayer. He taught it to the apostles as the prayer he confidently uses when he prays to God. When you pray it, imagine standing alongside Jesus addressing this prayer to his Father. The further challenge is for us to learn to pray the Lord's Prayer *in Jesus's metanoia*.

Jesus presents the Lord's Prayer ("Our Father") as a communal as well as an individual prayer. Teamwork remains essential for the success of God's project. Theologically, since it is the uniquely personal prayer of our Lord (see Luke 11:2–4), even when we pray it, it is Christ's prayer. That is, we pray it in him and through him. Teilhard would suggest that the best way for us to pray the Lord's Prayer is *as members of his Cosmic Body*. When we pray using these words, it is Christ praying to the Father in and through us.

In part 4, we explore Teilhard's *metanoia* in more detail and will see an even richer interpretation of the Lord's Prayer.

9

Faith as Love in Action

IN THE Sermon on the Mount, Jesus described *in words* what living in this higher consciousness (*metanoia*) looks like. In chapter 8 of Matthew's Gospel, Jesus begins to reveal the transforming power of this new consciousness *in action*. Jesus proposes not only a new mindset but also a new way of living, a new way to experience life more deeply.

Love is his primary driving force because it is the driving force of his divine Father. It is also the driving force of God's kingdom. Love is meant to be the driving force of our lives as well. The Gospel presents a new way of living based on a new kind of faith in God—an active faith.

In this spirit of compassionate love, Jesus will do countless healings, each one *an expression of love as an act of faith*. Healing through the energy of faith is a new and evolutionary idea, when we compare it to various ways faith is typically understood and expressed.

Various Expressions of Faith

Hebrew Faith. In the time of Jesus, faith was expressed essentially as *behavioral fidelity* to the tenets of the Mosaic Law. The Pharisees were good examples of such faith. They submitted their intellect and will to the Law. Today, some Christians believe that faith means behavioral fidelity to church law.

Catechetical Faith. In the *Catechism of the Catholic Church*, faith is described as "the adequate response" of believers to God's invitation welcoming them into his kingdom. The *Catechism* states, "By his Revelation, the invisible God, from the fullness of his love, addresses men as his friends, and moves among them, in order to invite and receive them into his own company. The adequate response to this invitation is *faith*."[1]

In the *Catechism's* next paragraph, its description of "adequate response" remains ambiguous. In fact, it requires only the response of "assent." It says, "By *faith*, man completely submits his intellect and his will to God. With his whole being man gives his assent to God the revealer. Sacred Scripture calls this human response to God, the author of revelation, 'the obedience of faith.'"[2]

Liturgical Faith is different. It is expressed during worship as an assent to and *belief in a series of doctrinal statements* as specified in the Nicene Creed. After reciting the Creed, the priest announces, "This is our faith! This is what makes us one!" Apparently, there are no required behavioral components to this type of faith, just a commitment of intellect and will to the Creed's theological dogmas. These creedal doctrines make no mention, as the *Catechism* does, of a God of love addressing humans as friends and inviting them into God's own company.

Gospel Faith, as portrayed in Matthew, Mark, and Luke, presents a striking contrast to the liturgical and catechetical expressions of faith. In the Gospels, faith is *an exercise of love power*. Faith is love in action. Faith gives life where life is weak or nonexistent. Throughout Jesus's public life, the only kind of faith he refers to is that which involves *the exercise of transforming power*. Typically, faith is manifested as an act of healing. Hundreds of times, Jesus heals based on his conviction that God's loving energy is at work in him and expresses itself through him *as faith*. His disciples are instructed to express their faith in the same active way (see Matt 10:1–10; Luke 7:1–23).

When Jesus sends his apostles to other towns, they are not only to announce the presence of the kingdom of God, but also to confirm their announcement of God's good news by doing physical and emotional healing of the sick (see Matt 10:1).

During Jesus's public life, the apostles perform healings alongside him as they travel from town to town. Only when they are unable to heal someone with a serious spiritual illness do they come to Jesus to complete a more difficult case. In one case, Jesus immediately rebukes a demon that the apostles cannot deal with (see Matt 17:16–18). Jesus explains that their inability to heal is their lack of *faith energy*. "If you have faith the size of a mustard seed, you will say to this mountain,

'Move from here to there,' and it will move; and nothing will be impossible for you" (Matt 17:20).

Jesus implies that faith energy can be used to do other things than heal. He will show that it can be used to transform a few loaves of bread and some fish into a meal for thousands. Or enable him to walk on water. Or to calm the winds and the sea. This active faith remains central to Jesus's teaching, and it remains central in the early church as the apostles continue to heal.

St. Paul says, "For in Christ Jesus neither circumcision nor uncircumcision counts for anything; *the only thing that counts is faith working* [i.e., made effective, expressing itself] *through love*" (Gal 5:6).

In the healing stories that Matthew relates in chapter 8, he is saying to his new convert readers, "I am taking you beyond what you and I were taught to do by the scribes and Pharisees. Jesus in his love calls us to live and act beyond the old ways. He is calling us to show love in action."

Faith Energy through Healing (8:1–17)

Each healing event shows how Jesus lifts Judaic religion and practice into a higher form of thought and behavior.

For example, on his way back from the Sermon on the Mount to Capernaum, Jesus encounters a leper and heals him by touch (see 8:1–2). According to Hebrew Law, touching a leper was not permitted and would incur ritual impurity. But Jesus touches the leper and heals him. Jesus demonstrates that the leper is not spiritually unclean. Rather, the sick man needs to be lovingly touched into health. Jesus is affirming that anyone who touches a leper with love and compassion does not become ritually unclean. Just to show that Jesus has no intention of overthrowing the Mosaic Law, he tells the cured leper to observe the law: "Go, show yourself to the priest, and offer the gift that Moses commanded, as a testimony to them" (8:4).

JESUS HEALS A CENTURION'S SERVANT (8:5–13)

As Jesus enters Capernaum, he meets a centurion. The centurion is a Roman officer in charge of a hundred soldiers. He is a powerful person. The military officer asks Jesus to cure his servant, and Jesus does so. This is the first time Jesus's disciples experience Jesus *curing at a distance*, without ever seeing the sick person. Jesus shows that he can cure sick people without needing to touch them or even be physically present.

Matthew is also presenting to his readers a Roman pagan who displays this new kind of faith—faith in action. Jesus says, "Truly I tell you, in no one in Israel have I found such faith" (8:10).

In the old mindset, a Jew would never help an enemy of Israel, especially one who represents the Roman army that subjugates and taxes Israel. But the God of love who cares for everyone comes to the aid of all who call upon him. Jesus's welcome of the Roman oppressor into the world of faith—and recipient of God's love—marks another evolutionary step.

Notice that both the leper and the centurion add the energy of their own active faith to that of Jesus. It is a combined active faith. Jesus heals most effectively when others share his active faith and believe that he has the power to heal.

This chapter in Matthew is filled with lessons on how to use active faith. He wants us to understand gospel faith because it is the kind of faith that Jesus invites and expects his disciples to develop. It is a new kind of faith, evolutionary in its implications. It is a faith that comes to bring a fuller experience of life.

JESUS HEALS PETER'S MOTHER-IN-LAW (8:14–17)

Jesus arrives at Peter's home, only to find Peter's mother-in-law sick. Without hesitating, Jesus heals her. "He touched her hand, and the fever left her, and she got up and began to serve him" (8:15). Here, Jesus expresses another aspect of faith energy: it is *spontaneous*. It is always ready to serve others. Once healed, she is capable of being a proper hostess. Jesus does his act of love by healing her, so she can in turn do her act of love by serving him. The kingdom that Jesus has come to reveal is one of mutual service, not simply one of obeying the Law.

JESUS HEALS MANY AT PETER'S HOUSE (8:16)

When the meal is over, they discover a line of people standing just outside Peter's front door. "That evening they brought to him many who were possessed with demons; and he cast out the spirits with a word, and cured all who were sick" (8:16). One more new expression of faith: *Jesus can heal emotional and spiritual illnesses* as well as physical ones. The many healings also point out that Jesus's faith energy is so strong that he can use it to heal one person after another.

Why does Jesus do all these healings? There is no indication that Jesus is trying to prove that he is divine or to impress people with his powers, though we can be sure that many are amazed. He seems to heal simply because he loves people and wants them to enjoy the fullness of life.

Based on Jesus's understanding of God as Oneness, his healings also reestablish community relationships that have been harmed. Once sick people are healed, they can contribute again to the life of the community, as did Peter's mother-in-law, the centurion's servant, and especially the leper.

Evolutionary Implications

In this chapter, Matthew reveals a most basic evolutionary advance, although he is unaware of it as an evolutionary event. It is the way Jesus portrays his understanding and application of faith. For the Jews, faith means fidelity to the Law. And the proper response of faith is obedience to the Law.

Jesus is evolving this passive notion of "faith as behavioral conformity to law." He takes it to an active stage where faith provides the energy for a creative loving response to specific situations. Faith is meant to bring more life.

In his demonstrations of active faith, Jesus also shifts the focus of our understanding of God. Jesus sees God, not as a Lawgiver, but as an attentive Loving Parent. Making this shift in our understanding of the nature of God enables "believers" (of whatever faith tradition) to do works of compassion, care, creativity, and collaboration.

For Jesus of Nazareth, faith has little to do either with giving assent to a list of doctrines or with obeying a religious law. For him, the faith that we practice is far more focused on *an inner conviction that each of us possesses a power for good.* We have confidence in our ability to make a positive difference in the world. It includes the conviction that God and the universe will support us in such actions. Jesus assures his disciples, "I will do whatever you ask in my name, so that the Father may be glorified in the Son" (John 14:13).

Jesus encourages his disciples again and again to develop this new kind of "faith in action" that releases energy to make a positive difference. Such love energy is already within them. They merely need to develop the mindset that gives them access to that energy. For Teilhard, it is a call to evolve.

For Jesus, the mission to do the healing actions of faith extends throughout time to all those who live his Way of faith. Jesus has access to all the Father's power to enable you and me to make a loving impact on the world today. He willingly gives that faith power to everyone (see John 14:12–14).

To use contemporary examples: Jesus in his many active expressions of faith may well be predicting the active kind of faith Dr. Jonas Salk would demonstrate when he believed he could find an inoculation to prevent polio. Or that Thomas Edison showed when he believed he could find a filament for his invention of the incandescent light bulb. Or that Albert Einstein had when he believed he could find a mathematical formula to explain his theory of relativity.

Out of a faith expressed as love in action, people have started schools for the blind, legal groups to protect immigrants, homes for abused wives and children, labor unions to ensure workers' rights, publishing houses, libraries, hospitals, orphanages, food banks, new forms of communication, and so on. Jesus shows us that faith is a way to enhance others' experience of life.

Jesus's faith is the kind of active faith that has the energy to accomplish good works, even seemingly impossible ones. The expressions of faith he calls us to develop include all actions that help the community experience life more fully.

Recognize your power to make a difference and release it on the world.

10

Forgiveness and Fullness of Life

Jesus Heals a Paralytic (9:2–8)

WHEN THEIR BOAT arrives at the familiar Capernaum shore, people are waiting for them. Here, Matthew presents an example of *collaborative faith*. He describes how group faith can help heal someone. A small group carries a paralyzed man lying on a bed. When Jesus sees *their* faith, he says to the paralytic, "Take heart, son; your sins are forgiven."

There are several new things to observe in this story. First, in the expression of active faith, Jesus recognizes *the faith of the people carrying the paralyzed man*—"Jesus saw *their* faith" (9:2). The paralytic himself may not have faith in the healing power of Jesus, but the stretcher-bearers do. That is enough for Jesus to heal. Honoring *the faith of a group of friends interceding* for a sick man is another expression of the gospel's evolutionary advance.

There will always be disciples with strong faith willing to help others who lack it. St. Paul recognizes that the special kind of faith needed to perform healings is a specific gift given to certain believers. He understands that members of the Christian community are each given different gifts. Among these gifts are the gifts of healing, teaching, preaching, comforting, mediating, counseling, organizing, and raising money (see 1 Cor 12:4–11). They are all ways of enriching the experience of life.

Second, in healing the paralytic, Jesus is, for the first time, openly dealing with sin and the forgiveness of sin. Sin is a major issue in Jewish religious tradition. Note what Jesus says: "Take heart, son; your sins are forgiven." He is announcing a fact; he is not at that moment doing the forgiving.

Although the English translation "are forgiven" is ambiguous, the original Greek text is clear. The Greek verb for "are forgiven" is in the *indicative perfect*, a verb tense that is used to describe *an act begun in the past, completed in the past, that keeps continuing*. The forgiveness of the man's sins is an event completed in the past. God the Father has long ago forgiven the sins this man committed. And the Father will continue to forgive the man's sins. Jesus is merely announcing the fact.

The idea that God is continually forgiving the sins that we commit—almost as soon as we commit them—is such a radically evolutionary idea about the nature of God that many cannot accept it. Even in the paralytic's story, the English translation may easily be interpreted as if Jesus was doing the forgiving at the moment. But the Greek text is quite clear. Jesus is simply announcing a fact that God's forgiveness of the paralytic is an act that happened in the past. Through the parable of the prodigal son, Luke's Gospel confirms without question the astounding revelation of God's continuing readiness to forgive.

The parable of the prodigal son (Luke 15:11–32) reinforces this idea of God forgiving our sins even before we ask for forgiveness. The prodigal son sins against his father the moment he takes his share of the inheritance and leaves home. The key question to ask is, *When did the father forgive his son?* The father's act of forgiveness happens long before the son comes home. The father is waiting for the son when the son is still far off. He requires no confession from the son and feels no need to hear the confession the son has prepared and is beginning to make. All has been forgiven already. Jesus presents the father in the parable as a symbol of our heavenly Father.

Significant to the parable of the prodigal son is Jesus's evolutionary perspective on forgiveness in that we may assume that God is always willing to forgive us. What is most important to the Father is that the sinner return home and become active in the Father's work on the estate again. Jesus is telling us not to spend our energy worrying that God might not forgive our sin. Such worrying is not where God wants us to spend our efforts. God expects us to realize that, like the prodigal son, we are always welcomed home. In the Father's forgiving love, we are set free to spend our effort on the Father's work in his kingdom.

Neither the Pharisees nor the audience present at the healing of the paralytic get Jesus's message about divine forgiveness. They believe Jesus did the forgiving. "They [the audience] glorified God, who had given such authority to *human beings*" (9:8). The scribes assert that Jesus announcing the forgiveness of sin is blasphemy, since only God can forgive sin.

Theologically, the sin of blasphemy occurs when someone presents oneself as divine or acts as though one is God. In Jewish theology, only God could forgive sin. To the scribes, when Jesus purports to forgive the paralytic's sins, he is acting as though he is God.

So, given the Pharisees' assumption, Jesus poses a question to them: "Which is easier, to say, 'Your sins are forgiven,' or to say, 'Stand up and walk?'" (9:5). In performing this miracle, Jesus is saying, "The Law says both the forgiveness of sins and miraculous healings are actions that only God can do. As the Son of Man, I am doing both actions, forgiving sin and healing sickness. Neither action is exclusive to God. Human beings can do both actions."

EVOLUTIONARY IMPLICATIONS

The scribes can only see Jesus's behavior as a contradiction or *violation of the Law* and a usurping of the unique privilege of the divine Lawgiver. For Jesus, however, mutual forgiving and healing among humans expresses a *fulfillment of the Law*. Jesus is presenting another evolutionary understanding of the true meaning of the Law. It is also a reminder of the central importance of mutual forgiveness in Jesus's evolved teaching and its special place in the Lord's Prayer. God will always concur with mutual forgiveness among humans. It is an affirmation that the heavenly Father is an unconditional lover.

Salvation and the Fullness of Life

The next two healing events are examples of active faith, the faith that heals and makes whole. Each event reveals something different about the way faith works.

The woman with hemorrhages believes Jesus can heal her *without him even being aware of it*—just by her touching the fringe of his cloak (9:20–23). And it works, except that Jesus does feel healing energy flow out of him and he tells her so. He also points out that it is *her faith* that made her well. Jesus isn't taking the credit for her healing; he attributes it to her faith.[1] This woman demonstrates one more way of using active faith to tap into love's healing energy.

In healing the synagogue leader's little girl who has died (9:18–19, 23–26), Jesus simply takes the dead girl by the hand and brings her back to life. Active faith, if strong enough, can *raise someone from the dead*.[2]

In these many healing events reported by Matthew, Jesus is reinforcing his new meaning of the word *salvation*. For him, in the kingdom of God, *salvation means enjoying the fullness of life*.

Bringing the fullness of life to others in whatever ways are available to us is a basic spiritual practice in Jesus's Way. According to Teilhard, in God's project, we are all assigned to bring the fullness of life to one another and to all creatures here on Earth. When we promise God, "Thy will be done on Earth," God, in effect, replies, "Then go, bring the fullness of life to one another in every way you can."

JESUS HEALS TWO BLIND MEN (9:27–29)

As Jesus is walking toward someone's home, "two blind men follow him, crying loudly, 'Have mercy on us, Son of David!'" (9:27). When he enters the house, the blind men come in after him (even though they don't live there). They are determined to get healed. They want to enjoy a fuller life. They are not going to let Jesus evade them.

So, Jesus engages them in a dialogue, testing their active faith. "Do you believe that I am able to do this?" They say to him, "Yes, Lord." Jesus directs his healing energy toward them and says, "According to your faith let it be done to you" (9:28–29). It is not simply Jesus doing the healing. Jesus is telling them that they will be healed to the degree that they actively believe they will be healed. Faith healing involves a partnership. Both the healer and the healed combine their faith to effect the healing.

EVOLUTIONARY IMPLICATIONS

In traditional Hebrew understanding, sickness was regarded as a form of punishment for sin by God. They believed it was fruitless to attempt to seek healing from a human physician since they assumed that sickness is imposed by God. Thus, no human could simply and directly cure a person.

Jesus turns the notion of "sickness as divine punishment" upside down. Evils like sickness, loss, accidents, and the like are inevitable in a complex, fallible world where we all must die. God does not have to produce sickness or any other evil. They simply happen. In doing healings, Jesus is teaching us that God is the loving Father who wants everyone to have the fullness of health. Therefore, acts of healing become a symbol and a validation of the kingdom of God at work. In God's project to renew the face of the Earth, all healing—physical, psychological, and spiritual—is of key importance to God's plan. Jesus is not only blessing healings performed by humans through active faith, he sees any form of healing as a special sign of God's active loving presence.

Jesus is affirming all the many different forms of healing that will happen in the following centuries. These emerging signs of God's active loving presence include the founding of hospitals, the practice of medicine and surgery, psychotherapy, nursing, pharmaceuticals, antibiotics, organ transplants, prosthetics, sanitation, nutrition, exercise regimens, vaccinations for disease prevention, hospice, and a host of other healing practices. All of them are designed to help bring about salvation, that is, the fullness of life.

11

Discipleship

Jesus Calls the First Disciples (4:18–22)

VERY EARLY in his ministry, Jesus is walking along the shore of the Sea of Galilee in the morning as groups of fishermen are sorting their catch or mending their nets. He says to two brothers, Peter and Andrew, "Follow me, and I will make you fish for people." The two leave their fishing nets behind and follow Jesus. A little farther on, Jesus comes up to another pair of brothers, James and John, mending their nets. He gives the same command to them. They too leave their nets behind and follow him.

One of the requirements of committed discipleship is an immediate and total response to Jesus's call. "Immediately they left their nets and followed him" (4:20). They "left their nets" means giving up their livelihood and careers, and "immediately" means they make no excuses nor ask for time to think it over. The response of the first four disciples is in contrast with other would-be followers, whose response is not immediate and total.

For example, one day, as Jesus and his small band of disciples are on their way, two men, who have been deeply impressed by Jesus's healing work, come up to him and ask to become his disciples.

The first of these, as Matthew notes, is a scribe. Scribes are essentially upper-class Jews who know how to read and write classic Hebrew. Many of the scribes are also teachers of the Law, for which they are revered and treated royally. So, when this eager scribe says, "Teacher, I will follow you wherever you go," Jesus tells him that, to become a traveling disciple with his group, he must give up his comfortable, prestigious life. Or, as Jesus puts it, "Foxes have holes, and birds of the air have nests; but the Son of Man has nowhere to lay his head" (8:20). We hear no more of this man. Evidently, when he hears Jesus's comment and the conditions of discipleship, his eagerness greatly diminishes.

The second enlistee seems eager but wants to delay his recruitment. "Lord, first let me go and bury my father." (Such a delay might consume several weeks, as the son would have to sit Shiva for seven days and, afterwards, take care of all the family's financial arrangements.) But Jesus says to him, "Follow me, and let the dead bury their own dead" (8:21–22). Jesus's response to the man—"Let the dead bury their own dead"—is a cryptic comment. Jesus is telling the man that as long as he remains primarily involved in family matters and views those matters as an essential concern, he cannot fully commit to working alongside Jesus. His heart remains divided.

This man realizes that to follow Jesus as a true disciple requires a total *metanoia* as well as a reenvisioning of what it means to serve the kingdom of God. Jesus is so single-minded that he needs people with him, as intimate disciples, whose commitment is immediate and total—like that of the four fishermen and Matthew.

The Call of Matthew (9:9–13)

If we lived in the time of Jesus, we would be surprised that Jesus personally *chose* Matthew to become a member of his intimate band. Jesus invites a man mistrusted by the Jewish community to become his trusted apostle. Matthew is considered a public sinner and a traitor to Judaism because he is a Jew collecting Roman taxes from the pockets of his own countrymen. However, unlike the two would-be disciples who offer excuses and delays for joining Jesus, Matthew immediately "got up and followed him" (9:9).

To celebrate his new calling, Matthew throws a dinner party for Jesus and his apostles. It is a big party, since "many tax collectors and sinners came and were sitting with him and his disciples" (9:10). By Mosaic Law, an observant Jew is not permitted to sit down and share a meal with anyone who is a public sinner—to say nothing of sitting with a group of them. Once again, Jesus is doing something new and unheard of. What he is really doing is *transcending the Mosaic Law by fulfilling it*. The Father wants all people—even those burdened by sin and ritual impurity—to have the fullness of life.

EVOLUTIONARY IMPLICATIONS

What is new and evolutionary about Jesus's choice of disciples is that they do not need to be educated, respected, wealthy, or upper class. None of the Twelve is versed in Hebrew. None of them qualifies as a scholar of the Law. None of them is a disciple of a recognized teacher, as Paul was of Gamaliel.[1] None of the twelve apostles enjoys any authority as a member of the priestly class or as a representative in the Sanhedrin. Jesus's apostles don't even have to be free of sin. They can even be rejects of Jewish society, like Matthew the tax collector. Jesus doesn't set any other conditions for being a disciple or to walk alongside him, except that their response to his invitation is immediate and total.

The Disciples of John the Baptist (9:14–17)

The scribes and Pharisees aren't the only ones who have difficulty with Jesus. The disciples of John the Baptist do as well. One day, the disciples of John come to Jesus, saying, "Why do we and the Pharisees fast often, but your disciples do not fast?" (9:14).

John the Baptist and his followers, despite their goodness, are still living and thinking in the old ways. Not only are Jesus's disciples expected to respond to their calling immediately and fully, they must also learn to think and act differently. They must undergo a *metanoia*.

To explain to them the difference between the Baptist's disciples and his disciples, Jesus uses three different images.

First, Jesus's disciples are like the *groom's friends* at a wedding feast enjoying themselves. One cannot be fasting and feasting at the same time (9:15).

The other two images are *cloth* and *wine*. Jesus is telling them that it is time to evolve beyond what John the Baptist is teaching. Jesus says,

No one sews a piece of unshrunk cloth on an old cloak,
for the patch pulls away from the cloak, and a worse tear is

made. Neither is new wine put into old wineskins; otherwise, the skins burst, and the wine is spilled, and the skins
are destroyed; but new wine is put into fresh wineskins, and
so both are preserved. (9:16–17)

The fresh "cloth" of Jesus's new Way cannot simply be sewn onto the
old cloth, nor can his new wine be poured into traditional containers.
Jesus's new Way will either tear apart the old cloth or split open the
old wineskins. Notice the evolutionary quality of the new Way in these
images. If the old way is like a cloth garment, so is the new Way. The
new Way "garment" cannot simply become part of an old garment; it
stands by itself. Yet it is still a garment. Similarly with the wine. Both
the old and the new wines are wines, but old wine containers have
limits. Just as new wine needs a new container, so the new Way needs
a new container, one that is fresh and resilient enough to hold it. The
new container is Jesus's new mindset (*metanoia*).

The Baptist's old wineskins—just like the Pharisees' old
wineskins—cannot contain Jesus's teachings. Jesus's new wine presents
God as an unconditionally loving Father. This new understanding will
burst asunder the old wineskin that presents God as a harsh Judge.

EVOLUTIONARY IMPLICATIONS

This chapter shows how Jesus's teaching and his Way has evolved
beyond the three traditional "containers": (1) the strictly legalist interpretation of the Mosaic Law of the scribes, (2) the rigorous practices of
spirituality demanded by the Pharisees, and (3) the simple repentance-
for-sin practices of John the Baptist's disciples.

Along with the evolutionary step Jesus's Way takes beyond the
Mosaic Law, a parallel evolution occurs in understanding the nature
of God. This new understanding of God as loving Father creates a new
"container." For the scribes, God is a supreme Lawgiver. For the Pharisees, God is a strict Judge. For the Baptist, God is a merciful Lord, but
still preoccupied with sin and repentance. Jesus transcends all three
images of God and offers instead a divine unconditionally loving Father
whose primary wish is for his children to enjoy the fullness of life.

Jesus describes this new understanding of God as a "fulfillment."
At that time, people had no word to describe the transformation of

any system as an evolutionary process. *Fulfillment* was one of the best words available to them.

Jesus tells us that in our prayer we are to address God as "Our Father." God, like a loving father, wants us to be healthy in body, mind, and spirit—to be full of life. In his healing of the sick, Jesus brings fullness of life to the diseased human body. In driving out demons, he brings fullness of life to confused minds. In his assurance of the Father's forgiveness, he brings fullness of life to the weak human spirit. The Father wants all three forms of life's "fullness."

The Harvest Is Great, the Laborers Few (9:35–38)

When Jesus saw the large crowds and envisioned the many who would never meet him or hear his message, he realized the need for more disciples, laborers who would bring the good news to all people.

Here, Jesus is calling for a new kind of "clergy." They are to be spiritual guides who understand God as Love. Such laborers in God's kingdom will have two basic roles: *teacher and healer*. These are the two main roles that Jesus lives out, and they are the two roles he asks of his disciples.

As teachers, his disciples are to announce the good news that God is an unconditional loving Father and that we are all brothers and sisters of "Our Father." As healers, they are to promote the fullness of life for all—physical, psychological, and spiritual—in whatever ways they can.

The two images Jesus uses to describe his disciples are "shepherds" and "laborers." Shepherds are totally responsible for the lives of their sheep. Most likely, they are poorly paid and get little or no time off from their work. Laborers, unlike owners of vineyards and farms, do all the menial and backbreaking work. They, too, are poorly paid and work long hours.

Jesus wants his disciples to be totally and permanently dedicated to the work of the kingdom of God—like shepherds and laborers.

EVOLUTIONARY IMPLICATIONS

In the old dispensation, the priests, scribes, and Pharisees proclaimed the Mosaic Law, emphasizing what was forbidden. Jesus fulfills (*evolves*) the Mosaic Law and emphasizes what is possible. His followers are to create whatever love makes possible. The old dispensation used fear and guilt as motivation; the new *metanoia* uses active faith and creativity spurred on by love to create the future.

In the old dispensation, the priests and teachers were revered as leaders and members of an exclusive upper class. Jesus says his disciples are to be like shepherds and laborers, at home among the poor, the lonely, the sick, the outcasts, the forgotten, and the sinners.

For Jesus, God's temple is not a building of inert stones, but one built of people—living stones. It will become a spiritual building as big as the planet. The kingdom of God is already alive and at work always and everywhere.

12

Explaining God's Project

The Discourse on Parables (13:1–53)

PARABLES ARE central to Jesus's method of preaching. He uses
parables to highlight certain qualities about the kingdom of God.
A parable is a teaching story containing one or more instructive points,
lessons, or principles. The parables in this chapter offer at least eight
different images to describe the kingdom of God: (1) the parable of the
sower; (2) the weeds among the wheat; (3) the mustard seed; (4) the
yeast in flour; (5) the hidden treasure, (6) the merchant in search of a
pearl; (7) a fisherman's net; and (8) a full storehouse.

Jesus's parables usually have three parts: they sketch a setting,
describe an action, and show the results. For example, "A sower went
out to sow [setting]. And as he sowed, some seeds fell on the path
[action], and the birds came and ate them up [results]" (13:3–4).

Although the meaning of these parables is often not explicitly
stated, their meaning is not intended to be hidden or secret but to
be quite straightforward and obvious. However, as Jesus sometimes
remarks, "People listen but they don't hear." In other words, they don't
"get" it. They haven't undergone the *metanoia*, the ways of thinking
and seeing that enable a person to grasp the meaning of these parables
and how they reveal certain characteristics of God's project for Earth.

Parables have a unique value in that their metaphorical language
allows people to more easily discuss or reflect on difficult or complex
ideas. For example, in the parable of the sower: Who is the sower?
What does the seed symbolize? What do the birds symbolize? What do

the thorns symbolize? What does good ground symbolize? What does the produce symbolize?

Jesus most often uses parables to reveal some truth, quality, or aspect of the kingdom of God. Since each of the many parables in this chapter has its own point,[1] we can infer one thing: Jesus is unable to capture completely the nature of the kingdom of God (God's project) in a single parable. To better understand the kingdom and its many processes, it helps to collate and organize the meaning or purpose of each parable, as with jigsaw puzzle pieces, and assemble them into a coherent whole.

Through the parables, Jesus describes the kingdom's inner dynamics. In other words, Jesus attempts to capture in active imagery how God works and what God is trying to accomplish in the world.

From his evolutionary perspective, Teilhard wants us to recognize how the revelations hidden in each parable can help describe a divine project that is continually transforming itself according to the laws of evolution.

THE PARABLE OF THE SOWER (13:1–9)

The first parable, of the sower and the seed, is broad and sweeping. For Teilhard, this might serve as an initial, general parable about the divine project and our human responsibility in it. God is the primary sower, but the sower may refer to anyone who brings the *"word of the kingdom"* (God's project) to others. The many different places where the seed falls shows that the good news of the gospel is being spread everywhere.

Jesus explicitly tells his disciples that the seed represents "the word of the kingdom" (13:19). One might also say this "seed" is the divine grace given to us to recognize and accept the good news of the gospel message. Humans are the "ground" that receives the word of God. We are not equally receptive to the seed (grace) nor equally productive in acting upon it: some of us are like rocky ground; others like thorns.

Clearly, God is focused on recipients who will work for the kingdom's growth and development. "This is the one who hears the word and understands it, who indeed bears fruit and yields, in one case a hundredfold, in another sixty, and in another thirty" (13:23). God's project requires the effort and creativity of countless people to help it grow to completion.

THE PARABLE OF THE WHEAT AND WEEDS
(13:24–30)

Jesus further refines his description of the kingdom of God with another parable about wheat and weeds. What about the seed that falls on good ground? Does it have any trouble growing? How does the kingdom of God deal with weeds growing among the wheat? Weeds also flourish in good soil.

First, those who till the soil for a living would have told Jesus that weeds take energy and nutrition from the soil. It is wise to remove weeds as early as possible, before they get deeply rooted, when it is easier to pull them out. Again, no farmer would harvest "the weeds first and bind them in bundles to be burned" (13:30). That would be an impossible task. Moreover, it would be hard to imagine an enemy with a bag full of "weed seed" planting them in a wheat field. The simple truth is that *weeds are simply present in most soil*. Weeds are everywhere, as any backyard gardener knows. This parable about wheat and weeds is symbolic. Jesus tells this parable to explain a familiar dynamic operating among humans in the divine kingdom (wheat fields) on Earth.

From Teilhard's perspective, this parable tells us that even the one who understands the word of God and puts it into practice will have to contend with "weeds." Perhaps, for someone committed to working for God's project, the weeds symbolize distractions, busyness, misunderstandings, prejudices, disagreements, accidents, illness, financial problems, and so on. *Such "weeds" are present in most people's lives.* In this case, the landowner in the parable (God) wisely realizes the danger if his workmen get focused on the weeds—those unavoidable diminishments that affect everyone—while missing the more important concern: growing the wheat. The slaves tending the field are mistakenly obsessed with getting rid of the weeds; the landowner is not. In God's project, God is not focused on the source of the weeds. Nor is God trying to evade or excuse the inevitable diminishments that we all experience in our service to God's project because of those weeds. Those diminishments will always be a part of even the most faithful servant's life. Rather, the parable reminds us that God is focused on the produce: "Gather the wheat into my barn." (13:30)

In his evolutionary understanding of God's work on Earth, Teilhard tells us we are not to get caught up in trying to eliminate life's inevitable diminishments ("weeds"). We all need to deal with them as we help to make a better, more loving world. Stay focused, Teilhard would advise, on moving the divine work forward ("gathering the wheat").

The Parable of the Mustard Seed (13:31–32)

The parable of the mustard seed is about producing visible results for the kingdom of God. It describes the way some visible results are achieved, expressed, and spread. Since Jesus puts his attention on the mustard seed and its small size, he may be focused on the *growth potential* of God's project that can be accomplished with only a small amount of faith:

> The kingdom of heaven is like a mustard seed that some-one took and sowed in his field; it is the smallest of all the seeds, but when it has grown it is the greatest of shrubs and becomes a tree, so that the birds of the air come and make nests in its branches.

For Teilhard, this parable offers another insight into the powerful visible impact that even a small amount of faith or love—the size of a mustard seed—can have in spreading the work and influence of God's project. "For truly I tell you, if you have faith the size of a mustard seed, you will say to this mountain, 'Move from here to there,' and it will move; and nothing will be impossible for you" (Matt 17:20).

The Parable of the Yeast (13:33)

For Teilhard, this parable emphasizes the hidden, invisible dimensions of God's kingdom and its unseen and unrecognized work in the world.

> The kingdom of heaven is like yeast that a woman took and mixed in with three measures of flour until all of it was leavened.

The yeast takes the grains of wheat ground into flour and fills them with growth energy. The yeast is the secret hidden ingredient that quietly penetrates the flour. In God's project, the kingdom has a secret ingredient that quietly penetrates the heart, permeates it, and expands it. For Teilhard, love, the inner drive to form caring relationships, provides the energy that keeps moving God's project forward. Yeast may also symbolize the active faith that Jesus talks about in his many scenes of healing.

From an evolutionary perspective, symbiotic bonding is one of the most common ways species' evolution happens. Symbiosis describes the process of two different things joining together to create a new, third thing. Although the Gospel writers know nothing about this evolutionary process, they understand the power of a symbiotic union. They know that when you knead together flour, water, and yeast, and put the mixture in a warm atmosphere, you create something new. The mixture grows and can be baked into bread. None of the individual ingredients by themselves can become bread. But in their symbiotic joining, they can. Love and faith are the yeast that interpenetrate our efforts for God and transform them with new energy.

THE PARABLE OF THE HIDDEN TREASURE (13:44)

For Teilhard, the image of finding a hidden treasure might reflect the joy that one discovers when one realizes that God has a project to transform the world and that one can join in God's work:

> The kingdom of heaven is like treasure hidden in a field, which someone found and hid; then in his joy he goes and sells all that he has and buys that field.

Those chosen ones who find the treasure are privileged to be called to participate actively in God's project. Finding that one's true purpose in life is to be part of God's project is worth selling all that one has. The first four apostles recognized the "treasure" in sharing that privilege. They left their nets (their entire livelihood) and followed him. They bought in, immediately and totally.

The Parable of the Merchant in Search of a Pearl (13:45–46)

Teilhard would point out the difference between treasure discovered almost by accident, as in the previous parable, and the *pearl merchant*, who, in this parable, is professionally and specifically looking for a pearl of great value.

> Again, the kingdom of heaven is like a merchant in search of fine pearls; on finding one pearl of great value, he went and sold all that he had and bought it.

Here, the pearl merchant symbolizes the kingdom of God. You and I represent the "pearls." If we can't find the kingdom by ourselves, the kingdom—and those working in it—will come in search of us.[2] Searching and being searched for are the key images in this parable. For Teilhard, those already actively involved in service of the kingdom (the merchant) are always looking not only for human "pearls," but also for whatever they can do creatively to further the scope and abilities of human endeavor. Finding some special thing (a pearl of great value) that can help move the human family one small step closer to God is a worthy objective—a pearl—in the kingdom.

The Parable of the Kingdom of Heaven (13:47–50)

The net is the focus of the next parable:

> Again, the kingdom of heaven is like a net that was thrown into the sea and caught fish of every kind; when it was full, they drew it ashore, sat down, and put the good into baskets but threw out the bad. (13:47–48)

The fishermen who pull the net into shore are secondary. This parable is all about the net and its contents. The net itself will gather all kinds of people—*fish of every kind*—into the kingdom. The point is that God does not exclude anyone from listening to the message or joining the flock. Only in the fullness of time—*when the net is full*—will there be a reckoning.

CONCLUSION (13:51–53)

An observation about all the parables of the kingdom is that God's work on Earth is *alive*. It is acting and producing results. Sometimes the action is evident, as in the growth and spread of the mustard tree. At other times it is quietly functioning in hidden ways, like yeast leavening the dough.

Jesus is not telling parables to entertain or to show how clever and creative he is. His parables are a training session for his disciples. At the end of the parables, Jesus summarizes the overall lesson his disciples should learn. Not surprisingly, he does it in the form of a parable. He pictures his disciples as scribes.

> Therefore every scribe who has been trained for the kingdom of heaven is like the master of a household who brings out of his treasure what is new and what is old. (13:52)

In Jerusalem, scribes were trained to administer the Mosaic Law. In the new dispensation, disciples are trained to work in the kingdom of heaven. They are to act like a skillful master who knows how to use all the tools and abilities at his command—*his treasure* (some translations say "storehouse"). Some of the valuable items in his storehouse will include skills, abilities, or resources he developed in the past (*what is old*) or abilities and resources recently acquired (*what is new*).

EVOLUTIONARY IMPLICATIONS

For Teilhard, this might suggest that wise disciples in God's kingdom take inventory of all the means they might have at their disposal to use to help fulfill God's project. Each of us has a storehouse of resources. It is important to do an inventory. Sometimes there are valuable things inside of us that we might have forgotten that we can use to help build the kingdom.

PART III

THE GOSPEL OF MARK

THE TRUE AUTHOR of the Gospel according to Mark is unknown. Early Christian tradition ascribes it to John Mark, a companion and Greek interpreter of the apostle Peter.[1] Tradition suggests that Mark assisted Peter and wrote this Gospel to preserve Peter's perspective on Jesus of Nazareth. Peter refers to Mark as a "son" (see 1 Pet 5:13).

Mark's Gospel is the earliest of the four Gospels, probably completed between the years 66 and 70. Most scholars agree that Mark wrote his Gospel for Gentile converts living in Rome.

In the Gospel's opening verse, the author states that he is bringing the gospel to his readers. For Mark, the gospel is not simply "good news" but "*the* good news." Mark uses the expression "*the* gospel" more often than any other New Testament writer besides Paul. Today we hear the expression so frequently that we seldom consider its meaning. What is "the good news" that Jesus brings us from God?

Unlike Matthew and Luke, Mark does not provide a genealogy of Jesus nor stories about his birth or youth. For Mark, everything important about Jesus begins at his baptism by John the Baptist in the River Jordan. Mark expresses great interest in the people of Galilee, since more than half of his text is devoted to Jesus's ministry in that northern-most portion of Israel.

Unlike Matthew and Luke, Mark's text contains no Beatitudes, no Lord's Prayer, no Golden Rule—and most surprisingly, in certain ancient manuscripts, no resurrection appearances. According to some scholars, this Gospel narrative in its original form ends abruptly: "So they went out and fled from the tomb, for terror and amazement had seized them; and they said nothing to anyone, for they were afraid" (16:8). Other early manuscripts add twelve more verses to Mark's final chapter, including an appearance to Mary Magdalene and the ascension (16:9–20).

The verses in Mark's Gospel narrating Jesus's deeds far outnumber those dedicated to his teachings. So, in exploring his Gospel for its evolutionary movement, we turn primarily to the miracles and works of Jesus. However, Jesus's teachings and parables, few as they are, also prove very important. By studying Jesus's words and actions, we can begin to deduce "the good news."

Mark presents his Gospel narrative from two perspectives: that of the *reader* and that of *the crowds listening to Jesus*. To us, the readers, Mark reveals in the first verse that Jesus is the Son of God. Yet, to Jesus's audience and those around him, Mark implies that Jesus wishes to keep his divinity secret from them.[2] Throughout Mark's Gospel account, Jesus conceals his divine identity in parables and actions so that even the disciples are puzzled and fail to recognize who he really is. For example, when Jesus calms the stormy sea, his apostles are filled with great awe and say to one another, "Who then is this, that even the wind and the sea obey him?" (4:41).

Mark is writing as if his readers are aware that Jesus is divine, but the people in his audience and even the disciples still don't realize it. We know the secret, but they don't. Mark tells us that the people in Israel at the time see Jesus as a heroic man of action, an exorcist, a healer, and a miracle worker. Eventually, they too come to realize that he is much more.

Mark is a great storyteller. His stories contain powerful visual details. He alone describes how John the Baptist looks and what he eats. "Now John was clothed with camel's hair, with a leather belt around his waist, and he ate locusts and wild honey" (1:6). When Jesus calls four fishermen to be his first disciples, Mark notes that they "were in their boat mending the nets" (1:19). In the healing of the paralytic, Mark specifies that there are four men carrying his stretcher. They break open the roof exactly above where Jesus is sitting amid the crowd—"they removed the roof above him; and after having dug through it, they let down the mat on which the paralytic lay" (2:4).

Mark tells the longest and most detailed version of Herodias's daughter's dance and the beheading of John the Baptist (see 6:14–29).

However, the story that dominates Mark's Gospel narrative is Jesus's passion and death. Early on, Mark announces the emerging plot to kill Jesus (see 3:6). Matthew and Luke don't mention the plot until much later (see Matt 12:14; Luke 19:47). Mark also anticipates the passion by including three separate predictions of it (see 8:31; 9:31; 10:33–34).

Teilhard's Perspective

As already noted in the introduction to part 2, "The Gospel of Matthew," Teilhard would look specifically for teachings and events that qualify as "evolutionary." He would search Mark's text for evidence of events that fulfill the six evolutionary criteria: are the teachings that accompany the actions of Jesus in Mark's Gospel

- different and genuinely new or novel compared to what went before?
- keeping essential elements or functions of what went before?
- more complex than anything within its class?
- irreversible, such that, once presented, it cannot be denied?
- transformative, but not destructive of what went before?
- manifesting new emerging properties?

As with the other Gospels, as we read Mark's text, Teilhard wants us to keep asking, "Does the material in this Gospel passage qualify as evolutionary?" "Is it taking the noosphere to a higher level of consciousness?" We focus on those sections of the text that meet Teilhard's criteria for perceiving it as evolutionary.

13

The Beloved Son

Thirteen Important Events (1:1–45)

MARK IS NOT a writer who wastes words. In the forty-five verses of his first chapter, after directly proclaiming that Jesus is the Son of God (1:1–3), Mark covers thirteen events in Jesus's story:

- the baptism offered to the public by John the Baptist (1:4–8);
- John's baptism of Jesus (1:9–11);
- Jesus's temptation in the desert (1:12–13);
- the beginning of his Galilean ministry (1:14–15);
- the call of the first four apostles (1:16–20);
- his first sermon in the Capernaum synagogue (1:21–22);
- the healing of a man possessed (1:23–28);
- the healing of Simon's mother-in-law (1:29–31);
- the healing of many at Simon's house (1:32–34);
- his custom of praying (1:35);
- his first preaching tour in Galilee (1:36–39);
- the cleansing of a leper (1:40–44); and
- his spreading fame (1:45).

Mark ends the chapter by saying that Jesus "could no longer go into a town openly, but stayed out in the country; and people came to him from every quarter" (1:45).

In this opening chapter, Mark reminds his readers three times that Jesus is the Son of God. First, as noted earlier, Mark himself asserts it in the opening verse: "The beginning of the good news of

Jesus Christ, the Son of God" (1:1). Second, he has God affirm it after his baptism by John: "And a voice came from heaven, 'You are my Son, the Beloved; with you I am well pleased'" (1:11). Third, when Jesus starts to heal the possessed man during the synagogue service, the devil himself acknowledges Jesus's divinity: the "man with an unclean spirit…cried out, 'What have you to do with us, Jesus of Nazareth? Have you come to destroy us? I know who you are, the Holy One of God'" (1:23–24).

Apparently, Jesus is caught off guard by this public revelation. Once he becomes aware that other evil spirits would keep announcing his divinity, he changes his approach. He continues to cure possessed people, but first orders the devils to be quiet about his identity. "He would not permit the demons to speak, because they knew him" (1:34; cf. 3:11–12). According to Mark, Jesus wants to keep his divine identity a secret from the crowds.

EVOLUTIONARY IMPLICATIONS

Having a "divine" person preaching was new in the history of religion. All known religions at the time were founded by human beings—wise men, holy men, and even ordinary people. These founders usually claimed to *speak for* the divine, but none of them claimed to *be* divine. This preacher, says Mark, is both human and divine.

Most religious prophets typically bring bad news to their people. They warn them that God is aware of their infidelity and evil ways and that they must repent and change their behavior. God will be their judge and punisher. In contrast, Mark assures his readers that Jesus is bringing the gospel—"*the* good news." The good news is that God is a loving God, a forgiving God, a healing God, a God that wants to share the fullness of life with us. And that is *news*.

The Holy Spirit in the Trinity (1:1–13)

In this first chapter, Mark indirectly introduces us to the divine Trinity. He asserts Jesus's divinity (*the Son*) in the opening verse (1:1). The voice of God (*the Father*) is heard at Jesus's baptism reaffirming Jesus's divine Sonship (1:11). The other important figure in the baptism scene is the *Holy Spirit*. "And just as he was coming up out of the water, he saw the heavens torn apart and the Spirit descending like a dove on him" (1:10). Presenting God as a Trinity of divine persons qualifies as evolutionary.

The central role the Holy Spirit plays in God's project is very new theology as well. John the Baptist is first to mention the Holy Spirit as the "gift" the Messiah will bring to the community. "I have baptized you with water; but he will baptize you with the Holy Spirit" (1:8). The implication is that the water baptism of John gets people to put on a new mind (*metanoia*) and realize that their sins are forgiven. This prepares them for the Spirit baptism of Jesus that will give people the positive energy to transform their lives and their world. This is the faith manifested by love in action.

Although "the Spirit of God" is often mentioned in the Hebrew Scriptures, the Jews interpret this expression metaphorically. For them, the "holy spirit" is simply the breath of God the Creator. Thus, when God "exhales," it manifests the Creator's grace or blessing. Jewish theology considered blasphemous the idea that there might be more than one divine being or person.[1]

For Mark, the Holy Spirit is not merely a gift or grace from God. The Holy Spirit is a personal force. For, immediately after John baptizes Jesus, the Holy Spirit asserts its power on the human Jesus. "The Spirit immediately drove him out into the wilderness. He was in the wilderness forty days, tempted by Satan" (1:12–13).

As Christian theology develops, it more clearly identifies the three divine persons, each of whom plays a distinct role in salvation history: the Father as Creator, the Son as Redeemer, and the Holy Spirit as Sanctifier.[2]

EVOLUTIONARY IMPLICATIONS

It is evolutionary enough for Mark to present Jesus being both human and divine. The idea that there are two divine persons—Father and Son—is already considered blasphemous to the Jews. Mark is now asking us to accept a third divine person, the Holy Spirit.

What is evolutionary here is the revelation that God is a community of three divine persons, a union of divine agents, each of whom plays an interactive role in fulfilling the divine plan for creation, God's project. The Son is doing the work assigned to him by the Father. The

Holy Spirit is guiding the Son, for example, in "driving" Jesus into the desert for a necessary retreat. There, he clarifies his purpose and mission before beginning his public life to proclaim—and demonstrate in action—a gospel of love given by a God whose name is Love.

What is also emerging as evolutionary, Teilhard suggests, is that the Trinity of divine persons forms a community of mutual love and union.[3] The Jewish God, Yahweh, appears to live as a solitary in "heaven." Yahweh has no one equal to him to love. He has only the chosen people to relate to, love, and care for. In contrast, in the community of the Trinity, its divine members are not alone, but share an infinite love with each other as peers. In addition, the love their union has for creation and humans is so powerful that they find a way to transform humanity so that countless people can enter, through Christ, into the Trinity's own divine level of life, love, and mutual union. Heaven will be full.

14

Jesus and the Religious Leaders

Jesus Confronts the Scribes and Pharisees (2:1–28)

IN HIS BRIEF second chapter, Mark summarizes Jesus's relationship to the scribes and Pharisees. Jesus encounters groups of them several times during his public life. In Mark's Gospel, the relationship between Jesus and these powerful religious leaders remains a central theme throughout his public life and at his death.

Mark presents a series of four encounters to highlight the differences between Jesus's perspective of God's kingdom and that of the Jewish religious and spiritual authorities. Teilhard might say that Mark's narrative clarifies how Jesus's morality and theology evolved beyond that of the scribes and Pharisees. In each of the four events, Jesus clarifies how his Way differs from the traditional Jewish understanding of God and of spiritual practice.

Teilhard might describe the relationship between Jesus and the Pharisees by comparing their different states of consciousness. For example, Jesus sees God's involvement with humanity as love centered—a level of consciousness much higher than that of the scribes and Pharisees. Jesus, who shares this love-centered perspective, sees what God is doing in the world very differently from the way the traditionally righteous people around him see it. Furthermore, this difference in perspective highlights four areas of ultimate concern.

The first of the four encounters between Jesus and the scribes and Pharisees focuses on the question, *Who can forgive sin?* (2:1–12). For example, in this scene he recognizes a strong faith in the stretcher-bearers who bring to him a paralytic man. Jesus says to the paralytic, "Son, your sins are forgiven" (2:5).

In the minds of the scribes and Pharisees, Jesus has committed blasphemy. They believe that only God can forgive sins and only God can do miraculous healings. To put an end to the discussion, Jesus does both. He forgives sin and does the healing. In effect, he dismisses the charge of blasphemy—by doubling it (see 2:8–11).

His second encounter with the scribes and Pharisees is about how to *relate to sinners*. It happens when these religious authorities see Jesus and his disciples enjoying dinner at the home of Levi son of Alphaeus (also called Matthew; see 2:15–17). Matthew is a tax collector and Jesus's newest apostle. Tax collectors are by definition "sinners." Several sinners—probably other tax collectors—are dining with Jesus and his men. Such association is not religiously allowed, since to eat with sinners is to contaminate oneself.

Mark points out that, in this instance, Jesus is confronted by a special group of professional people: "scribes of the Pharisees" (2:16). This special group is doubly righteous. Not only do they know and study the Law (as scribes), but they also practice it as perfectly as possible (as Pharisees).

Instead of bringing their challenge to Jesus himself, they choose to address their question to some of his disciples. They ask, "Why does he eat with tax collectors and sinners?" (2:16). Jesus overhears their question and answers it with a paradoxical statement: "Those who are well have no need of a physician, but those who are sick [do]; I have come to call not the righteous but sinners" (2:17). Jesus is, in effect, dismissing them and their question.

Teilhard would point out that Jesus's dismissive statement is also very important in that it is stating the essence of his mission. He is affirming clearly his mission or life's purpose: *to invite the sinners of this world into the kingdom of God so that they can work for its success.* Jesus is enlisting in his mission the very ones whom righteous people tend to avoid and reject. Jesus offers them new openings into the experience of life.

Note the difference between Matthew's and Mark's presentations of Jesus's life's purpose. According to Matthew, Jesus's purpose is, first, to bring his good news *to the Jewish people*. For Mark, it is much more focused—to bring the good news *to sinners*.

Because of this distinction, Jesus's attitude toward the scribes and Pharisees takes a different perspective in these two Gospels. In Matthew, Jesus engages the scribes and Pharisees in *debate*, as if he hopes to convert them, since they are part of the Jewish people to whom he has been sent. In Mark, Jesus's response to the scribes and Pharisees is more *dismissive*. As if to say, "My role is rather like that of a physician. My work is to help those who need healing. If you feel healthy, you don't need my services. You people don't spend your time with the sick, the crippled, the lepers, the possessed, the sinners. I do. They are the people I deal with every day. They are the people to whom I am sent. They are the ones to whom I am offering an invitation into a fuller and deeper life."

In the third encounter, the scribes confront Jesus on *the issue of fasting*, since fasting is a major part of their spiritual practices. But the scribes don't present themselves to Jesus as examples of those who fast. Cleverly, these scribes refer to John the Baptist's disciples who also practice fasting. "Why do John's disciples and the disciples of the Pharisees fast, but your disciples do not fast?" (2:18). Again, rather than engage the questioners, Jesus is dismissive. He knows they are not genuinely asking for an explanation; they are merely looking for ways to confound him.

Jesus responds with an image that, at first glance, appears to write them off. Yet, upon reflection, his response genuinely reveals who he is. Jesus presents himself as a bridegroom celebrating an ongoing wedding feast. Being at a wedding feast is a natural symbol for enjoying the fullness of life. This image explains why his disciples are not fasting. Jesus says to the Pharisees, "The wedding guests cannot fast while the bridegroom is with them, can they? As long as they have the bridegroom with them, they cannot fast. The days will come when the bridegroom is taken away from them, and then they will fast on that day" (2:19–20).

The fourth encounter with the Pharisees concerns doing *work on the Sabbath*. As Jesus and his group are walking through a field of grain on a Sabbath, a few of the disciples are hungry and begin plucking heads of grain off the stalks. The Pharisees claim this activity— harvesting grain—is "doing work," thereby violating the commandment that states that no one is to work on the Sabbath.

Jesus explains *why* God created the Sabbath precisely as a day of rest for humans. "Then he said to them, 'The sabbath was made

93

for humankind, and not humankind for the sabbath'" (2:27). God declares a Sabbath day each week to guarantee people a day of rest from labor. It is meant to be a day of freedom—a free day.[1] It is not meant to restrict what people can do or not do, as the Pharisees claim. On the contrary, Jesus is implying that, if on a Sabbath people want to take a walk or play games or go on a picnic, it is up to them. It is "their free day." If they want to do some work or pursue a hobby on the Sabbath, it is their right. If they want to eat some special food or enjoy a snack on the Sabbath, they are free to do so. The Sabbath is meant to be a day of freedom, not of restrictions.

Then, Jesus adds a final assertion: "So the Son of Man is lord even of the sabbath" (2:28). Jesus is claiming that he has the right to make decisions about the meaning and purpose of the Sabbath. He is claiming a divine privilege to revise the Jewish rules concerning permitted behavior on the Sabbath. The scribes saw this as another blasphemous action. Teilhard sees it as evolutionary.

EVOLUTIONARY IMPLICATIONS

Jesus affirms that his good news is very new. It brings a new perspective to all former customs and rules. Part of the good news is that God loves sinners as well as the righteous. God forgives sinners and is always ready to forgive. Moreover, God sent his Son to Earth precisely to convey this loving message to sinners. Jesus's disciples eat with sinners to express in action the good news of God's unconditional love. The good news is that God is not about making sure people keep the rules but about opening and deepening their experience of life.

The Pharisees and the disciples of John the Baptist follow a regular routine of fasting on certain days and at certain times. Jesus says there is no need to fast while the bridegroom is present. Thanks to the Eucharist, the "wedding feast" is always ongoing, and will continue until the end of time. So, is there ever a need to fast?

Perhaps the bridegroom's absence to which Jesus refers (2:20) is not to his physical presence as a human, but to his interior, spiritual presence—or "absence"—during those "dry" periods of personal prayer or when life is especially difficult and confusing.

For those serious about spiritual practice, there will be times when the presence of Jesus Christ seems to disappear, and his absence is felt very powerfully. Perhaps those are the times when such people may need to fast. Jesus seems to imply that they should fast as needed, not as required or prescribed by routine or an outside authority.

Jesus is also saying that God's commandments are not given to restrict our life, but to help us live together productively and to achieve the fullness of life. God declares the Sabbath to give us a day of rest from work, so that we can spend time with God as well as enjoy each other's company. Jesus feels free to do healings and exorcisms on the Sabbath because it enables those whom he heals to rejoin their communities as healthy productive members. It gives *more life* to them and to their community.

The Source of Uncleanness (7:1–23)

Here, Jesus is on the road journeying northward through Galilee toward Lebanon. The disciples stop at a market to buy some food for the group. They bring it back to their camp and begin to eat. The Pharisees note that the disciples are eating the market food without having washed either the food or their hands (7:2). Mark adds that Jews "do not eat unless they thoroughly wash their hands"; and "they do not eat anything from the market unless they wash it" (7:3–4).

In the Galilean countryside, there are no public washrooms where travelers can easily perform these rituals. Nor do they have fast food restaurants at every street corner with restrooms and running water available to all customers. So, lacking these amenities, the disciples skip the customary food-and-hand-washing ritual. And eat.

Observing this violation of tradition, a Pharisees team confronts Jesus directly: "Why do your disciples not live according to the tradition of the elders, but eat with defiled hands?" (7:5).

This infuriates Jesus. He now declares one of his very important theological principles:

> Then he called the crowd again and said to them, "Listen to me, all of you, and understand: there is nothing outside a person that by going in can defile, but the things that come out are what defile." (7:14–15)

Unfortunately, his own disciples fail to understand his point and he must spell it out to them. He does so privately.

> "Do you not see that whatever goes into a person from outside cannot defile, since it enters, not the heart but the stomach, and goes out into the sewer?" (Thus he declared all foods clean.) And he said, "It is what comes out of a person that defiles. For it is from within, from the human heart, that evil intentions come: fornication, theft, murder, adultery, avarice, wickedness, deceit, licentiousness, envy, slander, pride, folly. All these evil things come from within, and they defile a person." (7:17–23)

EVOLUTIONARY IMPLICATIONS

In his parenthetical comment—"Thus he declared all foods clean"—Mark identifies an evolutionary step in religious practice. Uncleanness or sinfulness does not come from simple external behavior or customary actions like eating prohibited foods or not washing hands before meals. Sinfulness always originates in one's heart. It may be expressed in external actions, but the stain of sinfulness is produced by the heart—by one's intention. Teilhard calls this an "activity of diminishment."[2]

Most diminishments we endure are not sins. Common diminishments include getting sick, being stuck in traffic, losing a job, losing a loved one, enduring a natural disaster, being betrayed by a friend, or being treated rudely. They are simply events through which we must pass. But how we choose to respond to such diminishments can come either from a good and loving intention or an evil one. In either case, these intentions arise from the heart. Teilhard calls actions that arise from good intentions "activities of growth." Some of these are choices we make to turn a diminishment into something good and productive.

In contrast, our choices to turn an unwelcome event into something defiling and destructive Teilhard calls "activities of diminishment." These are choices with evil intention that may lead to theft, murder, avarice, wickedness, deceit, envy, slander, and so on.

15

Parables

The Purpose (4:1–25)

CHAPTER 4 OF Mark's narrative is filled with parables. Jesus tells his apostles that he has a reason for teaching in parables. He is willing to explain a parable's meaning to them, but only to them:

> To you has been given the secret of the kingdom of God, but for those outside, everything comes in parables; in order that
> "they may indeed look, but not perceive,
>   and may indeed listen, but not understand." (4:11–12)[1]

The purpose of parables in Matthew and Mark is different. Mark's Jesus uses parables precisely to *prevent* the people from getting the message. Matthew's Jesus *expects* the crowds to understand a parable's message, but they don't (see Matt 13:13–19).

In Mark, what surprises Jesus is that even those closest to him don't get the point of a simple parable, such as the parable of the sower who went out to sow seed. Its meaning, at least to Jesus, seems rather obvious and easy to grasp. A disappointed Jesus says to the twelve, "Do you not understand this parable? Then how will you understand all the parables?" (4:13). Furthermore, how will they understand the workings of the kingdom of God, which the parables reveal? Jesus proceeds to explain to them the meaning of the parable of the sower (4:14–20).[2]

Mark then presents several other parables:

[Jesus] said to them, "Is a lamp brought in to be put under the bushel basket, or under the bed, and not on the lamp stand? For there is nothing hidden, except to be disclosed; nor is anything secret, except to come to light. Let anyone with ears to hear listen!" (4:21–23)

Teilhard notes that modern science has been providing such a lamp. For the last several centuries, advances in science have continued to reveal things about God's creation that previously had been "hidden."[3] Each year, new discoveries disclose to us more dynamic evolutionary movements happening on Earth. Paleontologists show us how living creatures on our planet have been growing in complexity and consciousness over many millennia — and even more so recently.

Biologists have shown how our planet forms a single organism and how humans are inextricably intertwined with Earth's every metal, mineral, and life-form. Humans cannot be separated from the rest of nature, for we are intimately part of it. We cannot survive without water and oxygen. We cannot stay healthy unless our bodies are nourished with vitamins, metals and minerals, calories, carbohydrates and protein from rocks, plants, and animals. Biologically, planet Earth is one huge living entity. We are not merely visitors on Earth. This is our home.[4] We are born from it. The Earth is part of our bodies and we are part of Earth's body.

These are some of the things that the light of science has shown us. These are revelations about God's creation that we would never know except for the painstaking work and research of thousands of scientists in physics, chemistry, biology, geology, archaeology, and many other fields. This knowledge enriches our minds and makes us more conscious of who we are. It is knowledge that God wants us to know and spread, not hide or deny. Such knowledge is not to be covered up or denied — put under a bushel basket or hidden under a bed. It cannot be kept secret. "For there is nothing hidden, except to be disclosed; nor is anything secret, except to come to light" (4:22).

And [Jesus] said to them, "Pay attention to what you hear; the measure you give will be the measure you get, and still more will be given you. For to those who have, more will be given; and from those who have nothing, even what they have will be taken away." (4:24–25)

If we pay attention to what we hear and see, what are we expected to "give" in return? And to whom are we to give it? Anyone reading this book is someone to whom God has given "much."

EVOLUTIONARY IMPLICATIONS

For over a century, certain people in the church have been trying to hide—or deny—many of the discoveries of modern science and the evidence for evolution. They fear it challenges biblical creation stories found in the first chapters of Genesis and, thus, jeopardizes the faith of ordinary believers. Today's high school students study physics, biology, and chemistry. They are daily exposed to the "light" of scientific evidence. Yet in catechism and early religious education, many are still taught to believe that, in the beginning, God created a complete and perfect world and that this perfect world was ruined by the first human act of disobedience committed by two adults who lived a carefree life in a beautiful garden.

Today, young people struggle to reconcile what they learn in school as scientific facts about human life on Earth with some things they are taught as religious truths. God is continually revealing God's mind and heart in creation. Science is teaching us how to decipher these revelations about our world that God is revealing. If you think of creation as a book written by God, then science is teaching us how to read God's creation language.

Instead of a confrontation between traditional Christian forces and the modern forces of evolution, Teilhard suggests we expand our religious vision and see "a providential and indispensable inter-fertilization" of science and religion. Consequently, "the guiding principles of Christianity may be expanded, without being distorted, to the dimensions of a universe which has been fantastically enlarged and integrated by modern scientific thought."[5]

For Teilhard, Christians should be more excited about the discoveries of science than anyone else. For such discoveries clarify for us more about God's nature, God's ways, and God's purpose in creating the universe. Teilhard also encourages Christians to become scientists—especially innovative scientists and researchers—for these are the men and women who continue lighting God's "lamp" to reveal the mysteries of creation.[6] Teilhard invites scientists to become mystics, for such people usually are the first to see and stand in awe of some new aspect of God that their "light" has discovered.[7]

"For to those who have, more will be given" (4:25). The more we are open to discovering new facts about our world, the more God will reveal to us. Those who refuse to welcome new knowledge and new abilities are closing themselves to God's self-revelation as it is happening in our time. "From those who have nothing, even what they have will be taken away" (4:25).

The Earth at Work (4:26–29)

For Teilhard, God has implanted an evolutionary drive in every element of creation. Notice how rain and soil engage with seeds, enabling them to sprout and grow. In this way, the earth produces nourishment for plants and trees and foods for grazing animals. Jesus has recognized this process in his parable of the growing seed:

> [Jesus] also said, "The kingdom of God is as if someone would scatter seed on the ground, and would sleep and rise night and day, and the seed would sprout and grow, he does not know how. The earth produces of itself, first the stalk, then the head, then the full grain in the head. But when the grain is ripe, at once he goes in with his sickle, because the harvest has come." (4:26–29)

This parable uses farming symbols to teach us about the growth of the kingdom of God. It is centered on three major stages in the life of the farmer raising crops. The three stages are *planting, waiting,* and *harvesting.*

The second stage—*waiting*—indicates that the farmer and the crops are two different realities. During the second stage, the farmer lives his own life; he "would sleep and rise night and day." Meantime, the earth has been doing its own quiet, hidden work on the crops, nurturing the seed without any help from the farmer. The seed grows and is transformed—"first the stalk, then the head, then the full grain in the head."

Everything that lives—plants, fish, animals, and humans—all begin as "seeds" of different kinds.

Teilhard would point out that Earth is doing its quiet, hidden work, nurturing humanity, as we gradually mature in complexity, consciousness, and love. We do not usually think of Earth as nurturing us, yet that is exactly what it does: *physically*, with air, water, calories, proteins, carbohydrates, fats, sugars, metals, minerals, vitamins, and so on; and *emotionally and intellectually*, with caring people, friends, neighbors, pets, entertainment, schools, workplaces, libraries, books, nature, and so on.

For Jesus, the parable is a story about the Father's relationship to us. The most important seeds the Father plants in us are the "seeds of love." In stage one, God, the loving Father, *plants* seeds of love in everyone on Earth. In stage two—*waiting*—God lets Earth and all its creatures (including us) nurture those love seeds as they grow and evolve. Like the farmer, God *watches* lovingly as humanity makes its way through its evolutionary stages of development—"first the stalk, then the head, and then the full grain in the head."

Evolutionary Implications

According to Jewish tradition at the time of Jesus, God was directly responsible for everything that happened to a person or to the people. If a person became sick, people believed that the sickness was caused by God. If a person became rich, people believed that God had made him or her successful. If the Israelite army won a battle, people believed it was God who brought the victory.

In contrast, Jesus is telling us that many things happen simply because they happen. On a farm, there are thousands of things that can happen to the "seed." Some of it may fall by the wayside or on stony ground. Most seeds find their way onto the soil. What happens to each seed depends on many forms of life interacting with it. Some soil is richer in nutrients than other soil. Some fields receive more rain than others. It is the same with people. Different things happen to different people.

God does not directly (and in every instance) command each of these helpful or unhelpful things to happen. Like the farmer, God continues watching us (the crops) lovingly. And he keeps blessing us with that love. For example, we may find that patience is growing within us so that we can endure a diminishment, or we may find surfacing within us the readiness to forgive someone who has wronged us. That's God at work. At other times, God's love puts a friend in our path that gives us a new perspective or a puppy befriends us, reminding us that God loves us unconditionally. This parable reveals some new and very different ways about how God relates to creation.

In this chapter, Mark recounts five more parables about the kingdom of God—the sower and the seed (4:3–9; 14–20), the lamp and lamp stand (4:21–22), the reciprocal measuring (4:24–25), the patient farmer (4:26–29), and the mustard seed (4:30–32). Each one reveals important aspects about the kingdom of God. Reflect on what would be missing in our understanding of God's project if one or other of these parables had been omitted.

16

Holy Week

THE STORY THAT dominates Mark's Gospel is the passion and death of Jesus of Nazareth. Early on in his narrative, Mark announces the emerging plot to kill Jesus. "The Pharisees went out and immediately conspired with the Herodians against him, how to destroy him" (3:6).

Mark also anticipates Jesus's passion, death, and resurrection by including three separate predictions of it. The first prediction: "Then he began to teach them that the Son of Man must undergo great suffering, and be rejected by the elders, the chief priests, and the scribes, and be killed, and after three days rise again" (8:31). In the second prediction, Mark adds the betrayal (9:31). The third prediction includes much more detail:

> See, we are going up to Jerusalem, and the Son of Man will be handed over to the chief priests and the scribes, and they will condemn him to death; then they will hand him over to the Gentiles; they will mock him, and spit upon him, and flog him, and kill him; and after three days he will rise again. (10:33–34)

Dramatic Moments (10:32 — 15:14)

The week that we now call Holy Week is a tumultuous time for Jesus and his followers. It begins with shouts of "Hosanna!" during Jesus's triumphal entry into the Holy City at the beginning of the week (see 11:10). It includes many dramatic confrontations with authorities

103

during the week (see chapters 10—14). Before the week is out, people will be demanding his execution (see 15:13–14). During the week, a total about-face occurs even among his followers. They shift from confidence to confusion, from public loyalty to hiding in fear, from support to betrayal, and from "Hosanna!" to "Crucify him!"

EVOLUTIONARY IMPLICATIONS

Mark's emphasis on the sufferings and death of Jesus highlights essential elements of Jesus's Way. Not only does Jesus model for us how to *live* our daily lives, he also models how to *suffer* and how to approach *dying*. In Jesus's Way, we learn how the energy spent in suffering and dying may be used to further God's project.

Teilhard brings a special perspective to these unwelcome events in life. He looks at what is happening to Jesus during these final days and hours in terms of *activities* and *passivities*. These are the two dimensions of life that can most affect the success of the evolutionary process—any evolutionary process.

Teilhard defines *activities* as those choices, decisions, and actions that a person consciously and freely chooses, makes, or performs. As examples of Jesus's *activities* during Holy Week, Jesus chooses to ride into Jerusalem on a donkey (11:7); to overturn the tables of the moneychangers in the temple area (11:15), where he will celebrate Passover (14:13–17); to institute the Eucharist at the Last Supper (14:22–15); to go to the Mount of Olives to pray (14:26); and to pray to his Father for a possible way out of his anticipated sufferings and death (14:35–36). For Teilhard, all these qualify as *activities*.

Teilhard calls *passivities* those happenings, external events, and decisions of others that we do not choose but must endure. In our lives, passivities outnumber activities by about a thousand to one, since they include all the vagaries of the weather, the traffic, and the combined actions and choices of millions of other people, seen and unseen.

Some passivities are positive, welcome, enjoyable, helpful, and growthful. Teilhard calls these *passivities of growth*. Other passivities are negative, unwelcome, harmful, and can hinder and weaken a person. Teilhard calls these *passivities of diminishment*.

In the Holy Week story, the man who donates the donkey is a welcome passivity for Jesus (11:2–6), as is the man who provides the Upper Room for the Passover meal (14:10–16). Either of those men could have refused to cooperate. Jesus may also have enjoyed, as a *passivity of growth*, the Hosanna parade into the Holy City (11:8–10)

In contrast, some of the *passivities of diminishment* Jesus endures during Holy Week include Judas's betrayal (14:10–11); Peter's denial (14:29–31, 66–72); the desertion of all his apostles (14:50); the false accusations of the high priests (14:55); the lies of the witnesses (14:56–60); the groundless guilty verdict of the Sanhedrin (14:60–64); the abusive mocking of the Roman soldiers (15:16–20); the painful crown of thorns (15:17); the weight of the cross (15:21); the physical pain of hanging from nails (15:24); and the crowds near the cross mocking him (15:29–32). These are things Jesus had to endure and undergo whether he wanted to or not.

In Teilhard's spirituality, *activities* and *passivities* constantly interact. A most important factor in such an interaction is the free choice (*activity*) a person can make in response to each *passivity*. One's free choice (*activity*) is especially important in response to an unwelcome event (*a passivity of diminishment*) that happens. In the face of a diminishing passivity, a person can respond by resisting, fighting, denying, blaming, cursing, seeking revenge, laughing, or crying.

There are other possible responses when undergoing an unwelcome diminishment. A person can turn the passivity into something good and useful. For example, the offended or harmed person can forgive, show understanding, or find a positive way to redirect the energy spent enduring the passivity.

For instance, Christians say that Jesus, while on the cross, offered his suffering and death to the Father to expiate our sins. Teilhard would say that, on the cross, Jesus transforms *passivities of diminishment* into *activities of growth*. Rather than "waste" the energy spent enduring these sufferings, Jesus consciously redirects that energy spent suffering to make reparation for humanity's offenses against God. He redirects his energy spent suffering by his intention and turns it into an *activity of growth*.

When we endure unwelcome suffering, that is, passivities of diminishment, we can redirect the energy we spend suffering *by our intention*. By our intention, we can make the unwelcome experience an activity of growth. Such an action may be directed to help build the kingdom of God. It also increases the amount of love and compassion produced on Earth.

A Fuller Meaning of the Cross

The strongest emphasis in liturgies and homilies about Jesus's suffering and death on the cross is that he died *for our sins*. Because of this emphasis, we can be led to think that the only reason Jesus suffered and died was to pay off our "financial" sin debt or, to use a different metaphor, to release us from the "prison" of sin. Consider either picture. In one metaphor, we have our bank debt erased and we now look at our account and see that we have no debt, but a zero balance. In the other metaphor, we have been released from prison and we now stand outside the prison walls wondering where to go. In neither case does the picture predict what we are to do in the future. Do God and Jesus have no plans for our freedom and our future?

ENERGY FOR THE FUTURE

Another, perhaps, more forward-looking purpose for Jesus's suffering on the cross is that he is making a *positive investment* on our behalf. He redirects the energy he spends suffering so that it enhances our spiritual growth. It also instills in us the energy to work toward the fullness of life and the freedom to love and serve one another.[1]

In his public life, Jesus enacts this forward-looking good news of the kingdom by his healing ministry. With each act of healing he performs (*activities of growth*), he gives more fullness of life to a person and to his or her family. Whenever he suffers diminishment, as on the cross, he redirects his intention so that we receive more fullness of life. Using the same two metaphors, he is putting money in our bank account and he is getting us (recently out of prison) a job and a place to live.

St. Paul recognized that Jesus's intention in redirecting the energy of his suffering involves two distinct stages. Paul understands Jesus redirecting his suffering energy, first, to *expiate* our sins, to wipe away our spiritual debt, and, second, to help bring about our collective *salvation*. His suffering energy is directed to the growth of the human race in love. It is aimed at helping humanity to become fully united and fully alive.[2] In this second stage, Jesus redirects his sufferings to enrich us in order to help bring about fullness of life for the human race.[3]

In the Gospels, there is evidence for this redirection of energy toward the fullness of life. For example: Jesus's prayer in Gethsemane

(Matt 26:39); the institution of the Eucharist at the Last Supper (Mark 14:24); Jesus's forgiveness of the thief on the cross (Luke 23:43); and his offering of his suffering to his Father (Luke 23:34; John 19:29–30).

Thanks to St. Paul, Teilhard recognized that, by our conscious choices, we can do as Jesus did. We have the power to redirect the energy we spend in suffering toward some noble purpose. We can transform our *passivities of diminishment* just as Jesus did. We can put our unwelcome suffering to good use by turning it into an *activity of growth*.

In imitation of his Lord, Paul does the same with his own suffering and diminishments. He redirects their energy in order to give more life to his communities. "I am now rejoicing in my sufferings *for your sake*, and in my flesh I am completing what is lacking in Christ's afflictions for the sake of his body, that is, the church" (Col 1:24, emphasis added). Paul is using an *activity of growth* to redirect the energy he spends in suffering. He uses his suffering to provide fuller life for the young Christian community.

In other words, Paul might say that Christianity is in the business of helping humanity flourish. Paul is reminding us that we can transform the energy we spend in suffering by an intentional *activity of growth* to help the community to flourish.

EVOLUTIONARY IMPLICATIONS

Although many people see the energy they spend in suffering as a waste, Teilhard sees the enormous amount of human suffering happening on Earth every day as a tremendous source of energy that can be redirected into positive projects. Sadly, most people are unaware of this potential. Teilhard recognizes the powerful value of suffering. For him, redirecting energy spent suffering can serve as an evolutionary force. In an essay on the constructive value of suffering, Teilhard wrote,

> Human suffering, the sum total of suffering poured out at each moment over the whole earth, is like an immeasurable ocean. But what makes up this immensity? Is it blackness, emptiness, barren wastes? No, indeed: it is *potential energy*. Suffering holds hidden within it, in extreme intensity, the ascensional force of the world. The whole point is to set this force free by making it conscious of what it signifies and of what it is capable. For if all the sick people in the world were

simultaneously to turn their sufferings into a single shared longing for the speedy completion of the kingdom of God through the organizing of the earth, what a vast leap toward God the world would thereby make![4]

The ability to transform suffering (an unwelcome *passivity*) into something that helps build the kingdom of God by using the *activity* of intention is radically new in theology. It is a powerful insight. Knowing how to put a constructive value on suffering allows us to enter more deeply into the mind and intentions of Jesus—and his union with the Father. It allows a new perspective on how Jesus endured the final days of Holy Week.

Today, as we reenvision these same diminishing events of Jesus with our understanding of how to redirect suffering energy, we can begin to comprehend some of what was probably going on in Jesus's inner life and choices. Using Teilhard's terms, we can imagine Jesus's inner *activities of growth* in response to the cruel *passivities of diminishment* he endures. In his prayer to the Father, we can imagine him redirecting the energy he spends in pain and humiliation. On the cross, he is using his intention to transform the world in love.

Such redirection of energy does not lessen the physical or emotional suffering one endures. He doesn't stop spending energy in his painful agony, he just changes its meaning. His positive intention gives his suffering new powerful meaning and purpose. Jesus does not waste the energy of his suffering. He transforms it into good.

This is such an evolutionary idea that most people today cannot grasp the possibility that, by love, all things can be turned into good. No event or experience need be wasted. Even the energy spent enduring suffering can, by a clear intention, help to build the kingdom of God.

Nowhere in religious history do we ever hear of a divine being willing, as Jesus was, to endure suffering at the hands of human beings. No people before the apostles could even imagine a God willing to be "humble" enough to endure humiliation such as this—even a shameful death. Teilhard believes Jesus was showing us much more than "God being willing to suffer." Jesus was teaching us *how* to suffer. More precisely, he was teaching us how to use suffering constructively.

Holy Week

Our challenge is to learn to transform our own personal suffering in life by redirecting the energy we spend in suffering to help accomplish important challenges or transformation that our community or our world needs.[5]

With this inner perspective we can now consider some of the events of Holy Week in Mark's Gospel.

17

The Upper Room

The Last Supper (14:12–25)

PREPARATIONS FOR the Passover meal go well. The disciples gather food and other necessities for the sacred ritual (see 14:12–16). That evening, they all gather in the Upper Room and sit down to begin the meal. But the atmosphere is not joyful. The disciples feel troubled (see 14:18–19). After Judas, the betrayer, leaves the Upper Room, the mood shifts. Jesus proceeds to a key moment of the evening.

As they are eating the traditional Passover food and drink, renewing the covenant God had made with Moses, Jesus makes a significant religious change in Passover theology. Instead of renewing the old covenant, Jesus establishes a new covenant with his followers. He transforms the Passover meal into the Lord's Supper.

He shows them a ritual they can reenact again and again to reaffirm the new covenant. It is designed to provide them with a continuous supply of food and drink for their spiritual health and growth. It is a totally new kind of nourishment. The food is his flesh, and the drink is his blood. This sustenance nourishes them with the fullness of life.

Recall the parable of the new wine breaking the old wineskin (2:18–22). Jesus's blood is the new wine; Moses's covenant is the old wineskin.

EVOLUTIONARY IMPLICATIONS

The Jewish Passover meal *looks backward*, commemorating a past event—the exodus from Egypt. The Lord's Supper looks *forward*. It is not focused on the past. It is all about the future.

As Christ's body of believers grows, they will need sustenance to keep progressing. This is what Jesus envisions during that supper. He institutes the Lord's Supper to bring the necessary nourishment of his body and blood into their regular meetings as they share this divine food with each other. As they eat his body and drink his blood again and again, they will continue to grow into the fullness of life (salvation). The members of his universal Body will eventually be transformed to become more like him in mind and heart.

St. Paul understands the Eucharist's future purpose. After recalling Jesus's words at the Last Supper (1 Cor 11:23–25), Paul adds, "For as often as you eat this bread and drink the cup, you proclaim the Lord's death until he comes" (1 Cor 11:26). The continual need for eucharistic nourishment will remain until Christ comes in glory at the end of time.

The Lord's Supper's purpose is to nurture the health and future of Christ's people. It is not simply a reminder of a past event, the Savior's passion and death. With the Eucharist, Christ is focused on the *future life* of his members. On the cross, Jesus refers to the completion of his *earthly work* as Jesus of Nazareth when he says, "It is finished" (John 19:30). But it is only the beginning of Christ's much longer *evolutionary work* of building his Cosmic Body and bringing that Body to its fulfillment. Only with the fulfillment of the kingdom of God on Earth will God's project be complete. Only then will the Cosmic Christ be able to say to the Father, "It is finished." The Eucharist remains central to the fulfillment of God's project.

For Paul, not only does the Eucharist nourish the members of the Body of Christ as they grow and are transformed, it also represents the entire mystery of Jesus Christ, from his incarnation to his final glory.[1]

As with St. Augustine, each time we celebrate the Eucharist, it is another Christmas. The Cosmic Christ in whom we all live is born again each day on Earth—on the altar during Mass. This is the great mystery of the Lord of the universe. Christ is the same, yet somehow new each day.

Jesus had come to Earth to become one with humanity. This is what his heavenly Father wanted Jesus to do with his life. Jesus is sharing that vision with his friends, as he speaks to them on that solemn night.

The Eucharist

It is interesting to note that the institution of the Lord's Supper is not shocking or amazing to the disciples. None of the Gospel writers even hint that the disciples are surprised at Jesus asking them to share his body and blood in a sacred meal. Early in chapter 6 of John's Gospel, Jesus had promised the crowds in Capernaum that he would give them his flesh to eat. He is the bread come down from heaven (John 6:51). He will also give them his blood to drink (John 6:53–56).

The disciples in the Upper Room remember clearly the day when Jesus first publicly announced this promise of divine food. After he had told the crowds that they would need to eat his body and drink his blood, almost everyone in the audience walked away, never to come back (see John 6:66). His faithful apostles and disciples remember this dramatic scene (see John 6:67–69).

Now, while sharing his final Passover supper with those who remain faithful to him, Jesus follows through on his promise to give his disciples his flesh to eat and his blood to drink, under the appearance of bread and wine.

> While they were eating, he took a loaf of bread, and after blessing it he broke it, gave it to them, and said, "Take; this is my body." Then he took a cup, and after giving thanks he gave it to them, and all of them drank from it. He said to them, "This is my blood of the [new] covenant, which is poured out for many. Truly I tell you, I will never again drink of the fruit of the vine until that day when I drink it new in the kingdom of God." (Mark 14:22–25)

Note here that Christian theologians have sometimes altered the scriptural words of Jesus for liturgical reasons. Today, for example, in the text of the Roman Missal, the institution of the Eucharist is made to appear that, at the Last Supper, Jesus is directly connecting the food gift of his body and blood to his death on the cross. The current *liturgical* text reads,

> Take this, all of you, and eat of it, for this is my Body, *which will be given up* for you.

None of the four New Testament authors describing the Last Supper's ritual even hint at a future suffering implied in the liturgical words "which *will be* given up." Here are the four scriptural versions of Jesus's words over the bread.

THE BREAD

Matthew: "Take, eat; this is my body." (Matt 26:26)

Mark: "Take; this is my body." (Mark 14:22)

Luke: "This is my body, which is given for you.[2] Do this in remembrance of me." (Luke 22:19)

Paul: "This is my body that is for you. Do this in remembrance of me." (1 Cor 11:24)

Regarding the consecration of the cup, the current *liturgical* text reads,

Take this, all of you, and drink from it, for this is the chalice of my Blood, the Blood of the new *and eternal* covenant, which *will be* poured out for you and for many for the forgiveness of sins. Do this in memory of me. (The italicized words do not occur in any of the New Testament texts.)

WINE

Matthew: "Drink from it, all of you; for this is my blood of the covenant, which is poured out[3] for many for the forgiveness of sins." (Matt 26:27–28)

Mark: "This is my blood of the covenant, which is poured out for many." (Mark 14:24)

Luke: "This cup that is poured out for you is the new covenant in my blood." (Luke 22:20)

Paul: "This cup is the new covenant in my blood. Do this, as often as you drink it, in remembrance of me." (1 Cor 11:25)

EVOLUTIONARY IMPLICATIONS

Teilhard would say that the Christian community must go through many stages of evolution in consciousness before the human family can renew the face of Earth in love. Jesus recognizes the enduring need for growth in his followers. So, he provides the food and drink for the long journey to fulfillment. At first, the disciples think the journey will end within decades of Jesus's resurrection. Later, expectations get revised to centuries, then to millennia.

Jesus's institution of the Eucharist as a liturgical rite also points to a long journey into the future for the young church. Paul recognizes that gatherings on the Lord's Day will have a long future. He writes, "For as often as you eat this bread and drink the cup, you proclaim the Lord's death until he comes" (1 Cor 11:26). Keep doing this—nourishing yourselves with his body and blood in your assemblies—until the end of time.

One of the most evolutionary changes witnessed in the history of religions is the institution of the Eucharist. It allows the followers of Jesus to be nourished daily with the body and blood of their risen and still alive Lord. In all other religions, the divinity remains distant and remote, inaccessible and unavailable, requiring great gifts and sacrifices with only the faintest hope of being heard. Jesus paints a totally different picture of God and God's kingdom. Jesus presents a welcoming, forgiving, loving God. God is present, nearby, all around us. In the Eucharist, God becomes totally immediate and accessible within our own bodies and minds. God's love becomes intimately available.

18

Passion and Death

Weakness of the Disciples (14:26 — 15:37)

THEY LEAVE THE Upper Room after sharing the Eucharist and
begin walking toward the Mount of Olives. Jesus again predicts
his imminent passion and the fact that they will all desert him (14:27).
Peter protests, as do all the others, that they will not desert Jesus (see
14:31).

Jesus spends some time in prayer. Mark tells us that Jesus is "dis-
tressed and agitated" and "deeply grieved" as he enters his prayer. Jesus
asks his three closest companions, Peter and the two brothers, James
and John, to join him and support him in prayer. But they fall asleep.
Jesus is disappointed. He finds them asleep, not once but three times
(see 14:37–38).

Just as Jesus has been expressing his disappointment in his three
dearest friends, Judas the betrayer appears. He brings a crowd of ruf-
fians, sent by the chief priests and scribes to ensure that Jesus is appre-
hended. Jesus is betrayed with Judas's kiss. Within minutes, they all
abandon him (see 14:50).

All these negative experiences are what Teilhard calls *passivities
of diminishment*. Jesus continues to endure them. He is arrested and
placed on trial before the formal assembly of the Sanhedrin. "Now the
chief priests and the whole council were looking for testimony against
Jesus to put him to death; but they found none. For many gave false
testimony against him, and their testimony did not agree" (14:55–56).
Jesus does not honor these false witnesses with a reply.

Finally, the high priest asks him a direct question: "Are you the
Messiah, the Son of the Blessed One?" To this he does reply.

I am; and

> "you will see the Son of Man
> seated at the right hand of the Power,"
> and "coming with the clouds of heaven." (14:62)

The high priest declares that Jesus's reply is an act of blasphemy. The council condemns him. Some begin to spit on him. Others blindfold him and strike him, saying to him, "Prophesy!" The guards also beat him (see 14:65). These events are humiliating passivities that Jesus is forced to endure.

Meanwhile Peter, the supreme apostle, stands in the courtyard denying his Master, not with a simple denial but with a curse. He swears, "I do not know this man you are talking about." But when the cock crows, Peter remembers Jesus's prediction. And he breaks down and weeps (14:71–72).

We can imagine that, while all the *passivities of diminishment* are being heaped on Jesus during the night and early morning, he remains in prayer with his Father, redirecting the energy of his unjust and humiliating suffering to bring new life to his people.

THE DIMINISHMENTS CONTINUE

The priests, elders, and scribes are determined to do away with Jesus once and for all. As Jews, they have no authority to declare the death penalty on anyone. That is Rome's prerogative. Only Rome can condemn a man to death. So the priests bring Jesus to Pilate, the Roman governor. They tell him that Jesus claims to be a king. Jesus does not defend himself against the charge. Pilate knows that the Jewish officials hate Jesus and, in fact, are jealous of him for his popularity with the people (see 15:10).

Pilate offers to set free one condemned prisoner. He proposes to the crowd the choice of Jesus or Barabbas, another man the elders hate. But they hate Jesus even more. They stir the crowd to start shouting for the release of Barabbas. When Pilate asks, "'Then what do you wish me to do with the man you call the King of the Jews?' They shouted back, 'Crucify him!'" (15:12–13).

Before he is crucified, the soldiers enjoy their sadistic pleasure with him. They go far beyond what they would normally do to a condemned prisoner. Instead of a private flogging, they do it publicly in the court-yard. They also invite other soldiers from the cohort to come, watch, and participate. They dress Jesus in purple, befitting a king. They twist some thorns into a crown and put it on his head. They mock him by saluting him, "Hail, King of the Jews!" (15:16–18). Mark adds that they "struck his head with a reed, spat upon him, and knelt down in homage to him" (15:19). Then, they lead him off to be crucified.

By this time, Jesus is so weak that he cannot carry his own cross. The soldiers commandeer Simon of Cyrene, "a passer-by, who was coming in from the country, to carry his cross" (15:21). At the place called Golgotha, they strip him and crucify him. They cast lots to see who will get each piece of his clothing (see 15:24).

Not only is Jesus in excruciating pain hanging from the cross, but he must also endure continual taunts from his accusers, from passersby, and even from those who are crucified alongside him (see 15:29–32). We are contemplating some of the basest and cruelest forms of human behavior.

EVOLUTIONARY IMPLICATIONS

Teilhard would see the many *passivities of diminishment* that Jesus undergoes as an expenditure of his energy of endurance. His passivities began the night before—with his loneliness in prayer, Judas's betrayal, abandonment by his dearest friends, the crudeness of the soldiers who took him to trial, the insolence of the guards slapping him, the duplic-ity of the high priests, the moral weakness of Pilate, the excess of the Roman guards' mockery, and the fickleness of the crowd so easily swayed. Add to that the physical pain on his skin from the rough wood he must carry, the shame of his nakedness in front of the crowd, and the incessant taunting of the Jewish leaders standing around the cross. Imagine the physical and emotional energy Jesus uses to endure these humiliating events!

One thing to recognize here is that, in his Way, Jesus is teaching us not merely *how to live* one's daily life but also *how to suffer* and *how to die*. Just as we spend our daily energy actively working to build the kingdom of God, we need to learn how to utilize the energy we spend in suffering and dying to help further God's kingdom. Teilhard says we can further God's project not only by our activities but also by how we

117

deal with daily passivities of diminishment as well as those endured while suffering and dying.

What does Jesus do with the energy he spends in suffering physical pain, emotional rejection, and spiritual pain? What is its purpose? Is it purely a waste? Can the energy spent enduring these things be used to benefit the growth of the kingdom of God? Teilhard answers yes.[1] That is what Jesus teaches us on the cross. The energy being spent in enduring passivities, just as the energy being spent in performing activities, may be directed to energize God's project *by one's intention*. In the kingdom, no energy need be wasted. Even the energy endured in unwelcome passivities may be directed to contribute to God's project. Teilhard sees Jesus doing precisely this. God's will is always to promote the growth of the kingdom. Jesus's prayer is, "Thy kingdom come. Thy will be done on Earth…." This is the meaning of all martyrdom. One willingly undergoes martyrdom to help the growth of God's kingdom, not merely to save one's soul.

In Teilhard's terminology, one acts and does good deeds to help accomplish God's work on Earth by one's *activities of growth*. One transforms *suffering* and *passivities* to help accomplish God's work on Earth by one's *activities of growth*. One *dies*—a *passivity*—to help accomplish God's work on Earth by turning it into an *activity of growth*.

19

The Seven Last Words

The Seven Last Words of Jesus

1. "Then Jesus said, 'Father, forgive them; for they do not know what they are doing.'" (Luke 23:34)
2. "Truly I tell you, today you will be with me in Paradise." (Luke 23:43)
3. "When Jesus saw his mother and the disciple whom he loved standing beside her, he said to his mother, 'Woman, here is your son.' Then he said to the disciple, 'Here is your mother.' And from that hour the disciple took her into his own home." (John 19:26–27)
4. "And about three o'clock Jesus cried with a loud voice, 'Eli, Eli, lema sabachthani?' that is, 'My God, my God, why have you forsaken me?'" (Matt 27:46)
5. "After this, when Jesus knew that all was now finished, he said (in order to fulfill the scripture), 'I am thirsty.'" (John 19:28)
6. "A jar full of sour wine was standing there. So they put a sponge full of the wine on a branch of hyssop and held it to his mouth. When Jesus had received the wine, he said, 'It is finished.' Then he bowed his head and gave up his spirit." (John 19:29–30)
7. "Then Jesus, crying with a loud voice, said, *'Father, into your hands I commend my spirit.'* Having said this, he breathed his last." (Luke 23:46, emphasis added)

Note that not all these seven sayings can be found in any one Gospel account of Jesus's crucifixion. The traditional ordering of the "seven last words" is a blending of texts from the four Gospels. Mark reports that, in Jesus's final moments before dying, he cries out *without speaking any specific words* (see Mark 15:37).

The First "Word"

Luke is credited with two of Jesus's sayings on the cross. They reflect Luke's Gospel themes of unlimited *forgiveness* and *salvation*—the fullness of life—for all.

On the cross, Jesus's first act is a prayer of forgiveness, as it often was during his public life before performing a healing. On the cross, he asks the Father to forgive everyone. In this first "word," Jesus pleads with the Father to wipe away all the sins of those who have caused him to suffer. He knows that the Father has always forgiven sins at his request.

This petition of Jesus from the cross covers everyone—from the betrayal and denial of Judas and Peter, to the indifference of Pilate and the wanton cruelty of the soldiers, to the cowardice of his hundreds of followers who deserted him, and even to the deep-seated hatred of the chief priests, scribes, Pharisees, and council elders. Jesus is asking his Father not to set any limits on his divine compassion and to forgive everyone.

EVOLUTIONARY IMPLICATIONS

Teilhard might comment that both Jesus and the Father could also foresee, through the ages, all the sins that would be committed, by action and omission. The Father knows that Jesus's request on the cross is for all people and all times.

God's forgiveness is deeply liberating. It is also a model for us. God's forgiveness sets us free to forgive others. Once we know that we are forgiven and loved by the Father, we can find the compassion within to show forgiveness to all who have offended us. If Jesus, in anguish on the cross, could forgive even the ones who hated him the most, can we not forgive those who have offended us? Forgiveness liberates both the forgiver and the forgiven.

The Second "Word"

The second "word" of Jesus highlights his pervasive theme of salvation. It is found especially in Luke. Jesus's intent is always to bring more life to humanity—richer life, deeper awareness, higher consciousness. More life comes to us as the result of adopting the gospel's way of thinking. The good news is that God is an unconditionally loving Father of all. True love always wants fuller life for those we love. The fact that Jesus would invite a criminal to join him in entering God's presence immediately upon death indicates that the kingdom of God is all-inclusive. He assured the criminal next to him, "Truly I tell you, today you will be with me in Paradise" (Luke 23:43). Life in the presence of God is not restricted to observant Jews. Even repentant hardened criminals may enter life in paradise.[1]

EVOLUTIONARY IMPLICATIONS

The gospel's message going out to the entire world is important to Teilhard. His understanding of God's evolutionary project requires the cooperation of all human beings, regardless of race, ethnicity, age, gender, state of health, or *religion*. For God's project to succeed, both themes—universal *forgiveness* and *salvation* (fullness of life for all)—remain essential building blocks of God's project on Earth.

For Teilhard, forgiveness of sins and redemption (one's debts being paid by Christ) are an essential step in God's project, but only a first step. Bringing about humanity's growth, vitality, and creativity toward the fullness of life is the larger and longer step in God's project. Only when we realize that Jesus on the cross contributes to *both steps* can we fully understand the significance of his suffering.[2] Teilhard writes, "Henceforth the world will be able to make the sign of the cross only with a cross that has become a symbol of *growth* at the same time as of *redemption*."[3]

According to Robert L. Faricy, a theologian who possesses a comprehensive understanding of Teilhard's thought, "Teilhard views

Christ's redemptive act not only as reparation for sin but also, and primarily, as an act of the laborious effort of the unification of the world."[4] Jesus's suffering becomes a laborious act of creative unification. On his cross, he carries "not only the weight of sin but the whole weight of the true progress of the world…toward the final synthesis of all things in Himself."[5]

The Third "Word"

The third "word" is really two words. It is about the importance of relationship and our need to care for each other. It is a quality Jesus not only preaches but also shows in his relationships. Even on the cross, naked and in unbearable pain, he displays concern for his mother's well-being after his death. This shows Jesus's humanity and the depth of his love for his mother and for the disciple into whose care he entrusts her.

EVOLUTIONARY IMPLICATIONS

For Teilhard, love and transformation always begin with the basic relationships among family and friends. Even though he challenges us always to keep the big objective in mind—keeping the human race evolving toward God—Teilhard never neglects to stress the importance of maintaining the flow of love among those we encounter daily at home, at school, at work, and in our neighborhood. Familial love marks the source of the river of love that will eventually reach out to everyone.[6] Jesus preaches a religion of face-to-face encounter among his followers—acts of forgiveness, compassion, and love are face-to-face events.

The Fourth "Word"

Both Mark and Matthew report the fourth "word" almost identically. Some authorities interpret this saying as an abandonment of the Son by the Father. Certainly, it represents the cry of one who is truly human and who feels forsaken. If you are being put to death by your foes and deserted by your friends, you might well feel deserted by God.

In this "word," Jesus speaks aloud the opening verse of the messianic Psalm 22: "My God, my God, why have you forsaken me?" Some scholars say that this "word" was spoken aloud like an antiphon, to clue those around him that he was praying Psalm 22.[7] People hearing the opening words of this psalm know that he is reliving *all* of its verses because those verses prophesy in detail the various forms of the Messiah's suffering.

Psalm 22 is about one who maintains trust in God, even when feeling abandoned by God. Abandonment is an emotion. Trust is a spiritual power that can exist and operate even when feeling deserted by God. Psalm 22 is a powerful, inspired song composed by King David that expresses the paradox that a sense of abandonment and trust can coexist in the same moment. The psalm ends on a triumphal and confident note. Jesus's trust is still grounded in God, "I shall live for him" (Ps 22:29). Here are some of the final verses of Psalm 22:

> I will tell of your name to my brothers and sisters;
>> in the midst of the congregation I will praise you....
> Future generations will be told about the Lord,
> and proclaim his deliverance to a people yet unborn,
>> saying that he has done it. (Ps 22:22, 30–31)

EVOLUTIONARY IMPLICATIONS

For Teilhard, life is fraught with pain and suffering. Diminishing experiences are unavoidable, even for Jesus. In Jesus's *metanoia* (a higher way of thinking), suffering is not something the loving Father wills for us, but something inevitable because of the way evolution works. Diminishments also happen because many human beings are immature and selfish. In this fourth "word," Jesus tells us to maintain faith and trust that God's work will get done, despite all the diminishments that befall us.

Evolution is a continual process of groping and growth. It is *inevitable* that, throughout this evolutionary process, there should be conflict, tears, bloodshed, suffering, death, destruction, natural disasters, injustice, immorality, and other forms of diminishment. Teilhard explains, "For evil appears *inevitably* with the first atom of being which creation 'releases' into existence."[8]

Teilhard lumps all these unwelcome events as "evils." He writes,

> If evil is rampant all around us on Earth, we should not be shocked but rather hold up our heads in pride....Our being must, indeed, be precious for God to continue to seek it through so many obstacles. And it is a great honor that he makes us able to fight with him, that his word may be accomplished.[9]

The Fifth "Word"

The fifth "word" is "I thirst." You may interpret that statement literally, as do the soldiers, who offer him something to drink. More likely, in saying, "I thirst," Jesus is merely fulfilling the prophecy that is expressed in Psalm 22 that he was just reciting.

> My mouth is dried up like a potsherd,
>   and my tongue sticks to my jaws;
>   you lay me in the dust of death. (Ps 22:15)

EVOLUTIONARY IMPLICATIONS

Jesus's thirst is so much bigger than having a dry mouth. For Teilhard, Jesus is thirsting on behalf of each member of his universal Body. Each one of us, in all the ages to come, is like the Samaritan woman at the well who asked Jesus to give her the "water of life." Jesus is thirsting for all of us. Teilhard wishes that we can all be as direct as the Samaritan woman and acknowledge our thirst for the living God and for the life that God wants to give us, *here and now*.

The idea that humanity could learn collectively to love more deeply and evolve in its ability to experience a fuller life on Earth is central to Teilhard's ideas about the growth and development of God's project. To say that humanity is incapable of evolving in love on Earth would be abhorrent to Teilhard. For him, if God created a human race that could experience growth in love only in heaven, after a life of suffering and anxiety on Earth, it would be a cruel divine joke.[10]

The Sixth "Word"

Traditionally, the sixth "word, "It is finished," is interpreted theologically as the announcement of the end of the earthly life of Jesus, in anticipation of his resurrection. It is viewed as a statement made to himself and to the Father: "I have done the work you gave me to do." It is a summation of his work on Earth, the completion of a massive task. A plan is completed. Salvation—the fullness of life—is made possible for all. He has shown the Father's love to humanity. He has become one of us and taken our place. In his human body, he has demonstrated both humanity's brokenness and God's love. He has made an offering of himself to God on behalf of humanity's future.

EVOLUTIONARY IMPLICATIONS

For Teilhard, this statement, "It is finished," means much more. It means that the *work of the human Jesus* is done, and he is now ready to begin the work of *Christ, the Risen Lord*. This is the work proper to the next stage in the divine plan. If anyone realizes that Jesus's greatest work is not yet accomplished, it is Jesus himself. Jesus realizes that his greatest challenge is not yet accomplished. He still has thousands of years of work to accomplish God's evolutionary project of transforming humanity and renewing the face of Earth.

Specifically, Jesus's role is to provide the Cosmic Body in which each of us will live and participate as active members, or cells, in that Christ body. We will all work together within Christ Jesus's Body to help accomplish the divine project. Only when humanity comes to learn to love the way the Father loves will the divine project be complete.

The Seventh "Word"

The seventh "word" Jesus speaks indicates that he is ready for total reunion with the Father. "Father, into your hands I commit my spirit." It is an expression of total surrender to the plan and to the will of God.

EVOLUTIONARY IMPLICATIONS

For Teilhard, Jesus, in his last seven "words," is weaving together the seven important qualities we all need if we are to help complete God's vision for humanity:

1. mutual forgiveness;
2. bringing to everyone a bit of the fullness of life;
3. valuing each personal relationship;
4. maintaining faith and trust that God's work will get done, despite all the diminishment that befall us;
5. thirst and longing for the success of God's project;
6. the confidence that we are accomplishing in our lives on Earth what we were meant to accomplish; and
7. the deepest confidence that we are always in a loving connection with God.

These are qualities that envision humanity's future on Earth requiring of us more than just a life of avoiding sin. They call for a life of action—perhaps even daring action—for God and for the work God wants to accomplish on Earth. These seven last "words" of Jesus can be summed up in his prayer to his Father that he taught us to say: "Thy kingdom come. Thy will be done on Earth."

PART IV

THE GOSPEL OF LUKE

THE GOSPEL ACCORDING to Luke is by far the longest of the first three Gospels. Although Luke recounts many of Jesus's miracles and parables found in Matthew and Mark, he provides several new ones. He also offers new insights into the future Christian community.

Luke's Gospel presents only the first part of his larger story. The second part is found in the Acts of the Apostles. In his Gospel, *Jerusalem* is the center of Jesus's life; it is where the church is born. In Acts, the message of Christ is proclaimed to the entire world. When Luke begins writing his account of Jesus and the church, Christian communities are sprouting up all over the Mediterranean and the church is beginning to develop its structure. Luke wants us to have the whole story.

Like Matthew, Luke begins his story with the baby Jesus. Matthew tells the story of Jesus's infancy from Joseph's perspective since he is writing primarily for Jewish Christians. Luke presents the story from *Mary's perspective* since he is writing primarily for *Gentile Christians*.

Many of Luke's Gentile readers have never been to Jerusalem, so Luke spends much of ten chapters (Luke 9:51–19:40) describing Jesus's journey *toward* Jerusalem. The rest of his Gospel story (chapters 20–24) takes place *in* Jerusalem, including Jesus's ascension.

Luke is unique in his emphasis on the *activity of the Holy Spirit*: Jesus is conceived by the Spirit (1:35) and anointed with the Spirit (3:22; 4:1, 14, 18); people are filled with the Spirit (1:15, 41, 67) and inspired by the Spirit (2:25–27); the Holy Spirit serves as a teacher (10:10–12); Jesus rejoices in the Holy Spirit (10:21); God gives the Holy Spirit to all who ask (11:13); and the disciples will be "clothed with power from on high" (24:49).

The presence and work of the Holy Spirit become even more dominant in the Acts of the Apostles, where the Holy Spirit guides the development and growth of the Christian communities throughout Asia Minor, Greece, Rome, and into Europe. The *metanoia* that we met in John the Baptist's preaching was needed to recognize the kingdom of God at work. In the early church, this *metanoia* is recognized as a direct grace or gift from the Holy Spirit (see Acts 11:15–18).[1]

Luke's Gospel places emphasis on *prayer and worship*. He frequently tells of Jesus's personal prayer.[2] Jesus also gives instructions on prayer (11:2–4), often encourages his disciples to pray,[3] and presents three parables on prayer.[4] For Jesus, the temple is a "house of prayer" (19:46).

Luke also emphasizes what Jesus calls his *"family"* (8:21). He is not talking about blood relations but spiritual bonds (see 8:3). Luke describes the commitment required to become a member of this spiritual family, the "cost" of discipleship, some basic requirements, and the rejection and even persecution that may result from one's fellowship with Jesus.[5]

Luke's Gospel often emphasizes Jesus's *concern for the excluded*. Among these are *Samaritans*,[6] *Gentiles*,[7] *tax collectors*,[8] *women*,[9] and *the poor*[10] compared to *the rich*.[11]

Each of these excluded groups were far from respected in Israel at that time. Jews hated Samaritans and Gentiles. They despised fellow Jews for becoming tax collectors for Rome. Women were considered second-class citizens. Poverty was considered a divine punishment, and the poor were pitied if not despised, while the rich were regarded as blessed by God. Each of these five excluded groups account for a significant number of members during the early generations of the Christian community.

In this part, we look at the role of the Holy Spirit, the importance of prayer, and Jesus's spiritual family. That Jesus included the excluded in his family is profoundly evolutionary.

20

The Holy Spirit

NO OTHER New Testament author mentions the Holy Spirit more than Luke. The Holy Spirit plays a significant role in his Gospel and in the Acts of the Apostles. Teilhard would note that Luke's presentation of the Holy Spirit as a divine force distinct from God the Father suggests a totally new theology. Whenever the Hebrew Scriptures mention the divine spirit, it is used metaphorically to express a blessing or gracious act of the Creator God. It is like what we might say to a troubled friend: "My heart goes out to you." For the Jews, God's "spirit" is not a being distinct from God but simply a term that expresses a "grace" or "blessing" flowing from God.

For Luke and for early Christians, the Holy Spirit emerges into their consciousness as a distinct divine being, manifesting qualities and abilities of a person. The Holy Spirit acts independently as a person, just as Jesus did as a human. Both operate under the guidance of God the Father.[1]

The Holy Spirit appears in many chapters of Luke's Gospel and throughout Acts, sometimes in surprising and unpredictable ways. Luke's writings present the Holy Spirit as a force influencing people's lives *from within.*

For Teilhard, the Holy Spirit is a prime mover in the evolutionary process. The Holy Spirit is primarily responsible for the success of God's evolutionary project for creation.[2] For Teilhard, the Holy Spirit is the "fertilizer" of love, union, and evolution in the universe.[3]

The Holy Spirit Permeates Jesus's Early Life (1:5–80)

In reading the first two chapters of Luke's Gospel, Teilhard would note the important role the Holy Spirit plays in the earliest stages of Jesus's life. God assigned to the Holy Spirit the task of enabling Jesus's incarnation. The Holy Spirit gives Jesus human life through the natural process of conception and gestation in a woman's womb. Jesus is conceived by the Spirit:

> The angel said to her, "The Holy Spirit will come upon you, and the power of the Most High will overshadow you; therefore the child to be born will be holy; he will be called Son of God. (1:35)

The angel Gabriel also tells Mary that Elizabeth is pregnant. Mary then takes the initiative and makes the three-day journey to Ain Karim to help Elizabeth in her final months of pregnancy.

Luke emphasizes that, even before Jesus's incarnation, the Holy Spirit has already been at work in the lives of Zachariah and Elizabeth. Both have been filled with the Spirit (see 1:15, 41, 67). In his vision, Zachariah the priest is told that his son John "will be great in the sight of the Lord. He must never drink wine or strong drink; even before his birth he will be filled with the Holy Spirit" (1:15).

Zachariah's wife, Elizabeth, receives the Holy Spirit when Mary, pregnant with Jesus, approaches her. "When Elizabeth heard Mary's greeting, the child leaped in her womb. And Elizabeth was filled with the Holy Spirit" (1:41). We may assume by his leaping that the baby John in Elizabeth's womb also receives the Holy Spirit.

When the baby is to be named, Zachariah, John's father, says he is to be called John. The Holy Spirit then inspires Zachariah to praise God in his prophecy (see 1:67–75):

> And you, child, will be called the prophet of the Most
> High;
>   for you will go before the Lord to prepare his ways,

to give knowledge of salvation to his people
>> by the forgiveness of their sins.
By the tender mercy of our God,
>> the dawn from on high will break upon us,
to give light to those who sit in darkness and in the shadow
>>>> of death,
>> to guide our feet into the way of peace. (1:76–79)

In the prophecy, note that the "knowledge of salvation" will give light even to the Gentiles, that is, the Holy Spirit will be given also "to those who sit in darkness and in the shadow of death" (1:79).

When Mary and Elizabeth first meet, both she and Elizabeth are inspired by the Holy Spirit to praise God. Elizabeth is inspired to reveal to Mary that Jesus is the Lord. When Elizabeth feels the Spirit, she "exclaim[s] with a loud cry, 'Blessed are you among women, and blessed is the fruit of your womb'" (1:42).

Mary, too, is inspired by the Spirit to sing God's praises. The theme of her song is that God has blessed the lowly ones—the forgotten people, the humble women, the poor, and the excluded (see 1:46–49).

Furthermore, Mary is inspired to announce that the child she will bring into the world will begin a movement that will last unto "all generations." And this child will be a blessing "to Abraham and to his descendants forever" (1:55).

SIMEON AND ANNA (2:22–38)

In Luke's second chapter, the Holy Spirit is at work in two elderly people in the Jerusalem temple. One is a devout man named Simeon:

The Holy Spirit rested on him [Simeon]. It had been revealed to him by the Holy Spirit that he would not see death before he had seen the Lord's Messiah. Guided by the Spirit, Simeon came into the temple; and when the parents brought in the child Jesus, to do for him what was customary under the law, Simeon took him in his arms and praised God. (2:25–28)

Simeon is inspired by the Holy Spirit to announce that Jesus's light will encompass the whole world (see 2:32).

On the same day, we meet one more woman touched by the Holy Spirit. Luke identifies her as "a prophet, Anna the daughter of Phanuel, of the tribe of Asher" (2:36). After seeing Jesus, Anna becomes his first disciple, announcing him in the temple. She "began to praise God and to speak about the child to all who were looking for the redemption of Jerusalem" (2:38).

The Twelve-Year-Old Jesus (2:41–52)

Luke alone recounts the story of the twelve-year-old Jesus coming from Galilee to Jerusalem to celebrate the Passover Feast. In pointing out his age, Luke implies that Jesus has just celebrated his bar mitzvah. To prepare for it, Jesus would have been studying the Bible for the past year or more with his local rabbi in Nazareth. Instead of returning to Nazareth from Jerusalem with his community's caravan, Jesus is inspired—undoubtedly by the Holy Spirit—to join the teachers in the temple as they debate fine points of the Law (see 2:49).

Evolutionary Implications

Luke presents the Holy Spirit as an identifiable actor in human events and as someone distinct from the Father Creator. Luke introduces the Spirit as a new way of explaining divine involvement in human affairs. For Luke, it is inaccurate to say that God *controls* every act of every person. This is what the Jews believed. Rather, for Luke, God's way of being involved in the world is to let people find their own way. When needed, God inspires, guides, urges, and nudges. God *manages and guides* rather than controls. The inner guidance comes from the Holy Spirit.

We also notice that the adolescent Jesus is aware that he has a "Father" different from the paternal figure of Joseph. Luke hints that the young Jesus still needs to mature in many ways before he is ready to take up his assigned role in God's project. "Then he went down with them and came to Nazareth, and was obedient to them....And Jesus increased in wisdom and in years, and in divine and human favor" (2:51–52).

The Holy Spirit at the Beginning of Jesus's Public Life (3:21—4:44)

The Holy Spirit continues to manage God's divine project. The Spirit was with Jesus at his baptism in the River Jordan, throughout his desert retreat, his encounters with the devil, and in his public ministry.

We read at his baptism, "When Jesus also had been baptized and was praying, the heaven was opened, and the Holy Spirit descended upon him in bodily form like a dove" (3:21–22).

After his baptism, "Jesus, full of the Holy Spirit, returned from the Jordan and was led by the Spirit in the wilderness, where for forty days he was tempted by the devil" (4:1–2).

Then, in his public ministry, Jesus says, "I must proclaim the good news of the kingdom of God to the other cities also; for I was sent for this purpose." So he continues proclaiming the message in the synagogues of Judea (see 4:43–44).

Finally, Luke notes in Acts that after Jesus is taken up to heaven, he continues to give "instructions through the Holy Spirit to the apostles whom he had chosen" (Acts 1:2).

EVOLUTIONARY IMPLICATIONS

Luke informs us that the Holy Spirit plays a major role in the life of Jesus, and that the Holy Spirit will play a major role in the development of the Christian assemblies in the early church.[4] We see this repeatedly in the Acts of the Apostles.[5]

Although baptism of new converts is essential for membership, most Christian communities never really become powerfully active and charismatic until new converts receive the Holy Spirit.[6] Even the apostles don't get truly fired up for Christ until the Holy Spirit enflames them at Pentecost (see Acts 2:1–13). As recognition of the Holy Spirit's energizing work grows in their Christian community life and during their eucharistic assemblies, their experience of the Spirit reshapes their understanding of theology, liturgy, and spirituality.

Prayer and the Holy Spirit

Luke presents Jesus's advice to his disciples to remain persistent in prayer. But the nature of God's response to our various petitions comes as a surprise:

> Ask, and it will be given you; search, and you will find; knock, and the door will be opened for you....If you then, who are evil, know how to give good gifts to your children, how much more will the heavenly Father give the Holy Spirit to those who ask him! (Luke 11:9–13)

According to Jesus, the Father doesn't give you what you ask for. Rather, *the Father always gives the same gift, no matter what you ask for.* If you pray to get a job; the Father gives you the Holy Spirit. If you pray to be cured of your illness; the Father gives you the Holy Spirit. If you pray for patience with your children; the Father gives you the Holy Spirit. It appears that the Holy Spirit is the universal gift of the Father.

There will be times when that gift of the Holy Spirit is critically important:

> When they bring you before the synagogues, the rulers, and the authorities, do not worry about how you are to defend yourselves or what you are to say; for the Holy Spirit will teach you at that very hour what you ought to say. (12:11–12)

EVOLUTIONARY IMPLICATIONS

Regarding the focus of our prayer life, Luke might advise us to devote time and attention to the Holy Spirit and look to the Holy Spirit for inner guidance. The Holy Spirit wants to provide us with the "fire of love" that flows between the Father and the Son. This is the fire that not only changes the way we think, but also totally transforms us. The Holy Spirit is the source of never-ending inner and outer evolution.

When we reflect on the many references to the Holy Spirit and the Spirit's importance in our lives and the lives of all people, it is surprising that we do not turn to the Holy Spirit more each day. Catholics, for example, pray the Lord's Prayer and the Hail Mary frequently, but seldom direct their prayer to the Holy Spirit. In our tradition, there is a classical, yet *evolutionary* prayer to the Holy Spirit that Teilhard would encourage us to make personal:

> *Come, Holy Spirit. Fill the hearts of your faithful.*
> *enkindle in us the fire of your love.*
> *Send forth your Spirit and we shall be created.*
> *And You shall renew the face of the earth.*

21

On Prayer

Jesus's Personal Prayer

LUKE'S FIRST example of Jesus's own prayer is at his baptism by John in the Jordan River. Jesus prays for guidance, and the Holy Spirit fills him with peace (symbol of the dove). It also evokes a special blessing of approval from the Father:

> Now when all the people were baptized, and when Jesus also had been baptized *and was praying*, the heaven was opened, and the Holy Spirit descended upon him in bodily form like a dove. And a voice came from heaven, "You are my Son, the Beloved; with you I am well pleased." (3:21–22, emphasis added)

In Luke's Gospel, Jesus prefers to pray in private. For example, during Jesus's public life and after having performed healings and miracles, Jesus would go off alone to pray (see 5:15–16).

For Luke, Jesus is the model for us of the importance of private prayer and reflection, especially before major decisions. One big decision Jesus needed to make was to select the twelve people who would receive the special calling as his "apostles":

> He went out to the mountain to pray; and he spent the night in prayer to God. And when day came, he called his disciples and chose twelve of them, whom he also named apostles. (6:12–13)

EVOLUTIONARY IMPLICATIONS

Even Jesus, who is one with the Father, needs to pray in order to discern his Father's will before making big decisions. If Jesus needs to connect with the Father to perceive the Father's will, how much more do we need to do it? We often say to God, "Thy will be done on Earth." Yet, it is the Holy Spirit that inspires us in prayer to discern God's will for us in today's decisions.

Special Prayer Times (9:29–31)

Jesus experiences some very special moments in personal prayer. At times, he allows a few of his favorite disciples to accompany him. One time, when Peter, James, and John were with Jesus on a mountain, he was transfigured before their very eyes. "And while he was praying, the appearance of his face changed, and his clothes became dazzling white" (9:29).

PRAYER AND ACTION (10:21–24)

Not all of Jesus's experiences are as impressive as the transfiguration or about big decisions like starting his public life. Sometimes his prayer is spontaneous and joyful. For example, Jesus selects seventy-two disciples. He sends them out in pairs to announce the good news in the towns and villages that he will eventually visit. After their successful missionary work, they return and tell Jesus about the healings and exorcisms they were able to perform. He gave them the authority to do those amazing things and now he is "rejoic[ing] in the Holy Spirit" with them that his gift of healing worked wonders (see 10:21). What does it mean for Jesus to rejoice in the Holy Spirit?

EVOLUTIONARY IMPLICATIONS

For Luke, it is the task of the Holy Spirit to transform the people on Earth. Jesus sent out seventy-two disciples to proclaim the kingdom of God. Undoubtedly, many were not "the wise and intelligent" ones but were more like children—"infants" in a spiritual sense. Can you imagine the Holy Spirit imparting the power to heal and to drive out demons to these ordinary folks?

It is the will of the Father that all his disciples, even the lowly ones, can reveal the power of God's kingdom by their active deeds. Such work requires a certain depth of prayer and active faith.

It is seldom emphasized but clearly implied that when the crowds of sick people were very large, the twelve apostles also had lines of people coming to each of them for healing. Apparently, they were able to continue healing the sick just as they had been able to do when they went out in pairs on mission. In one instance, when the apostles were healing alongside Jesus, a man came to Jesus with his epileptic son and said that the apostles tried to heal his son but were unable to do so (see Matt 17:14–18).

Martha and Mary (10:38–42)

At one time, Jesus and his group visit the home of Martha and Mary, two women who are close friends of Jesus.

This scene has often been interpreted as Jesus approving the "contemplative life" (Mary) over the "active life" (Martha). If so, it is the only time in the New Testament where contemplation is preferred over action.

A more realistic interpretation of the scene would be that Jesus has been giving a talk to a group of people in the house, perhaps sharing some important teaching or insight. Mary, sitting near Jesus, has been listening to his teaching, and gaining insight from his words. In this context, Mary appears to be an attentive student or an eager learner, rather than a person rapt in contemplative prayer.

Regarding Martha, Jesus may merely want her to join the group of attentive listeners. Luke describes Martha as "distracted." Martha would say that she is not distracted but is attentive to Jesus. She stays focused, not by listening to him, but by taking care of preparing food for him and his large group. There is no sign of servants doing the cooking. Martha knows that as soon as Jesus finishes his lesson everyone will be eager to eat. Someone must get the food ready. That someone is she.

The "better part" that Mary chooses is not because she is lost in contemplative prayer. Rather, she is growing intellectually and spiritually by listening attentively to the master teacher.

EVOLUTIONARY IMPLICATIONS

Teilhard might suggest that Mary is learning more about the mindset of Jesus, how he perceives the world and how she should act in response to certain events. We might imagine Martha whispering to Jesus, "Don't worry, Master. I won't miss a thing. Mary will tell me in detail about your teaching after your group departs tomorrow."

Jesus Encourages Prayer (11:1–13)

Luke begins chapter 11 with an exhortation to prayer. Jesus teaches his disciples his own prayer. It is the Lord's Prayer. Note that Luke offers a shorter version than the one in Matthew's Gospel. Matthew's version is the one we use today. Some authorities claim that Luke's version, being shorter, is probably more primitive and accurate, while Matthew's version has most likely been liturgically enriched.

In both versions of the Lord's Prayer, the two halves are similar. In the first half of both versions, we promise Our Father that we will work to make the kingdom of God happen on Earth. In the second half of both versions, we ask the Father for the physical and spiritual support needed to keep our promise.

Both Matthew and Luke present the Lord's Prayer as a prayer in preparation for action or service. In Luke, Jesus uses a clever story to make his point (see 11:5–8). At midnight, when almost everyone is asleep, a man knocks on his neighbor's door asking for some bread to feed surprise guests who have just arrived and are hungry. The neighbor resists, but the man keeps at it until the neighbor relents, opens his door, and gives the man the bread he needs. The usual lesson: persistence wins on Earth. Jesus's lesson: persistence in prayer also gets results from heaven (see 11:9–13).

GOD'S UNIVERSAL RESPONSE TO PRAYER

Jesus tells people to ask in prayer for the gift of the Holy Spirit. You don't have to pray for the basics of food, clothing, and shelter, he says (see 12:29). Your Father doesn't need to be reminded that you need these things (see 12:30). "Instead, strive for his kingdom, and these things will be given to you as well" (12:31).

In Teilhard's language, the Father calls you to work for the fulfillment of the divine project. Let the success of God's project remain the focus of your prayer and of your action. Let it be the desire of your heart. "For where your treasure is, there your heart will be also" (12:34).

Jesus tells his disciples to pray for their enemies and bless those whom they would least likely bless. "Love your enemies, do good to those who hate you, bless those who curse you, pray for those who abuse you" (6:27–28).

Prayer becomes very important during times of persecution. "Be alert at all times, praying that you may have the strength to escape all these things that will take place, and to stand before the Son of Man" (21:36).

Jesus prays for his disciples, especially when he knows they will be facing difficult times. During the Last Supper, he prays especially for impetuous and impulsive Simon Peter: "Simon, Simon, listen! Satan has demanded to sift all of you like wheat, but I have prayed for you that your own faith may not fail; and you, when once you have turned back, strengthen your brothers" (22:31–32).

Jesus advises his disciples to pray for strength, especially when they are to be brought to trial. He is entering his own final day of suffering, humiliation, and death. On the Mount of Olives on the night before his death, he says to them, "Pray that you may not come into the time of trial" (22:40). On that same fateful night, Jesus himself prays with great intensity:

> "Father, if you are willing, remove this cup from me; yet, not my will but yours be done."…In his anguish he prayed more earnestly, and his sweat became like great drops of blood falling down on the ground. (22:41–44)

When Jesus gets up from prayer, he walks over to the disciples and finds them sleeping "because of grief." He says to them, "Why are you sleeping? Get up and pray that you may not come into the time of trial" (22:46).

EVOLUTIONARY IMPLICATIONS

The Jews are a praying people and a worshiping community. Jesus, first, encourages his followers to be good Jews in their prayer lives. Is there any evolution in the way Jesus teaches prayer? One obvious difference is that Jesus teaches us to call God "Our Father." Nothing in the Jewish tradition suggests that people address God by such an intimate name. In fact, Jesus says they may call God "Daddy."

Second, Jesus advises that prayers be kept simple and direct. There is no need to add all manner of adjectives and flourishes. No need to string lots of words together the way the Pharisees do. Just knock and ask. And don't give up. God always gives the Holy Spirit in response to our prayer. The Spirit teaches us how to cope.

Parables on Prayer (18:1–14)

Jesus also offers two parables on prayer. The first is the parable of the widow and the unjust judge (see 18:1–8). It is about the need to pray always and not to lose heart.

The second is a parable comparing the prayer of the self-righteous Pharisee to that of a tax collector "standing far off, [who] would not even look up to heaven, but was beating his breast and saying, 'God, be merciful to me, a sinner!'" (18:9–14). God prefers simple, honest prayers. "All who humble themselves will be exalted" (18:14).

EVOLUTIONARY IMPLICATIONS

Humility was not a prominent virtue among traditionally religious Jews, but it becomes central to Jesus's teaching.

22

The Spiritual Family

The Concept of Family (8:19–21)

ACCORDING TO MARK, while many of the locals in Capernaum think Jesus is a holy person, the Pharisees spread the word that he is possessed by the devil (see Mark 3:22). Others say that "he has gone out of his mind" (Mark 3:21). These confusing reports reach Jesus's home village of Nazareth, and so Jesus acquires a mixed reputation in Galilee. The rumors upset members of his extended family. "When his family heard it [the rumors], they went out to restrain him" (Mark 3:21).

Both Mark and Luke relate the story about a worried contingent of Jesus's relatives from Nazareth, including his mother Mary. They make the trip to Capernaum to see what they can do regarding their kinsman, Jesus. Perhaps they hope to keep him from embarrassing his family and neighbors any more than he has already. Perhaps they can convince him to return to Nazareth.

They arrive at Jesus's home in Capernaum only to find the house filled with people listening to him. The house is so crowded that they can't get inside to talk to him. "Standing outside, they sent to him and called him." People pass the message along until it gets to Jesus. Those sitting around him say to him, 'Your mother and your brothers and sisters are outside, asking for you'" (Mark 3:31–32).

In reply, Jesus clarifies for the crowd who God really is—the loving Father of us all. He redefines the concept of family as it is understood in the kingdom of God: Jesus replies, "My mother and my brothers are those who hear the word of God and do it" (Luke 8:21).[1]

We don't know what the Nazareth contingent does after hearing Jesus's reply. We do know that he doesn't go back home with them.

EVOLUTIONARY IMPLICATIONS

In effect, Jesus tells the crowd, "I am God's Son and I declare that your Father in heaven proclaims all of you to be my brothers and sisters." It is the kind of good news no one has ever preached to them before Jesus. Teilhard would suggest that this message is evolutionary.

Jesus is not just gathering a team of people to work with him. He is building a spiritual family. What makes them a family is not a "blood" connection but a shared belief in the importance of the kingdom of God and a commitment to work toward the accomplishment of God's divine project. It is a "spiritual" family.

Jesus's Spiritual Family

Luke tells us that the core group of Jesus's spiritual "family" travel everywhere with him. The twelve apostles are always with Jesus as "he went on through cities and villages, proclaiming and bringing the good news of the kingdom of God" (8:1).

In addition, Luke points out that there are always women in the entourage. They have taken the responsibility to obtain and provide daily food necessities for the group. Luke notes that the women "provided for them out of their resources" (8:3). The women are using their own money.

Luke also mentions that some of these are "women who had been cured of evil spirits and infirmities: Mary, called Magdalene, from whom seven demons had gone out, and Joanna, the wife of Herod's steward Chuza, and Susanna" (8:2–3). Luke writes about the women in Jesus's group "soon after" the event with the sinful woman at Simon the Pharisee's house (see 7:36–50). Perhaps this woman also joined Jesus's band of faithful disciples.

EVOLUTIONARY IMPLICATIONS

During this period, extended families—men, women, and children—might have traveled together, for instance, as in a group of people from Nazareth making a three-day pilgrimage to Jerusalem to celebrate Passover (see 2:4). However, it was unusual for a group not related by blood, like Jesus's team of men and women, to travel together from town to town like nomads.

Were these men and women accompanying Jesus learning to see themselves as a new kind of family, with a primary allegiance to each other and to Jesus, rather than to their own kinfolk in their own hometowns?

True Followers of Jesus (9:23–25)

Jesus makes clear the cost to become his follower as well as what rewards might come to a faithful follower:

> Then he said to them all, "If any want to become my followers, let them deny themselves and take up their cross daily and follow me. For those who want to save their life will lose it, and those who lose their life for my sake will save it." (9:23–25)[2]

EVOLUTIONARY PERSPECTIVE

Luke wrote these verses (9:23–25) many years after Jesus walked to his death carrying his cross. In Jesus's day, carrying a cross meant crucifixion. Criminals carried their own cross only *once*, on the day they died hanging from it. Many decades later, when Luke is composing his Gospel, the image of "taking up one's cross *daily*" has developed a very specific meaning. It means more than accepting one's everyday pains, problems, deprivations, and losses. Rather, "the cross" means *accepting the responsibilities and challenges of being an unconditionally loving person living in Jesus's Way.*

Like their master during his life, Christians are expected to spend their lives focused on relieving the burdens of others, including the burdens of sin, guilt, sickness, mental illness, spiritual oppression, poverty, hunger, homelessness, victimhood, physical handicaps, social exclusion, and imprisonment. Caring for others is the hallmark of

Jesus's life and remains the hallmark of each Christian's life. That is what it means to "live in Christ."

Relieving the burdens of others—whether physical, mental, spiritual, financial, or social—remains the challenge of Christians today. This responsibility includes parents, teachers, nurses, physicians, pharmacists, therapists, social workers, nursing homes, rehabilitation centers, pharmacologists, orthopedic inventors, financial planners, social security specialists, spiritual directors, confessors, and others.

Thirty or forty years after Jesus's death, many Christians are being persecuted for their faith. That persecution is ongoing. Daily persecution is their cross. An early Christian could always opt to worship the Roman emperor to avoid persecution and "save your life." But that would mean giving up your life in Christ as one who is dedicated to relieving the burdens of others. The Christian commitment is a total giving of self to *live* in Christ and to *love* as Christ loved.

Commitment (9:57–62)

Some would like to be included among Jesus's close followers, but they are not committed enough to pay the price of being a true follower. It is not uncommon for such would-be followers to approach Jesus. He usually recognizes them and makes them aware of the cost. Luke provides three examples of would-be followers:

> As they were going along the road, someone said to Jesus, "I will follow you wherever you go." And Jesus said to him, "Foxes have holes, and birds of the air have nests; but the Son of Man has nowhere to lay his head." To another he said, "Follow me." But he said, "Lord, first let me go and bury my father." But Jesus said to him, "Let the dead bury their own dead; but as for you, go and proclaim the kingdom of God." Another said, "I will follow you, Lord; but let me first say farewell to those at my home." Jesus said to him, "No one who puts a hand to the plow and looks back is fit for the kingdom of God." (9:57–62)

EVOLUTIONARY IMPLICATIONS

Interestingly, the last two would-be followers merely want to delay their commitment in order to perform customary family duties, such as arranging the burial of a parent or celebrating a formal farewell ceremony with family and friends. However, once you agree to follow Jesus completely, your fellow disciples become your new home and your new family. This is a message Jesus already gave to his own mother and other relatives when they came to Capernaum to bring him back to Nazareth. He told them, "My mother and my brothers are those who hear the word of God and do it" (8:21).

Believers in Jesus's Way are not merely joining the ranks of a religious organization. They are joining a spiritual family whose members are totally committed to one another and to Jesus. Jesus feels the urgency of working full time on God's project. Organizing weddings, funerals, and farewell parties with kinfolk—events that often last for days—are distractions from the work to bring about the kingdom of God.

To manage and protect one's money, to safeguard one's property and one's possessions takes a tremendous amount of time and attention. "So therefore, none of you can become my disciple if you do not give up all your possessions" (14:33). When Jesus calls a person to be a disciple, he expects the response to be immediate and total.

Jesus tells two parables about people who plan to do something but don't take the time to calculate the cost. They don't consider whether they have the resources and the ability to carry out their plan (see 14:29–32). He is talking about would-be disciples who haven't planned or realized the cost to undergo a complete *metanoia*.

Prejudices and False Assumptions (6:39–42)

Luke presents a parable to his disciples about failing to undergo the necessary *metanoia*, especially when it calls for letting go of old prejudices and false assumptions. People who are unconsciously prejudiced are likely to judge the behavior of others from within their own misperceptions. Jesus says, "Why do you see the speck in your neighbor's eye, but do not notice the log in your own eye?" (6:41).

Why is this self-cleansing of one's eyes important? Jesus explains, "A disciple is not above the teacher, but everyone who is fully qualified will be like the teacher" (6:40).

EVOLUTIONARY IMPLICATIONS

Apparently, having a clear mind and an undistorted perspective is required of any disciple of Jesus. A disciple's *metanoia* must be total if he or she is to proclaim the true gospel message. Otherwise, it is likely to be misrepresented through bias, prejudice, or unwarranted assumptions. Most of us spend our lives, especially early on, influenced by unhelpful beliefs, attitudes, and values held by family members, neighborhood friends, and peer groups. We absorb these assumptions unconsciously while growing up. Such distortions of reality hinder our ability to clearly "see" the kingdom of God at work. They are like wooden logs in our eyes interfering with our ability to see things clearly. Becoming conscious of these powerful influences, recognizing the distortions they cause, and patiently eradicating them become important tasks of our spiritual and personal evolution.

Who Belongs to Jesus's Family? (9:49–50)

There is always the question of *belonging*. Who is really a follower of Jesus? Apparently, some of the disciples notice a person casting out demons in Jesus's name but they do not recognize him. He isn't part of their group. They try to stop him. They wonder if this man is a rival of Jesus. They tell Jesus about him.

With Jesus's answer, we see another often-unnoticed aspect of the kingdom of God. Jesus says to the ones that want to stop the man from doing exorcisms: "Do not stop him; for whoever is not against you is for you" (9:50). He's on our team.

BLOOD FAMILY AND SPIRIT FAMILY (12:49–53)

It is important to understand why Jesus makes a distinction between living with the mindset of your blood relatives and undergoing a *metanoia* in order to live in Jesus's family.

Followers of Jesus cannot divide their allegiance between family obligations and working for the kingdom. In these verses, Jesus recognizes the inevitability of a "collision" between family values and kingdom values. Typically, family values include "family first," protecting family property, ensuring financial inheritance through generations, seeking revenge—legally or nonlegally—for offenses against a family member, maintaining social privilege, buying and selling property, celebrating family customs, and attendance at family events. The new values adopted by those who have experienced a Christian *metanoia* would doubtless collide with many traditional values their families hold.

In effect, Jesus says, "Many families won't like it if you become my disciple. If you don't live by their values, they will disown you and betray you" (cf. 21:16–19).

EVOLUTIONARY IMPLICATIONS

For traditional religions to blend with social structures, they have to adapt to the family and social values of their members. A traditional religion, in order to survive and thrive, often lets itself be co-opted by society's values. Jesus's disciples have become a conspiracy of love working for the kingdom. In the *metanoia*, the new way of thinking that Jesus proposes, his followers clearly appreciate the collision of values.

Jesus puts it succinctly: "Those who try to make their life secure will lose it, but those who lose their life will keep it" (17:33). People try to make their life secure by making multiple allegiances—to family, tribe, political party, religious affiliation, and so on—in hopes that one or another group will protect them. For Jesus, the only way to experience the fullness of life is to be totally committed to a life of service to others in his Way. Or, as Jesus puts it in John's Gospel, "This is my commandment, that you love one another as I have loved you" (John 15:12). Note that this is not a suggestion but a "commandment."

In his redefinition of family, Jesus presents a most striking evolutionary dimension. St. Paul presents his Christian converts with the same family idea, indicating that followers of Jesus through baptism become members of Christ's universal family.[3]

23

The Prodigal and the Samaritan

The Mercy of God (15:1–32)

LUKE 15 PRESENTS a series of parables about the kingdom of God. Each one focuses on God's desire to save what seems to be lost. In the first story, a man loses one of his sheep, and he goes in search of it until he finds it (see 15:3–7). Then he shares his joy with his friends. Jesus explains that this is how it is in the kingdom: "I tell you, there will be more joy in heaven over one sinner who repents [undergoes a *metanoia*] than over ninety-nine righteous persons who need no repentance [*metanoia*]" (15:7).[1]

The next parable tells about a woman who misplaces one of her ten silver coins and sweeps her house thoroughly until she finds it. After finding it, she rejoices with her friends (see 15:8–10). Again, Jesus states, "I tell you, there is joy in the presence of the angels of God over one sinner who repents [*metanoia*]" (15:10).

Then Jesus tells the much longer story of the man with two sons. This parable is traditionally titled "the Prodigal Son" (15:11–32). This story is not about lost sheep or lost coins, but about a lost son — something far more important than an animal, or what today might be a misplaced twenty-dollar bill.

Some say that the prodigal's story is the most important parable in Luke's Gospel. It is a story about the kingdom of God and saving what has been lost. When a sheep gets lost or money is misplaced, the proper way to save it is to go in search of it. When a person becomes lost, it is not a

149

simple matter of going to find the person. It is more like a waiting game, hoping the person will have a moment of realization and feel the desire to be found. In the case of the prodigal son, Luke describes that moment for the son as an awakening. "But when he came to himself…" (15:17).

In the story, the father represents God, and the two sons represent different qualities in a human family. The younger son symbolizes the wayward ones, the elder one stands for the consistently faithful ones. Both are loved by the Father, but to each one the Father expresses his love in different ways.

Toward the faithful and dependable elder son, the Father's love is steady and quiet. "Son, you are always with me, and all that is mine is yours" (15:31).

Toward the wild and self-centered younger son, the Father's love is generous, trusting, and forgiving. "The younger of them said to his father, 'Father, give me the share of the property that will belong to me.' So he divided his property between them" (15:12).

The relationship between the two sons is quite different. The younger son thinks only of himself. He dismisses his responsibilities toward his father, his brother, and the family farm. He desires only to get away from dull and boring farm life and be off to the exciting big city with lots of money to spend. He is totally self-absorbed.

For many reasons, the elder son harbors strong feelings of resentment toward his younger brother. First, the younger son outrageously demands to get his share of the inheritance *now*, something that would normally come to him only after the father's death. By greedily taking his inherited money during his youth, the younger son betrays family tradition, and worse, instead of investing his inheritance wisely, word reaches the family that the younger son has squandered every penny.

Yet the Father welcomes home the wayward, repentant son as if he had never abandoned the family and wasted half of the inheritance. The elder son is so furious at this that he refuses to participate in the homecoming party. "He became angry and refused to go in" (15:28).

Neither son has experienced the *metanoia* of the kingdom of God. Yet the Father loves them both.

Evolutionary Implications

If you are among the faithful and dependable workers in God's kingdom, the lesson to learn from this story is that you will be tempted to be angry and resentful toward those whom God has prodigiously forgiven and welcomed home. God forgives your anger and your unforgiveness of others.

If you are among the wasteful, wild, and self-centered members of God's family, the lesson to learn is that God is always forgiving because you are God's child and loved unconditionally.

This story communicates that the mercy of God is without limits, no matter what the sin. This fact alone makes the point that this story is an evolutionary step Jesus has taken beyond the Jewish tradition.

What is more important and evolutionary is to ask, *At what point in the story does the Father forgive his wayward son?* It is probably in the moments after he hands over half of the family wealth to his son and waves goodbye. We can infer that the Father always remains concerned about the welfare of his prodigal son. The father is not looking for repentance and restitution. All he wants is his son back under his care. He is always on the lookout for him. We know that as soon as the repentant prodigal sets off for home, his father is already out on the roadway waiting and looking. "But while [the son] was still far off, his father saw him and was filled with compassion; he ran and put his arms around him and kissed him" (15:20). The father refuses to hear the son's prepared confession (see 15:21–22). *The father had long ago forgiven the son's sins.*

In the father's mind, there is no expectation that the prodigal will have to pay for his infidelity to the family. In fact, the very opposite happens. The father immediately puts a family ring on the youth's finger. This ring signifies that the wayward son once again has the power to make decisions for the family. As far as the father is concerned, the prodigal's reinstatement into the family is total and complete.

Unfortunately, the elder son is not so forgiving. That is the difference between God's perspective and our human way. God wants everyone to be in heaven; many are eager to keep certain people out.

If Jesus is using this story to teach us about the true nature of the Father in heaven, he is showing a new level of divine mercy and forgiveness that humans have never dreamed of. Jesus is presenting a God who loves us unconditionally and wants to be one with us in love. The divine Father is a God *who forgives us even before we ask for forgiveness.*

151

Unlimited Compassion (10:29–35)

Just as the Father's forgiveness is unconditional, Jesus wants his followers' compassion to be unconditional. The second great commandment is "to love your neighbor as yourself." One day, a man asks Jesus, "And who is my neighbor?" Jesus replies with the story of the Good Samaritan.

Like a seasoned storyteller, Jesus first sets the scene. "A man was going down from Jerusalem to Jericho, and fell into the hands of robbers, who stripped him, beat him, and went away, leaving him half dead" (10:30).

Next, Jesus gives two examples of people who don't qualify as good neighbors. Both a priest and a Levite notice the half-dead Jew lying on the side of the road, but they "passed by on the other side" (10:31–32). We can imagine that they both feel a momentary urge to help the wounded fellow, but they squash it immediately. Perhaps, they rationalize their reluctance to help as we all do at some time or other: "I'm busy." "I'm in a hurry." "I don't have the time." "There is nothing I can do to help." "Let someone else deal with it." "I don't want to get dirty or get blood on my clothes." "I don't want to become ritually impure by touching him." "If I walk away, I won't have to look at him."

Then along comes a stranger, a man from another town and from a community that the Jews dislike. The Samaritan notices the wounded Jew. He "came near him; and when he saw him, he was moved with pity. He went to him and bandaged his wounds, having poured oil and wine on them" (10:33–34). This act of kindness probably goes above and beyond the call.

The Samaritan does not then get back on his animal and ride off. Instead, he picks up the wounded man, puts him on his animal, "brought him to an inn, and took care of him" (10:34). That little phrase—"and took care of him"—indicates that the Samaritan does not just leave the wounded Jew with the innkeeper and continue on his journey. The Samaritan stays with him overnight.

"The next day he took out two denarii, gave them to the innkeeper, and said, 'Take care of him; and when I come back, I will repay you whatever more you spend'" (10:35).

The Samaritan's compassion costs him time and money, but he is generous with both. He loves his neighbor as himself.

EVOLUTIONARY IMPLICATIONS

Jesus is giving his followers a clear example of fulfillment of the Golden Rule. Almost all religious traditions promote a limited version of the Golden Rule: "Do *not* do unto others what you would not want them to do to you." Jesus's version of the Golden Rule is positive and unlimited: "*Do* unto others what you would want them to do unto you." The Samaritan provides a good model of Jesus's positive and unlimited version. He does for another what he would have wished someone would do for him if he was the wounded man on the side of the road.

A religion that teaches unlimited forgiveness and unlimited compassion, as Luke presents in these two parables, has made an evolutionary step in its spirituality and ethics.

PART V

THE GOSPEL OF JOHN

NINETY PERCENT of the Gospel according to John is unique to John. For example, none of the other evangelists tell about

- the wedding feast at Cana (2:1–11);
- the cleansing of the temple (2:14–16);
- Jesus's secret late-night meeting with Nicodemus (3:1–21);
- his intimate conversation with the Samaritan woman at the well (4:1–42);
- his healing of the outspoken cripple at the pool of Bethesda (5:1–18);
- Jesus's discourse on the "Bread of Life" (6:26–40);
- the woman taken in adultery (8:1–11);
- the parables of the good shepherd (10:1–21);
- the raising of Lazarus (11:1–44);
- the allegory of the vine and branches (15:1–15);
- the private dialogue between Jesus and Pontius Pilate (18:33–38); and many more.

Many of these events and stories reveal evolutionary implications about Jesus and his teachings. We explore only some of them in this chapter.

The stories in John that are similar in the other Gospels are often *told quite differently*. For example: According to John, Andrew is the first to meet with Jesus after Jesus is baptized. Andrew spends the day with Jesus and afterward recruits his brother, Simon Peter, as a disciple (1:35–51). John adds details to the feeding of the five thousand. Andrew tells Jesus, "There is a boy here who has five barley loaves and two fish. But what are they among so many people?" (6:9). After this miracle, the crowd "were about to come and take him by force to make him king" (6:15).

Again, during the storm at sea, when Jesus walks toward them on the water, Jesus never gets into the boat as he does in Mark's version (see Mark 6:51), nor does Peter walk on the water as he does in Matthew's version (see Matt 14:28–31). For John, walking on water is not the important miracle. Rather, it is the fact that, even though they are miles from shore, "immediately the boat reached the land toward which they were going" (John 6:21).

John's Gospel was authored much later than the other three—as many as twenty years later. It probably emerged from within one of the less persecuted and more intellectual Christian communities in Asia Minor. Its isolated location enabled the faithful there to develop a much more sophisticated theology than that of the other three evangelists. The first three frequently deal with more critical practical problems like persecution from Greeks, Romans, and fellow Jews.

John's Evolutionary Advances

John's Gospel presents an entirely new potential in its evolutionary purpose. John's Gospel shows Jesus's Way as evolving beyond the theology of Hebrew Scriptures. But of greater interest is the evidence suggesting its marked theological advance *within the early Christian communities*. In other words, John presents an evolution within an evolution.[1]

The first three Gospels—Matthew, Mark, and Luke—are called Synoptic because they share the same viewpoint on Jesus's teaching. (In Greek, *synoptic* means "with the same eyes.") John's Gospel enters a new level of evolutionary development in the Christian community. John sees Jesus's teachings with even "newer eyes."

The Gospel of John

When we reflected on the Synoptic Gospels, we used Teilhard's six evolutionary criteria to show how Jesus's teachings evolved beyond those of the Mosaic Law. As we reflect on Jesus's teachings in John, we apply the same six evolutionary criteria, but this time to show how Jesus's teachings in John have evolved beyond those presented in the three Synoptic Gospels.

As we read John's text, Teilhard would suggest asking the six questions in a new way. Are passages in John's text

- different and genuinely new or novel compared to what is in the Synoptic Gospels?
- keeping essential elements or functions of the Synoptics?
- more complex than anything within its class in the Synoptics?
- irreversible, such that, once presented, the new insights cannot be denied?
- transformative, but not destructive of the Synoptics?
- manifesting new emerging properties beyond the Synoptics?

For example, consider how much further John takes Jesus's teaching on love than the Synoptic writers. In the Sermon on the Mount in Matthew's Gospel, Jesus proposes love as a higher value than justice. Jesus replaces the Mosaic principle of "An eye for an eye, a tooth for a tooth" with the Golden Rule.

In the Synoptics, Jesus evolves the Golden Rule. Instead of using the traditional "negative" expression of the Golden Rule, "Do not do unto others what you would not want them to do to you," he makes it "positive": "Do to others as you would have them do to you" (Matt 7:12). In this open-ended version, the Golden Rule becomes evolutionary.

In John's Gospel, Jesus raises the positive Golden Rule to a higher level. It becomes, "Love one another *as I have loved you*" (15:12; cf. 13:34). We are to love one another as Jesus loved us. In case the breadth and depth of this "commandment" is not clear, Jesus adds, "No one has greater love than this, to lay down one's life for one's friends" (15:13).

Correct, Clarify, Complete

John's Gospel also corrects, clarifies, and completes the other three Gospels in several ways. For example,

(1) It "corrects" the true origin of Jesus (1:1–9).
(2) It "clarifies" the institution of the Eucharist by revealing its fuller meaning and purpose as the "Bread of Life" and its centrality in the lives of his followers (6:22–51).
(3) It "completes" the description of the kingdom of God by showing the trajectory and goal of God's project (1:12–13).

An example of correction is the true origin of Jesus. John's Gospel begins with *a prologue* that presents Jesus as the preexistent "Word of God" (*Logos*) made flesh (1:1–18). Matthew merely traces Jesus's lineage back to Abraham. Luke traces it further back to Adam. In the very first line of his Gospel, John asserts that Jesus is God's "Word."[2] As God's Word, Jesus is and was with God from the beginning, even before creation. This assertion fulfills the six evolutionary criteria listed above.

Moreover, during Jesus's farewell address at the Last Supper (13:1 — 17:33), John presents a *theological evolution* in the following texts:

(4) his early announcement of the centrality of the Eucharist in the lives of his followers (6:22–51).
(5) a more developed "theology of the Holy Spirit." While Luke mentions specific actions of the Holy Spirit far more often than John, only John provides the explanatory theology (14:15–28; 15:26–27; 16:4–15).
(6) a clarification of the Trinity, which identifies the distinctive roles of the Father, Son, and Holy Spirit— within their Oneness (14:8–31).
(7) In the *development of the kingdom of God,* Jesus specifies that the goal of God's project for creation is to achieve our oneness in Christ and our oneness with the Father (17:10–11, 20–24).

(8) For the first time, Jesus uses the image of the vine and the branches to describe how he will provide a continuous source of life to his disciples (15:1–15).

(9) The Father's desire to be "one" with the disciples is just as deep as the Father's desire to be "one" with the Son (17:10–11, 21–24).

Each of these nine points shows how John's Gospel has furthered the evolution of Jesus's teachings beyond that of the Synoptics. He has elevated them to a new level. Each point fulfills the six evolutionary criteria. And there are many more points in John that qualify as evolutionary beyond the Synoptics.

For instance, only in the security of the maturing Christian community circa 90 CE can John dare to tell the almost unbelievable story of Jesus's intimate and solitary encounter at Jacob's well with a Samaritan woman of questionable morals (see 4:1–42). In Jesus's time, such a one-on-one meeting and conversation alone with a woman from a rival tribe would be taboo for any Jewish man—no matter how thirsty he might be.

For similar reasons of intimacy with women, the Synoptics would not have been able to tell the story, as John does, of the woman taken in adultery (see 7:53—8:11). However, these events give future Christian missionaries the courage to travel to strange countries and use every loving and compassionate means to bring the good news of Christ to others.

Authorship

Biblical scholars find it difficult to identify the authorship of this Gospel. Since the approximate date of the Gospel is placed in the 90s, it is most unlikely that any of the original apostles are still alive. Many biblical scholars believe the Gospel text was compiled by a small team of John's disciples. Its elegant and unique Greek stylized writing suggests that it was *not* composed by John himself, an uneducated Jewish fisherman from Galilee.

Furthermore, the earliest extant Johannine manuscripts show signs of having been edited. For example, the story of the woman taken in adultery (7:53—8:11) is missing in some ancient manuscripts and positioned in different places in others.

Another possible argument for team authorship is that some passages of the Gospel narrative don't make sense. For example, the text has Jesus saying, "You look for an opportunity to kill me" (8:37), to Jews *who believe in him* (8:31). In another chapter, John's Gospel tells us that "Mary was the one who anointed the Lord" (11:2), but the anointing event isn't reported in the text until the following chapter (12:3). At the Last Supper, Jesus says to the group at table, "Rise, let us be on our way" (14:31). However, instead of departing, the group remains in the Upper Room. Jesus continues with his discourse for two more chapters. And last, the final two verses of chapter 20 read like the end of John's Gospel (20:30–31), yet the manuscripts add another chapter.

It would take an entire book to explore and analyze the evolutionary implications of John's Gospel. For our purpose, it is enough to cite and discuss some of the more outstanding passages. We will look at the magnificent hymn-like Prologue (1:1–18), the secret conversation with Nicodemus (3:1–21), the discourse on the Bread of Life (6:26–40), the woman taken in adultery (8:1–11), and elements of Jesus's farewell discourse at the Last Supper, which take up almost five complete chapters (chapters 13—17).

24

From Beginning to End

The Word Became Flesh (1:1–18)

> In the beginning was the Word, and the Word was with
> God, and the Word was God. He was in the beginning with
> God. All things came into being through him, and without
> him not one thing came into being. What has come into
> being in him was life, and the life was the light of all people.
> The light shines in the darkness, and the darkness did not
> overcome it. (John 1:1–5)

JOHN BOLDLY makes Jesus equal to God. He asserts that Jesus
existed before creation, living in the mind and heart of the Creator
(1:18). Jesus Christ is in God and is God yet is a person distinct from
the Creator.

Stay with those first few verses and imagine them as John might.
We are in the realm of metaphor, of course. But it is the only kind of
language that a mystic can use. Picture God the Creator in the eternal
silence uttering a divine Word causing the Big Bang. John assures us
that, even before God spoke, the Word that made creation happen, the
Word itself, had been alive in God's mind and heart. Picture the Word
in God's mind before it is uttered. Imagine the Word in God longing
to be spoken aloud, longing to become materialized!

If you or I create something, it is a *self*-expression, albeit a partial
self-expression since nothing you can create could ever be a full and
total expression of who you are. In God's mind and heart, however,
God's Word can never be a partial self-expression. It must always be a

full and total divine self-revelation. God's Word, when spoken, must be fully divine.

Imagine the Word proceeding from deep within God's mind and heart; coming out of God's mouth. As soon as God utters the creative Word, creation—the universe—comes into existence. Creation comes into existence *through* the Word. "All things came into being through him [the Word], and without him not one thing came into being" (1:3).

However, as we now know from science, creation first bursts out in fragmented forms at the Big Bang—subatomic particles and photons of light. How could all these myriad fragments be the fullest expression of God?

We humans know this "fragmented" experience. We express all our thoughts in fragments. Suppose you have an idea or thought or feeling. That thought, or feeling, feels complete in your mind. However, when you try to express it outwardly, you can only do it using a series of words. What are words but fragments of speech that make up a sentence or a paragraph? You often need many fragments of speech to express your mind's entire insight fully. Furthermore, you must organize these many fragments coherently into intelligible sentences, and those sentences into clearly organized paragraphs. This organization of the fragments to express your thoughts is a process, and it takes time.

The first fragmented elements that God speaks at creation are inert, lifeless, made up mostly of protons, electrons, neutrons, and photons. These subatomic particles need to be organized in order to realize the meaning they have in God's mind. And the gradual organization of divinely uttered fragments takes eons of time. Creation has been working at the process—of coming together—for almost fourteen billion years.[1]

In an evolutionary process through matter, the Word of God eventually emerges in creatures in basic signs of *life*—sensation, perception, cognition, self-awareness, and finally in self-reflective consciousness. The Word of God gives *life* to creation.

The Word of God also gives *light* to creation—light in a physical sense in photons; light in an intellectual sense in self-reflective consciousness, insight, and creativity; and light in a moral and spiritual sense in the formation of conscience, community, and the awareness of God.

EVOLUTIONARY IMPLICATIONS

In John's Gospel, we are not looking merely for evolutionary development beyond the theology of the Hebrew Scriptures. John has evolved far beyond Judaism. In John's Gospel, we are witnessing *theological evolution within Christianity itself*. Some scholars may claim that John's theology is merely a natural development of the other three Gospels. But one can find theology in John's Gospel, for instance, in his Prologue, that cannot be simply inferred from the other three Gospels.

By the same token, there is material in Paul's letters, such as describing the mystical Body of Christ, that cannot be simply inferred from material in Matthew, Mark, and Luke. It is new theology emerging in the growing church—a new understanding.

John's Gospel reveals that Christian theology has begun to mature. Creative minds have been reflecting on Jesus's life and teachings for decades. The faithful have been pondering the meaning and identity of Jesus for almost sixty years. Indeed, John's mystical perspective presents "high" theology.

The Eucharist (6:27–69)

An example of John's high theology applies to the Eucharist. The other three Gospel writers present the institution of the Eucharist as a ritual to be reenacted again and again in memory of Jesus. John develops the meaning, purpose, and significance of the Eucharist and presents it as the Bread of Life (see 6:27–69).

Being in Jesus's presence and listening to his word is life-giving nourishment. "Whoever comes to me will never be hungry, and whoever believes in me will never be thirsty (6:35). Jesus's instructive teachings are a kind of "bread," nourishment for the mind. But Jesus's very body is the Bread of Life. "Those who eat my flesh and drink my blood have eternal life, and I will raise them up on the last day; for my flesh is true food and my blood is true drink" (6:54–55).

St. Paul explains how the Eucharist serves as the creative lifeblood that nurtures the daily life of the Christian community (see 1 Cor 12:12–31). But early Christians had to wait, perhaps thirty years, for

John to develop the theology behind this transformational process. In John's Gospel, Jesus explains how the personal and communal process works:

DIVINAZATION

> Those who eat my flesh and drink my blood abide in me, and I in them. Just as the living Father sent me, and I live because of the Father, so whoever eats me will live because of me. (6:56–57)

Without this confirmation of John's theology, Paul's mystical Body of Christ can be interpreted as a mere metaphor—like membership in a corporation or citizenship in a country. John's theology asserts the physical and spiritual reality of the Christ Body. In fact, we live in Christ's Body, much as living cells function in any organism. This participation in Christ's Body also allows us to "think and act" with the mind of Christ.[2]

From Teilhard's perspective, John's presentation of Jesus's farewell address during the Last Supper describes the final divine unification of all things—the accomplishment of God's project. It is what Teilhard called the Omega Point[3] and St. Paul called the *Pleroma* (see Col 2:9; Eph 4:13).[4] Jesus prays to the Father that all humanity, not just the people around him at the Last Supper, be sanctified in the truth and become one with him and his Father. Jesus envisions a long future of believers:

> I ask not only on behalf of these, but also on behalf of those who will believe in me through their word, that they may all be one. As you, Father, are in me and I am in you, may they also be one in us, so that the world may believe that you have sent me. (17:20–22)

EVOLUTIONARY IMPLICATIONS

In the time of Jesus, Jews claimed to be "children of Abraham" because they could trace their bloodline back to Abraham.

Jesus is initiating a new "bloodline." Through the eucharistic meal, his followers will receive a spiritual blood transfusion. Collectively, they will gradually evolve into a new kind of being as each one becomes more and more like Jesus. John describes this process of becoming one with him and the Father (see 17:20–22).

To indicate this oneness, John uses the image of the vine and the branches. Jesus is the vine, whose roots send their lifegiving energy into its branches. Those living in his Way generate delicious fruit.

Paul uses a different image to express this intimate union. For him, those who follow Jesus's way—who eat his flesh and drink his blood—become part of a much larger, cosmic-sized Christ. They become members—eyes, arms, legs, etcetera—of this grand Christ Body. A more contemporary image to describe those who follow Jesus's Way is as "living cells" in his universal Body. Only in John and Paul do we find this evolution of theology.

Note that among the early church fathers, the *ecclesia*—the community of believers—was considered the "real" Body of Christ, while the Eucharist was seen as the "mystery" or the "mystical" Body of Christ. Somewhere in Christian history a switch occurred, probably when the reality of the Eucharist was being called into question. Today, we say that the Eucharist is the "real" Body of Christ, while the people of God are called the Mystical Body.[5]

25

Born from Above

Nicodemus Visits Jesus (3:1–15)

APHARISEE, A LEADER of the Jews named Nicodemus, comes to Jesus one night and they have a dialogue. Nicodemus begins, "Rabbi, we know that you are a teacher who has come from God; for no one can do these signs that you do apart from the presence of God."

Jesus's first response is, "Very truly, I tell you, no one can see the kingdom of God without being born from above."

Nicodemus says to him, "How can anyone be born after having grown old?"

Jesus answers, "Very truly, I tell you, no one can enter the kingdom of God without being born of water and Spirit. What is born of the flesh is flesh, and what is born of the Spirit is spirit" (3:2–6).

Jesus goes on to explain how the Spirit is like invisible wind on a windy day (3:8). The wind blows where it wants to blow. Because the wind is invisible, you can't see it, but you can feel it. You can't predict when it will blow or the direction from which it will come. When you are born of the Spirit, the Spirit takes over your life. Once you agree to let the Spirit manage your life, it will move you wherever it chooses to move you. You may feel a movement—a push—within you, but you do not know where it comes from. Nor do you know when it will come or where it will lead you. Everyone born of the spirit is familiar with this experience.

Nicodemus says to him, "How can these things be?"

Jesus answers him, "Are you a teacher of Israel, and yet you do not understand these things?…If I have told you about earthly things [like how the wind blows] and you do not believe, how can you believe if I tell you about heavenly things [like being born of the Spirit]? (3:9–12).

Jesus then introduces another topic that baffles Nicodemus. He feels overwhelmed and makes no response. Jesus says,

No one has ascended into heaven except the one who descended from heaven, the Son of Man. And just as Moses lifted up the serpent in the wilderness, so must the Son of Man be lifted up, that whoever believes in him may have eternal life. (3:13–15)

Jesus claims that he has descended from heaven, and is therefore a heavenly being who can also claim the title "the Son of Man."

Nicodemus recognizes the image of the serpent in the wilderness. When the Hebrew people were wandering in the desert, many were being fatally bitten by poisonous snakes. Moses asked God for a snakebite cure. God told Moses to mold a bronze serpent and put it on a staff. If anyone bitten by a snake comes to the bronze serpent and believes it will cure him, that person will be cured. That is, he or she will be given life again.

In using this striking image, Jesus is predicting his own death to Nicodemus. Jesus will be like that bronze serpent on the pole. When he is lifted up on the cross of his crucifixion, those who look upon him on the cross and believe in him will be given life, even eternal life.[1]

EVOLUTIONARY IMPLICATIONS

What is implied in having "eternal life"? Jesus has come, not merely to teach us how to think and act, but to introduce us to life in abundance (John 10:10). He came to open and deepen our experience of life. It is a continuous process that grows throughout life as we learn to see more clearly the kingdom of heaven at work all around us. So, what could the gift of "eternal life" mean, but an endless growth and deepening of the experience of life? A continuance of what we began on Earth.

In a static universe, eternal life may mean a shift from a troubled life on Earth to a peaceful life in heaven, or from a chaotic life to a life of rest, or from a dangerous life to a safe and secure life with God.

In an evolving universe, the idea of eternal life takes on a richer meaning. Even in heaven, our minds and hearts will continue to stretch and expand, as we experience more deeply and comprehensively what life in God can be. And with that ever-expanding experience of life in God, our experience and capacity to love will also continue to grow forever.

God's Love for the Cosmos (3:16–17)

Jesus then moves on to another new topic with Nicodemus.

> For God so loved the world that he gave his only Son, so that everyone who believes in him may not perish but may have eternal life. Indeed, God did not send the Son into the world to condemn the world, but in order that the world might be saved through him. (3:16–17)

Nicodemus, overwhelmed by this assertion, can make no reply. For us, Jesus's words are central to John's evolutionary perspective.

Here, early in his Gospel, John introduces us to the *God of love*. God doesn't love just humans, God loves the entire cosmos. *Cosmos* (all of creation) is the Greek word for the English *world* used here. God loves everything that the divine Word uttered in creating the universe (1:2–3).

To what degree does God love the physical world? God loves creation so much that "he gave [the world] his only Son." Jesus is telling Nicodemus—and us—that God loves creation as much as God loves his Son. God wants nothing and no one in creation to perish. God's will is that all creation "may have eternal life."

In the following statement (3:17), John tells us that God has no wish to condemn the world. God's wish has always been that all will enjoy the fullness of life—eternally. After all, the universe is the self-expression of the Creator. It came to exist when the Word of God uttered it. How could God not love his Word and the universe that his Word expresses?

In fact, Teilhard might argue that creation is an ongoing self-expression of God materialized.

EVOLUTIONARY IMPLICATIONS

Teilhard would connect these two verses (3:16–17) with the opening verses of the Prologue (1:3–5). What else is creation but the Word of God expressed outwardly in fragmented matter? Is creation not the thought within the heart of God that is being expressed outwardly in material form? How can God not love all the divine Word that is being uttered?

In this multibillion-year evolutionary process, God continues to love the fragmented creation into a living wholeness. God is gradually and organically loving creation into oneness, as it originally is in the Word of God in the divine mind and heart. God continues to love creation throughout its eons of evolutionary collisions, confusions, conflicts, destructions, deaths, and emerging potential.

Jesus shares with us his Father's desire for creation to return to its original oneness as the divine Word he spoke in the beginning. Jesus shows us the Way to live in order that we can help bring about that original oneness. Jesus nourishes us with his divine flesh and blood to guarantee the success of God's project for creation. By assimilating us into himself as parts of his divine Body, he remakes us into his Word, the Word that was dwelling in the mind and heart of the Father before the Father spoke it.

The Aramaic Jesus pictures God as Oneness. As the Risen Lord, he is bringing creation full circle, from original Oneness through fragmentation back to original Oneness. He is managing God's project, since he is the Word that created the universe.

This is the reality that John and Paul "see." It is also what Teilhard envisions but integrates far more than John or Paul could have imagined. Teilhard integrates into this first-century vision of John and Paul the evolutionary process that creation has been going through for almost fourteen billion years.

Light of the World (3:19–21)

Just as the previous verses are connected to the "life" spoken of in the Prologue, the final verses in the dialogue with Nicodemus are connected to the Prologue's "light" of the world.

Not only is Jesus the light of the world, his disciples are also to serve a similar role (see Matt 5:14–16). Eventually, as the light from members of Christ's Body lights up the world, the deeds of all people will become visible. Forgiving and compassionate people will be attracted to the light.

EVOLUTIONARY IMPLICATIONS

As more people adopt the Way of living that Jesus teaches, it will gradually transform the human community. For this reason, Jesus creates a mission-centered spiritual community, so that they can spread the "light of the world" over the planet and transform it.

The transformation process happens, first, person by person. "No one can see the kingdom of God without being born from above" (3:3). According to Teilhard, this individual *metanoia* will become so widespread that a collective *metanoia* will happen, and humanity will be transformed in the conscious recognition that we are all one in Christ and one in God.

26

Discipleship

Some Unusual Disciples (4:1 — 5:15)

JESUS TAKES an evolutionary step in choosing his disciples when announcing the Beatitudes in Matthew's Gospel (see Matt 5:3–12). Instead of enlisting the rich and well educated as disciples, Jesus chooses the poor, the weak, the humble, and the outcasts. He proclaims that these often-excluded ones are members of his team. He will entrust to them the task of spreading the good news of God's love. They will show people how to live in that love.

The other evangelists present some ordinary people as disciples, like the four fishermen, Peter, Andrew, James, and John. They also mention an outcast tax collector, Matthew, as a disciple. But these disciples are all healthy, male Jews. In contrast, John presents disciples who are female and non-Jew, thus expanding the field of apostles further. According to his Gospel, the very first disciple who spreads Jesus's good news to her townspeople is the Samaritan woman at the well—a non-Jewish woman. John writes,

> Then the woman left her water jar and went back to the city. She said to the people, "Come and see a man who told me everything I have ever done! He cannot be the Messiah, can he?" They left the city and were on their way to him. (4:28–30)

The woman Jesus chooses to be his disciple is one who has gone through five husbands and is at present living out of wedlock with another man. She is the first missionary to her non-Jewish people.

171

Many Samaritans come to believe in him because of the woman's testimony (see 4:40–42).

In the chapter immediately following, John tells us that Jesus chooses another disciple, a helpless cripple. This man proclaims Jesus to the Pharisees (see 5:1–14).

A Man Born Blind (9:1–34)

John relates the story of another unusual disciple, a man born blind who preaches to the Pharisees. He says to them, "He put mud on my eyes. Then I washed, and now I see….He is a prophet" (9:15, 17).

The Pharisees first claim that the man was not born blind and maybe never was. But the man's parents refute that claim. His parents, however, refuse to say how their son regained his sight, though he must have told them the story of his miraculous healing (9:22–23).

A second time, the Pharisees call the man who had been blind and say to him, "Give glory to God! We know that this man [Jesus] is a sinner" (9:24). The healed man is a bold disciple. He will not back down. Listen to his remarkable retorts:

> "I do not know whether he is a sinner. One thing I do know, that though I was blind, now I see." They said to him, "What did he do to you? How did he open your eyes?" He answered them, "I have told you already, and you would not listen. Why do you want to hear it again? Do you also want to become his disciples?" Then they reviled him, saying, "You are his disciple, but we are disciples of Moses. We know that God has spoken to Moses, but as for this man, we do not know where he comes from." The man answered, "Here is an astonishing thing! You do not know where he comes from, and yet he opened my eyes. We know that God does not listen to sinners, but he does listen to one who worships him and obeys his will. Never since the world began has it been heard that anyone opened the eyes of a person born blind. If this man were not from God, he could do nothing." They answered him, "You were born entirely in sins, and are you trying to teach us?" And they drove him out. (9:25–34)

This man is not afraid to testify about Jesus in the face of the scornful authority of his questioners. He is even willing to be excommunicated from his community's synagogue to testify to the truth (9:34).

WOMEN DISCIPLES

John also tells us about two sisters who live in Bethany—Martha and Mary. They are clearly disciples of Jesus. They often welcome him into their home. Their testimony is clearly seen in the poignant story of Lazarus's death and his resurrection by Jesus (see 11:1–44).

In Christian tradition, another brave woman disciple, Mary Magdalene, holds a revered position. She is the first to announce the resurrection of Jesus to the apostles. She is commissioned by Jesus himself to make the announcement.

> Jesus said to her, "…But go to my brothers and say to them, 'I am ascending to my Father and your Father, to my God and your God." Mary Magdalene went and announced to the disciples, "I have seen the Lord"; and she told them that he had said these things to her. (20:17–18)

Thus, a woman is the first to whom the risen Jesus reveals himself. She becomes the first disciple commissioned by Jesus to publicly announce his resurrection. Jesus appears to the male disciples only later that day (20:19).

EVOLUTIONARY IMPLICATIONS

Before Jesus, no Jewish religious leader enlisted women, especially women of questionable morals, to be prominent disciples. Nor had any earlier religious leader chosen or inspired the crippled and the blind to announce a new understanding of the kingdom of God.

27

The Holy Spirit and the Trinity

Heavenly Things (3:1–15)

L UKE MENTIONS the Holy Spirit far more often than John. However, John offers a more developed theology of the Holy Spirit.[1]

When the brilliant and powerful Nicodemus comes to meet Jesus secretly at night, this Pharisee greets Jesus as a teacher. He says, "Rabbi, we know that you are a teacher who has come from God; for no one can do these signs that you do apart from the presence of God" (3:2).

Jesus clarifies by saying, "Very truly, I tell you, no one can enter the kingdom of God without being born of water and Spirit. What is born of the flesh is flesh, and what is born of the Spirit is spirit" (3:5–6).

Consequently, John introduces a spiritual *metanoia* as a necessary condition for perceiving the workings of the kingdom of God.[2] Unless Nicodemus goes through a complete change of mind and heart—enters a new mindset—he can't consciously enter the kingdom of God.

What John makes clear that the other evangelists don't is that the Holy Spirit is the one who brings people into the new mindset that enables them to recognize the kingdom of God among them. Today, we might describe this *metanoia* as a new state of consciousness induced by the Holy Spirit.

Jesus is so familiar with this spiritual mindset that he is amazed that it is unknown to Nicodemus, the devout Pharisee. "Are you a teacher of Israel, and yet you do not understand these things?" (3:10). And, a few verses later, "If I have told you about earthly things and you do not believe, how can you believe if I tell you about heavenly things?" (3:12).

It is consoling that Nicodemus eventually becomes a follower of Jesus, although a secret one. He appears again at Jesus's death, bringing spices for his burial (19:39).

EVOLUTIONARY IMPLICATIONS

Already in this early dialogue with Nicodemus, Jesus is teaching new theology about the Holy Spirit. The first step in understanding the teachings of Jesus is to undergo a personal transformation that is so powerful that it is like being born again.

The *metanoia* of Jesus also involves a *metamorphosis*. A radical change in one's way of thinking (*metanoia*) involves a corresponding change in one's way of being and acting. It also requires that one sees oneself in a new way, as a new kind of being—*metamorphosis*. The clearest way to describe this process is to say it feels like being reborn with a new mind and a new body.[3] One is born first of water (a human birth) and then of Spirit (a spiritual rebirth). First, one is born of human parents. Then, while still living, one dies and is reborn in Christ.

Being reborn in Christ is indeed a *metamorphosis* since one begins living in a new body—a cosmic-sized body that is Christ's Body. Living in Christ is a totally new way of seeing oneself and the significance of one's choices and actions. The spiritual person realizes that he or she is no longer living merely as an individual human life on Earth, but as a cell in a much larger, eternal, divine Body.

The Holy Spirit is the divine person who facilitates this death and rebirth, and who reminds us that we are living primarily as members of Christ's Body. It is easy to forget that we are not just humans living a human life. We need to be reminded, repeatedly, that we participate in a divine life, and that divine person in whom we live is bringing about the kingdom of God—with our help.

The Abiding Spirit (14:15–26)

Not only does the Holy Spirit foster and nurture the spiritual *metanoia* in each person, but the Spirit also becomes an abiding presence in each one. Here is Jesus at the Last Supper:

> If you love me, you will keep my commandments. And I will ask the Father, and he will give you another Advocate, to be with you forever....You know him, because he abides with you, and he will be in you. (14:15–17)

From these three verses we learn several things:

- The Holy Spirit is given to us by the Father. The Spirit is a *gift* from the Father.
- The Holy Spirit takes up his dwelling place in us. He sets up his *home* permanently—forever—in us and among us.
- He will continue to act within us as an Advocate or *helper*.
- As we develop sensitivity to the Holy Spirit's presence, we come to know him and develop a *familiarity* with him since he is living within us and is active in us.
- John also tells us that Jesus said that, wherever one of the Trinity is present, all three divine persons are present. "Those who love me will keep my word, and my Father will love them, and we will come to them and make our home with them" (14:23).
- A characteristic of the Holy Spirit is that he will be a *teacher*. Since Jesus doesn't have the time to explain everything we need to know about the kingdom, the Holy Spirit will continue to instruct us. He will not only refresh in our minds the teachings of Jesus that we may forget but he will also teach us new things that we have never heard before. "The Advocate, the Holy Spirit... will teach you everything, and remind you of all that I have said to you" (14:25–26).
- The Holy Spirit will also come to our defense, as an

inner lawyer and a *speaker of the truth.* "The Spirit of *truth* who comes from the Father, he will *testify* on my behalf" (15:26–27).

It is important that Jesus leave his disciples so that they can learn to fend for themselves. Otherwise, they will continue to lean on him for answers and to save them when they get into trouble. As long as Jesus walks among them, they will not learn to turn to the Holy Spirit within them to discern how to live in the world and how to deal with the difficult situations that arise.[4] "It is to your advantage that I go away, for if I do not go away, the Advocate will not come to you; but if I go, I will send him to you" (16:7).

Jesus knows so much more about the kingdom of God that the disciples need to learn. But, like a good teacher, he realizes that they are not yet ready to absorb this knowledge. It will have to be learned gradually. In years to come, the Holy Spirit will continue to be their tutor, their source of knowledge, their guide (see 16:12–15).[5]

From this passage, we learn five more theological facts about the Holy Spirit:

- He possesses the fullness of truth.
- He will tell you what he hears from the Father.
- He will advise you how to prepare for the future.
- He will glorify Jesus.
- He will take all the knowledge Jesus possesses and give it to you.

EVOLUTIONARY IMPLICATIONS

John presents a theology of the Holy Spirit that is totally new and evolutionary. The Holy Spirit is a distinct divine person. To prove it, the Holy Spirit will serve many functions that only a person can carry out. The Holy Spirit will be a teacher of new knowledge, one who reminds them of knowledge they have already received from Jesus, a tutor, an advocate, an inner guide, a lawyer, a speaker of the truth, and so on. The Spirit is not a thing or an it. The Spirit is a person. (Since the word for "spirit" is masculine in both Greek and Latin, we refer to the Spirit as "he.")

We do nothing to earn the Holy Spirit's help. The Spirit is a permanent gift from the Father. Since the Spirit is making a home in us, our role is to become familiar with this divine guest and learn to recognize his voice, his urgings, and gentle nudging. For Teilhard, the Holy Spirit will teach us how to live evolutely.

The Holy Trinity (14:8–31)

During this same lengthy farewell address, John's Gospel is first to present a clarification of the Trinity, identifying the distinctive roles of the Father, Son, and Holy Spirit—within their Oneness—in the development of the kingdom of God.

Jesus clearly acknowledges that he and the Father are one. As we profess in the Nicene Creed, the Father and the Son are two persons. The Son is "one in being" or "one in substance" with the Father. The two divine Persons dwell completely in each other.

> Whoever has seen me has seen the Father. How can you say, "'Show us the Father'? Do you not believe that I am in the Father and the Father is in me? The words that I say to you I do not speak on my own; but the Father who dwells in me does his works. Believe me that I am in the Father and the Father is in me; but if you do not, then believe me because of the works themselves. (14:9–11)

A few verses later, Jesus adds the "person" of the Holy Spirit to the Father and Son.

> And I will ask the Father, and he will give you another Advocate, to be with you forever. This is the Spirit of truth, whom the world cannot receive, because it neither sees him nor knows him. You know him, because he abides with you, and he will be in you."(14:16–17)

The Holy Spirit is one with the Father and the Son because the Spirit knows everything that the Father and Son know. "The Holy Spirit, whom the Father will send in my name, will teach you everything, and remind you of all that I have said to you" (14:26). "All that the Father has is mine. For this reason I said that [the Spirit] will take what is mine and declare it to you" (16:15).

The Holy Spirit within us speaks not merely for himself but for the Trinity. Metaphorically, the three divine persons have a shared heart, mind, and will. We might be able to separate conceptually their functions in God's project for creation, but they always act in concert with one mind, heart, and will. Jesus says of the Holy Spirit, "For he will not speak on his own, but will speak whatever he hears" (16:13).

EVOLUTIONARY IMPLICATIONS

For Teilhard, no matter how much work the Trinity must do to complete the divine project and fulfill the kingdom of God, Jesus is very clear that we are expected to be fully and actively involved in the success of God's project. The Holy Spirit will inspire us with an inner vision suggesting ways we are to contribute. "He will declare to you the things that are to come" (16:13). Since it is in Christ Jesus's cosmic body that the work of God's project is happening, the Spirit will explain Christ's work to us and how we fit into it. He will "take what is mine and declare it to you" (16:14).

PART VI

TEILHARD'S
METANOIA

28

The Hermeneutic Challenge

THROUGHOUT THIS BOOK we faced two challenges. The *first* challenge was to show that *the Gospels are evolutionary documents.* We did this by showing how Jesus elevated the Mosaic Law to a genuinely new level. He did not do away with the Mosaic Law, since that would have been a revolutionary act. *Revolution means to reject and replace.* Rather than rejecting Hebrew Scripture's core teachings, Jesus built his message upon them. In his Sermon on the Mount, he raised teachings of the Mosaic Law to a higher understanding and practice. *Evolution works with what is there and takes it to a higher level.*

Regarding this first challenge, we identified the higher ways of thinking and behaving (*metanoia*) that Jesus introduced—ways that had the power to change the mind, the heart, and the behavior of the human family. We called this higher stage "Jesus's Way."

Teilhard would have described the first-century *metanoia* as "an evolutionary leap in the noosphere." But Teilhard was looking for more, and he discovered it. He recognized in Jesus's words and teachings the potential to reveal and achieve further steps in the evolution of the noosphere. Teilhard realized that Jesus had introduced *a way for humanity to continue to reach ever-higher stages of consciousness.*[1]

For believers to pursue future evolutionary movements consciously, they need to undergo an additional *metanoia*. This new way of thinking and acting is the mindset shift—the *metanoia*—proposed by Teilhard.

A Higher *Metanoia*

The *second* challenge, our present hermeneutic task, is to show that *Jesus's proposed way of living allows for the continual evolution of humanity*. Not just one evolutionary step, but a continuing series of them.

For Teilhard, God is not simply the producer of creation, in the way a human might author a book, carve a sculpture, or paint a portrait. Once completed, a book, sculpture, or portrait remains unchanged. Creation, however, is a dynamic, evolving reality. For Teilhard, creation is God's ongoing love project. Its goal is the mutual loving union of everything in the universe. And it is far from complete.

For Teilhard, God didn't just set the universe in motion, then sit back and watch the process unfold. The universal Christ, who is at work in our lives today, shows that God remains fully involved in the successful completion of the divine project. We might view God as its project manager and Jesus's Way as the process designed to effect the successful completion of the project—the fullness of life for all in a cosmic Oneness.

For Teilhard, Jesus's Way remains a way of thinking, living, and loving that continues to drive evolution forward until all come to enjoy the fullness of life. For Jesus, love is the driving force behind the kingdom of God as expressed in Jesus's commandment: "Just as I have loved you, you also should love one another" (John 13:34).

His Way welcomes and embraces all levels and kinds of love that help humanity to enjoy life to the full. His Way begins with— and is founded on—*compassionate love* for the poor, the sick, the forgotten, the oppressed. It also includes *forgiving love* toward relatives, neighbors, strangers, enemies, and oppressors. These are very tangible descriptions of individual acts of caring love, beautiful in themselves. Yet there are many more creative ways to show love. Ways that artists, musicians, writers, and filmmakers can express love and evoke love. Ways that relationships can make a loving impact. For example, teams of research scientists can help heal human disease and planetary distress, or groups and organizations can bring healing and wholeness where there is sickness, hunger, or political unrest.

Many ways of showing love have yet to be discovered.

Since God the Creator is unconditional Love, Teilhard realizes that God's total creation—starting at the Big Bang—must be an expression of that unconditional love.[2] Love and creation's evolution must be connected at the deepest levels. This essential inextricable union between love and evolution toward the fullness of life generates several other insights. For example, since evolution is itself a universal force, love must be

- a cosmic energy;
- at play even at the atomic, molecular, and cellular levels;
- the most universal, the most tremendous, and the most mysterious of the cosmic forces;
- the basic energy guiding evolution; and
- what keeps driving evolution forward and upward.[3]

Teilhard makes other fundamental connections. Because the universe comes forth from a "creator" (one who brings things into existence):

- Love itself must be a creative force.
- Humans are destined to create as well as to love.
- Love always wants to share itself.

Three Realizations

Teilhard realizes that the ways of showing love that have yet to be discovered will most likely emerge through the creative work of relationships, human teams, and groups large and small. He offers three realizations—or operating principles—that apply to love, creativity, and evolution. All three are based on *relationships*.

- The most basic way to *love* is to form relationships or unions.
- To *create* is to form unions, since a unified team is always something new and often capable of creating things that none of the team members alone can create.
- To *evolve* begins by forming unions, because unions often possess new, emergent properties and abilities.

185

Insightfully, Teilhard recognizes that "God creates by uniting."[4] Relationships provide for a fuller experience of life. Teilhard sees that this principle—creating by uniting—holds true at every level of existence. Subatomic particles join to form unions that we call atoms. Over a hundred of these atoms are identified in the table of chemical elements. Atoms join with other atoms to form unions called molecules—millions of different ones, each with unique properties and potential. Molecules join to form unions called compounds. Compounds join to form unions called cells. Cells join to form all the living things on Earth. Humans join to form teams that creatively reshape Earth. We carry a creative God in our hearts, and God drives us to create ever-new ways to join, to show love, and to experience life in more abundance (see John 10:10).

Creative love is operating at all levels of the universe. It is a sacred reserve of energy. It is the lifeblood of evolution. "Love is the primal and universal psychic energy." Like an underground river, it "runs everywhere beneath our civilization." It is the driving force in the growth and development of the noosphere. "In science, business, and public affairs, people pretend not to know it, though under the surface it [love] is everywhere."[5] Creative love is limitless.

Teilhard sees Jesus's Way as encouraging humans to explore an ever-wider range of creative love. Such explorations in creative love contribute to advances in government, education, medicine, communication, technology, and all forms of research. These are just some of the areas providing opportunities for more creative ways to show love. Love provides energy to empower any project, large or small, that offers the possibility of fuller life for the human community and the natural world. For Teilhard, Jesus's Way fosters not only the continued evolution of Christianity but also the continued evolution of humanity.[6]

In his writings, Teilhard teaches us how to "see" creation the way he sees it. His *metanoia* invites us to develop the new eyes we need if we wish to see things the way he does. His *metanoia* enables us to perceive things we have never noticed before. With our new eyes, we will be able to glimpse God's Spirit at work among us. Each of us will be able to experience the kingdom of God growing in our neighborhoods. We will recognize God's project expressing an expanding drive to life like that of a mustard plant. We will be able to recognize evidence of God's project penetrating and permeating the hearts and minds of people all over the planet, the way yeast permeates rising bread dough.

With Teilhard's *metanoia*, we will be able to comprehend how discoveries, inventions, innovations, and ideas occurring daily in science and technology can foster God's evolutionary work among us. In his way of thinking, Teilhard sees a revitalized Christianity as the vehicle for the integration of evolutionary science and religion:

> Christianity has acquired a new value....It provides the fire that inspires man's effort...it is seen to be the form of faith that is most fitted to modern needs: a religion for progress— the very religion of progress of the earth—I would go so far as to say the very religion of evolution.[7]

Teilhard believes that his *metanoia* will allow today's believers to integrate continually the present and future findings of modern science into their theology, spirituality, and ethics.[8] By entering this new mindset, he suggests, we will realize and "see" that scientific discoveries are part of God's divine revelation. In ever-new ways, we will recognize these discoveries as manifesting ways that the kingdom of God is actively at work in our midst. "I am convinced that an Epiphany of this sort would be for Christianity the signal for a vast movement of interior liberation and expansion."[9]

With this *metanoia*, we would realize that God is revealing the divine nature through research in each of the sciences. We would see an aspect of God's self-revelation reflected in the DNA molecule. For instance, biologists researching the DNA molecule are using genetic coding to show how all living species, including humanity, are connected in a deep oneness.

All forms of life on Earth—not just humanity—can find their place on a single tree of life, even though that tree spreads out in myriad evolutionary branches. The tree of life continues to give rise to countless species in an endless variety of shapes and sizes—from dinosaurs to daisies, from cedars to chipmunks, and from parrots to persimmons. God made creation so that, like its Creator, it would be driven from within to create—expressing itself in life, duplicating itself, improving itself, transforming itself—with amazing fecundity.

As another example, astrophysicists keep giving us additional perspectives on Earth's place in our galaxy. The Hubble spacecraft's cameras, sending images back from outer space, display in living color the immense grandeur of the universe. Seen from space, our planet

Earth is clearly a single complex living organism made up of countless interacting elements.

Whether we focus on microscopically small molecules in a chemistry laboratory or on our planet as part of a very large expanding universe, Teilhard says that science's eyes are giving us glimpses of the Creator's intent and Christ's ongoing work of transforming humanity.[10]

Teilhard's primary focus is on the Christ who lives today. It is the universal Christ, in whom we all live and move and have our being, that Teilhard wants us to learn to see.

This Christ Body contains within itself not only humans but also everything in the universe, from the smallest bacterium to the largest galaxy. This cosmic Body also gives existence and continues to pulse life into everything. Once we can see everything that exists as living and interacting within the Body of the Cosmic Christ, the new *metanoia* becomes easier to live out and pass on.

To grasp Teilhard's vision of Christ alive today, he proposes a way of seeing that is far more complex and richer than the first-century *metanoia* that the apostles experienced. The apostles had merely to learn to re-envision and reinterpret the Mosaic Law in a new way in order to shift their perspective on the nature of God from a punishing monarch to a loving father.

Teilhard calls us to his more comprehensive *metanoia*, a mindset that can both believe in a Cosmic Christ as well as enthusiastically embrace all that science has discovered about the universe and all that it will discover in the future.

In Teilhard's *metanoia*, believers need to recognize a larger potential meaning in Jesus's teachings. Teilhard wants us to view the kingdom of God from the Cosmic Christ's perspective. To recognize the implications of Jesus's teaching for our age and future ages, believers need to think in ways that were impossible for the apostles. It is an evolutive mindset that we today must strive to make our own.

Teilhard informs us that God created an evolving universe, and the divine loving communal presence—Creator God as Father of us all, Christ Jesus, and Holy Spirit—permeates it. The Trinity is invested in human progress and its outcome. Jesus assured his apostles and assures us of his continuing involvement in the transformation of the world. Teach them to "obey everything that I have commanded you. And remember, I am with you always, to the end of the age" (Matt 28:20).

God's Evolutionary Project

Today, people easily abandon the literal reading of traditional biblical stories, such as Adam and Eve in the Garden of Eden. These stories may contain important truths about human life, but they are not factual events. They are divinely inspired products of religious imagination designed to teach lessons to people who lived in a certain historical civilization. Creative imagination is a special tool not only for communicating religious truths but also for communicating scientific truths.

Evolutionary scientists also use imagination to weave stories about how early humans lived and interacted. They admit that our prehistoric past is shrouded in mystery. No paleoanthropologist knows in detail how our earliest ancestors spent each day. Bits and pieces of ancient fossils cannot reveal the different ways males and females related. They can't tell us how religion, music, dance, art, or humor were valued. Nor do they know how the daily rituals of eating, dressing, bathing, child rearing, or work roles were expressed. There is no observational evidence to confirm—or deny—their stories.

What can be agreed upon, both from the Adam and Eve story and today's evolutionary scientific story, is the truth that *the human species as we know it and experience it is flawed, individually and collectively.*

It makes little difference whether one believes religiously that, in the beginning, the parents of humanity were "perfect" as in the Garden of Eden; or, scientifically, that those parents were an evolving branch of the phylum of the great apes. Humanity, as we know it and as the people in Jesus's day knew it, is flawed, imperfect, and immature.

The fact that our nature is still flawed is empirically verifiable. Simply observe human interactions over a period of time. It becomes clear that self-interest typically takes precedence over ensuring the happiness of others. The primacy of self-interest is daily manifested in individuals, families, ethnic groups, races, and nations.

Jesus's healing stories call attention to his larger mission. His overall mission was not the healing of a few people suffering from physical or mental ailments in Israel. Once he became the Risen Lord, his long-term objective became *to heal the flawed nature of humanity.* For Teilhard, God is using the continual evolution of humanity to do it.

Jesus recognized this healing task as a gradual process, just as the experience of entering fuller life is a gradual process. To begin the process,

Jesus assigned disciples to share the good news everywhere that the great healing project was underway. They were to give instructions on his Way of love. His Way provided a model for living that would help bring humanity to its destined maturity and health. In Teilhard's language, the work of God's kingdom is an evolutionary project.

To heal humanity and open it to a fuller experience of life, Jesus introduced a new level of loving—*agápē*, or unconditional love. This love formed the centerpiece of his teaching and his Way.

> Whoever wishes to become great among you must be your servant, and whoever wishes to be first among you must be slave of all. For the Son of Man came not to be served but to serve, and to give his life a ransom for many. (Mark 10:43–45)[11]

People living *agápē* love do not seek personal advantage over others or fear loss for themselves. Unburdened by greed and anxiety, they can calmly assess a situation and act for the good of others. In unconditional love, people act, not to glorify their ego, but to find joy in the happiness of others and to rejoice in being able to contribute to God's project.

The healing process begins in each of us when we realize that the aim of human life is for each and all of us to be one with God and with one another in loving union. Jesus made this point clear in his prayer to the Father:

> I ask not only on behalf of these, but also on behalf of those who will believe in me through their word, that they may all be one. As you, Father, are in me and I am in you, may they also be in us, so that the world may believe that you have sent me. The glory that you have given me I have given them, so that they may be one, as we are one, I in them and you in me, that they may become completely one, so that the world may know that you have sent me and have loved them even as you have loved me. (John 17:20–23)

Before this supreme union with God can be realized through the evolutionary process, the present challenge is for all humans to work toward becoming one with each other in love. In his teaching and modeling, Jesus gives us the way to achieve this union and oneness among us. We begin by learning to live in him (as if we were him) and following his Way of unconditional love. It is a simple formula that transcends all religions, and it does not require swearing allegiance to any specific theological dogmas.

Spreading his Way was the assignment Jesus gave to his disciples. They were to teach people how to continue healing flawed humanity and to show people how to become one in loving union. They were to do it by modeling unconditional love.

Apparently, Jesus's evolutionary assignment was almost lost. In recent centuries, people were taught to believe that, by dying on the cross, Jesus had healed flawed humanity, once and for all. But, as each of us can testify from our personal experience, though our sins may have been forgiven, our tendency to sin remains. Obviously, humanity is still flawed and immature. God's love project for us is far from complete. The human family still has a long way to go before we can say that we humans have "become completely one," as Jesus and the Father are one.

Teilhard proposes a *metanoia* for God's project that we need to enter into, in order to get back on track to allow Christ to heal us and to bring us the fullness of life.

29

The Principles of Teilhard's *Metanoia*

HERE ARE NINE of Teilhard's principles that shape his new way of thinking—his evolutionary *metanoia*:

1. The discoveries of modern science must form an important foundation for any contemporary theology, spirituality, or morality if it is to be true, relevant, and inspiring.[1]
2. Love is the very nature of God.[2] The universe is God's love project.[3] God loves creation with an unconditional love.[4]
3. God created an evolving universe.[5] Evolution is happening continually on every level of being—and it is moving in the direction of ever-increasing complexity and higher *consciousness*.[6] *"Complexity-Consciousness" is the law giving evolution its direction and purpose.* It is also a law of love.[7]
4. Bringing evolving creation to its fulfillment is God's project[8] as well as God's purpose for creating the universe.[9] The moral call here is to be willing to try anything that offers hope for advancing God's project.[10]
5. The success of God's project for creation depends on each one's conscious and creative activity to keep that divine plan evolving and developing in the direction God wants for creation.[11]
6. Each one, according to his or her resources of love

192

energy,[12] is morally obliged to nurture the evolutionary process.[13] This is humanity's purpose on Earth.[14]

7. A planetary mind and heart—the noosphere—has arisen and is evolving.[15] At present, God's project is focused on the continual evolution of knowledge and love in the noosphere.[16]

8. To know, love, and serve the universe with a passion is our role on Earth.[17] We love and serve it through creativity and collaboration.[18] Thus, we must learn to love the "invisible" and to love the "not-yet."[19]

9. We do all of this by seeing ourselves as members and cells of Christ's cosmic body, living with, in, and through him.[20]

These are some of the salient principles that govern the way Teilhard thinks about and perceives reality. They are fundamental assumptions he holds about the nature of God, God's involvement in the world, and our expected response. They are thoroughly Christian and scientifically valid from his perspective. It would take an entire book to develop them more fully. Each one deserves much meditative reflection.

Each principle introduces us to important aspects of the cosmic horizon that Teilhard perceives. This set of principles forms the basis for how Teilhard sees creation and makes sense of all that is happening as it is happening, not only on Earth but also throughout the universe. Like St. Paul, he sees everything happening *in Christ Jesus*.[21]

Teilhard is operating within this loving, hopeful, optimistic, and even mystical mindset when he reads the Scriptures. Would that we might begin to see in the sacred writings the evolutionary potential that he sees there.

The Fullness of Life

For all who seek to enter Teilhard's *metanoia*, the apostles' *metanoia* is a wonderful starting point for three reasons. First, it raises people from seeing God primarily as a Just Judge to seeing God as a Loving Father. Second, it raises people from living in fear of punishment for sin to acknowledging God's mercy toward the sinner, especially God's readiness to forgive sins even before we ask for forgiveness.[22] Third, it sets people free to spend their energy loving and forgiving each other.

Teilhard's *metanoia* then transforms the apostles' *metanoia* into a new higher love-focused mindset *appropriate to an evolutionary universe*. While acknowledging that Jesus saves us from the punishment for sin, Teilhard sees Jesus as primarily showing us *the way to the fullness of life*.

Jesus's true life's purpose is to help us experience the fullness of life. That's why he heals people—to give them a fuller life here and now. Every healing act that Jesus performs reinforces his primary message: God is offering us the fullness of life. "I came that they may have life, and have it abundantly" (John 10:10). Jesus is showing us how, by our service to others, we help each other toward a fuller life. In this way, we grow together *as a species* in evolutionary stages into the fullness of life.

For Teilhard, the fullness of life comes to us in continuing steps. One does not jump in a single step from selfishness to unconditional love for others. Neither does the growth from childhood to adulthood happen in one step. Each new level attained reveals an ever-increasing complexity of things accompanied by ever-deepening levels of consciousness about them.

Teilhard offers us a way to integrate religious and scientific pursuits into a single shared pursuit of the fullness of life. His way enriches both ways of thinking. As we welcome more fullness of life and help provide it for others, we expand our consciousness to see Christ's Way and scientific discovery working together to provide more fullness of life.

Science assures us that all levels of life are interwoven. We cannot think or feel without a physical body and a physical brain. And we cannot enjoy spiritual consciousness or pray without a body and a brain. We nourish our brain with food and drink, so that we can think. Our brain doesn't require much food to keep working. Teilhard once remarked that eating one slice of bread gave him enough energy to come up with several ideas and insights.

Jesus often uses the metaphor of money to explain certain aspects of God's kingdom. If I look at the amount of money I possess as a symbol of the amount of the fullness of life I enjoy, I can say that, as a first step, Christ's redemptive action brings me from a debt-laden condition (due to sin) into a debt-free condition. Financially speaking, I go from sin to forgiveness, from a bank account in deep debt to a bank account of zero (debt paid). But a loving God would never leave me with no financial potential. God provides me—and each of us—with some "capital" to work with. We get a body, mind, and spirit plus abilities and talents to invest on God's behalf.

In the parable of the talents, the master entrusts his servants with his money and expects them to invest it on his behalf (see Matt 25:14–30). With the grace-filled investments God gives to us, God expects us to develop an ever-greater ability to show love to one another and to nurture creation. In the parable of the talents, the returning master does not take back the talents he has entrusted to his servants. He leaves his money with them to keep investing it—to multiply it even further. They become part of his investor group.

Our talents, shared for the benefit of others, also allow us to develop an ever-greater capacity to receive God's love. When we maintain the perspective of God's divine investment in us, it reveals a richer meaning of salvation—not only forgiveness of sin, but also the fullness of life, what Jesus calls building the kingdom of God on Earth.[23]

What the Gospels reveal—and we learn to see—is that Christ's true work operates on an ever-expanding continuum of love and life. His primary mission and challenge is not merely forgiving our sins but rather, with our help, bringing God's love project to a successful conclusion.

If we stay exclusively focused on our personal sins and their forgiveness, we remain self-focused. In Teilhard's *metanoia*, we shift our focus outward. In the new mindset, we thank God for our existence, our abilities, and our opportunities *to bring life to others*. We focus on how we can contribute to God's project. We become attentive to God's work and find divine purpose for our daily lives.

We might describe God's evolutionary project as *bringing the fullness of life to all creation*. To accomplish this work, God needs the help of humans. Jesus's Way shows us how to invest our talents to create more love and life among our fellow humans, especially among those most in need. The creative and caring ways of Jesus remain just as relevant today for advancing the world as they did for his first followers.

For Teilhard, Jesus's Way provides a system to support continual evolution. He would suggest three key insights to promote successful evolution:[24]

First, *love provides the source of energy for God's project,* since love is the most powerful force that keeps evolution moving forward.[25] One of the other abilities of love is that it provides us with "faith in the future."[26] Love keeps us going when the going gets rough.

Second, *to increase love's output of energy, we are to expand our loving connections with others* locally and world-wide.[27] When groups of people work together for a shared purpose, the ability of the group is often greater than the sum of what each can accomplish alone.

Third, *always aim for higher, more open, more inclusive states of consciousness.*[28] In Jesus's words, this point might be described as approaching life with the openness of a childlike mind. "Truly I tell you, unless you change and become like children, you will never enter the kingdom of heaven" (Matt 18:3). Jesus is telling us to be open-minded and curious, like a child. Ask questions, be willing to learn, try new things, explore, test your limits. If you have ever been with a curious four-year-old in a new place, you know the child will bombard you with questions. When you enter Teilhard's *metanoia*, act like that curious child.

30

The Evolution of Human Consciousness

Human Evolution

THE JEWS and early Christians seemed to believe that the human race began with a pair of perfect humans—Adam and Eve—living a carefree life in a blissful garden called Eden. Then, with one act of curious disobedience, they caused the downfall of humanity.

Today, paleoanthropologists show that humanity (*Homo sapiens*) first emerged on Earth, not as a pair of perfect humans, but rather as conscious but primitive groups of people living in caves in various places on Earth. According to evolutionary principles, every new species is "born," that is, *it emerges from something that went before.* The group of protohumans (in the order of primates) from which *Homo sapiens* evolved (or was "born") had already migrated to different parts of the world. Thus, it is possible that humans emerged simultaneously in different parts of the planet.[1]

The first humans were underdeveloped planetary beings *in process* toward ever-higher degrees of consciousness.[2] Although these early humans enjoyed self-reflective consciousness, they learned much about living just by watching animal behavior.

Animals provided early humans with examples of hunting, fishing, and food gathering. From observing animals, humans learned about family life, social life, teamwork, protecting their young, feeding each other, washing themselves, grooming one another, and caring for their sick or wounded. Our ancestors watched animals use tools, gather food, store it, and preserve it. Humans share all these instinctive abilities—and go beyond them.

In the earliest days as *Homo sapiens,* humans took a mental evolutionary step. Primitive men and women developed creativity and ingenuity *consciously.* Over time, using these self-reflective abilities, they taught themselves to craft tools and weapons, harness fire, communicate with words, count, draw pictures, make jewelry, grow crops, and honor their dead. They learned to take risks, explore, and venture outward beyond their safe places. Most important, they learned to love and care for each other in different ways. They found certain herbs and roots useful in curing illness and alleviating pain. They discovered that cooked food was tastier and easier to digest.

Scientific evidence shows that, as hundreds and thousands of years passed, humans continued growing steadily in consciousness. They developed language, formed hunting teams, improved farming skills, defined community roles, and organized tribal structures.

As civilization developed, humans kept expanding their ability to show love and compassion with an ever-widening embrace. For example, Jesus healed individuals, one by one. Today and every day, we heal hundreds and thousands at a time in hospitals all over the globe. We have created vaccines—stunning achievements—to keep people worldwide from being infected by illnesses such as whooping cough, polio, diphtheria, measles, mumps, chicken pox, pneumonia, smallpox, rubella, influenza, hepatitis, and certain forms of cancer. We have devised antibiotics to cure various bacterial illnesses. We use stem cells to reduce inflammation, strengthen bones, and rebuild body parts. We provide mental hospitals, orphanages, and residential homes for the elderly sick. We operate Medicare and Medicaid for seniors and the poor. Jesus predicted we would do more healing than he did and greater things than he did (see John 14:12). And we are doing just that.

Teilhard encourages us to keep searching Jesus's teachings to find relevance for developing a forward-reaching consciousness.[3] As a first stage, Teilhard wants us to learn to recognize the Gospels as evolutionary documents and to experience the apostles' *metanoia.* However, he is much more interested in us reading the Scriptures from within his new mindset, his next-stage *metanoia.*[4]

Jesus Christ was and is always concerned about manifesting the kingdom of God among us. Certainly, he wants us to keep recognizing the kingdom of God—and God's project for creation—as it is revealing itself in our world today. Jesus Christ wants us to develop transformative ways of thinking and loving. Today, more people are demonstrating the kingdom of God at work on Earth. Some do it consciously. Many more do it unconsciously. But God's work keeps getting done. The growth and development of the noosphere is proof of this accomplishment.

For example, fifty years ago over half the people in the world were poor and undernourished. According to the World Health Organization, twenty-five years ago the concerted effort of nations reduced that percentage by more than half, to 23 percent. Today, the number of undernourished people stands at 13 percent. Such significant improvement represents the power of a worldwide collective conscious commitment to making a positive difference in world hunger.

Such planetary commitment is the result of humanity itself undergoing a *metanoia*. Today, we think globally rather than merely personally or nationally. If we could eliminate national and tribal warfare, the percentage of undernourished people could quickly be reduced to near zero. Teilhard would say that this concern for the health of all humanity is a clear evolutionary leap from a century ago.

An Evolutionary Pope

Without explicitly referring to evolution, Pope Francis repeatedly emphasizes Jesus Christ as "forever young and a constant source of newness."[5] The pope recognizes and expresses a foundational insight of Christian theology that many have forgotten. He refers to St. Irenaeus's affirmation: "By his coming, Christ brought with him all newness."[6] The pope explains,

> Whenever we make the effort to return to the source and to recover the original freshness of the Gospel, new avenues arise, new paths of creativity open up, with different forms of expression, more eloquent signs and words with new meaning for today's world.[7]

Would that Teilhard had lived long enough to hear Pope Francis proclaim the gospel as "a constant source of newness." He would have delighted at the clear affirmation of his fellow Jesuit, Pope Francis, and his evolutionary way of thinking.

Many believers may find it impossible to grow into Teilhard's evolutionary mindset. Some continue to see themselves surrounded by evil and immersed in a society in perpetual chaos. They want to escape life on Earth. Such believers tend to interpret Jesus's suffering and death simply as providing for them "an evacuation plan to the next world." Or as Fr. Richard Rohr puts it: "We become preoccupied with those last three hours of Jesus's life, when we get the blood sacrifice that gets us humans saved, our ticket to heaven punched."[8] John the evangelist sees Earth differently. When Jesus came into this world, he came not as a stranger. He came to Earth as to *his home* (John 1:11).

Other believers today insist that the gospel message would become totally distorted if they were to try to integrate the findings of contemporary science—evolutionary and otherwise—into Christian theological doctrines. Many believers typically avoid dealing with scientific discoveries by emphasizing Jesus primarily as a historical figure, who appeared on Earth at a certain point in history, was brought back from the dead, and was taken up to heaven by the Father, after making his ultimate sacrifice for our sins. Such people find it hard to envision Christ as a cosmic figure permeating all history, past, present, and future. To quote Richard Rohr again, in reply to such believers,

> Christian scripture, in fact, gives us Jesus' place in that [cosmic] history counted in billions of years if you look for it—in the prologue to John's Gospel, for example, or in the Pauline hymns or the letters to the Colossians and Ephesians, or in the opening of John's first letter. All speak of Christ existing from all eternity. We just don't see those references used often. They've never been unpacked for the majority of Christians, and we don't have theology to know how to see it.[9]

"Unpacked" Scripture

That "unpacked" theology waits there in the New Testament. It may be found in Paul's letters as well as those of John. For example,

Paul in effect tells his Colossian community that their first mistake is that they are trying to fit Jesus into a religious system. Jesus does not fit *into* a system; Jesus Christ *is* the system.[10]

For St. Paul, the universe is the Body of Christ. Teilhard takes Paul's insight to the next stage. For him, the universe in evolution is also the evolving story of the Body of Jesus Christ.

Teilhard wants to show how planet Earth and the people on it have their roles to play in this magnificent story. When you make the connection, as Teilhard does, between God's project for creation and the Body of Christ, you realize that God's project is to build the Body of Christ. God's project is the Christ Project.[11]

Teilhard finds in the writings of Paul and John clear grounds for encouraging this second *metanoia*, which is actively promoting the conscious loving unity of the entire human family on Earth. Whether we are Christian, Jewish, Muslim, Hindu, or of any other religion—including nonbelievers—our earthly task is the same in God's divine project, namely, *to love and serve one another.*

The power of actively providing loving service to each other is the evolutionary secret that Jesus reveals to us. "This is my commandment, that you love one another as I have loved you" (John 15:12). It is the only way all humanity will experience the fullness of life. The earthly task of mutual service remains in effect until the end of time.

In his eschatological discourse in Matthew 25, Jesus tells his apostles three parables about getting ready for his return. These parables are not addressed to the crowds. All three are directed to people of faith, those who believe that Jesus is the Savior of the world. To these believers, Jesus explains how doing good works—showing love and care for each other—is the clearest way to prepare for eternal life with God. Learn to love ever more deeply on Earth in order to get ready to live with the God of Love forever.

These three parables remind us that living a life of loving service includes three levels: how to live lovingly day to day; how to make our unique contribution to God's project; and how to be spiritually ready and alert.

First, the parable of the sheep and goats (Matt 25:31–46) is about ordinary compassion. It emphasizes each one's daily responsibility to care for our brothers and sisters in their immediate needs for food, clothing, understanding, and companionship.[12]

Second, the parable of the talents (Matt 25:14–30) is about human activities that make a positive difference in the world. We are called to creatively invest our resources and abilities on behalf of the kingdom of God.

Finally, the parable of the wise virgins (Matt 25:1–13) emphasizes the need for spiritual readiness. Most scripture scholars agree that the "oil" of the wise virgins represents their good works. This is the reason why some of their extra supply cannot be given away.

What you and I contribute to the building up of the kingdom of God is important to Jesus because building up the kingdom of God is the primary purpose for which he came to Earth. "[Undergo *metanoia*], for the kingdom of heaven has come near" (Matt 4:17).

The role of loving service toward each other transcends any religion, since it is central to all of them. The fundamental spirituality and moral life of every major religious denomination is based on the Golden Rule—treating others the way you would want them to treat you.

From a much wider perspective, loving service may be offered, consciously or unconsciously, within a religious consciousness or independent of one. In all cases, love can provide the force behind every evolutionary advance made by humanity. Loving service to one another will never go out of date, even in eternity, since mutual love and union is the essence of the Trinity and permeates the milieu of God's kingdom.

From Teilhard's perspective, we can no longer read the Gospels with a self-serving focus. We can no longer simply ask, "What has Jesus done *for me*?" The question now is, "What can I do for God? How can I show loving service to my neighbor? What can I do, alone and in union with others, to help reveal and accomplish God's love project while I live?"

EVOLUTIONARY IMPLICATIONS

Here are some suggestions for ways the principles of Teilhard's *metanoia* may be actualized in behavior. For example, principle 4 says,

4. Bringing evolving creation to its fulfillment is God's project as well as God's purpose for creating the universe. The moral call to us is to be willing to try anything that offers hope for advancing God's project.

This principle reflects the teaching of Jesus. According to the parable of the talents (Matt 25:14–30), Jesus has no use for the steward who buried his talent. This fearful man is unwilling to take a risk in serving his master. Through the parable, Jesus is telling us that he wants the fullest commitment of everyone on his team, if his Father's vision for creation is to be fulfilled. Jesus is not promoting reckless behavior but well-reasoned risk-taking. Use your creativity boldly.

In the next two principles, Teilhard spells out this path of conscious creativity within a shared loving purpose:

5. The success of God's project for creation depends on each one's conscious and creative activity to keep that divine plan evolving and developing in the direction God wants for creation.
6. Each one, according to his or her resources of love energy, is morally obliged to nurture the evolutionary love process. This is humanity's purpose on Earth.

If we review the public life of Jesus in our imagination, we realize that Jesus was practicing these Teilhardian principles. He lived a life of service for others in the ways in which he was capable, given his time in history. Teilhard practiced these principles, living a life of service in his unique way. Both Jesus and Teilhard call us, in turn, to find our unique ways of being of service to our fellow humans today. We are to do it creatively, innovatively, and even daringly.

These Teilhardian principles present a definite moral imperative. They go beyond certain traditional moral attitudes, such as those that caution people not to get involved, to focus on avoiding sin, and to view life on Earth simply as a preparation for life in heaven.

Teilhard's principles move in a different direction. They invite us to get immersed in the world's activities and to promote human advances. We are not to be obsessed with sin nor are we to mind getting our hands dirty with work. As a geologist, Teilhard always has his hands in the dirt, digging for fossils. From his perspective, you and I are put on Earth to make a positive difference with our effort and creativity.

If enough people commit to a future grounded in gospel values, it guarantees that evolution will continue to keep moving forward and upward. Such transformed people will also continue to transform Earth with patient, compassionate, joy-filled love.

Conclusion

If an evolutionary drive is behind all things physical, psychological, and spiritual, then it was clear to Teilhard that a God whose name is Love created a universe in continual evolution from the start. That awareness became a new basis for his theological reflection. For Teilhard, a world in continual evolution toward a higher unity in love provides the only true basis for theological reflection.

As we reenvision traditional Christian doctrines in the light of evolution, it will expand and enrich our understanding of heaven and hell, life and death, sin and suffering, redemption and sanctification, conscience and consciousness, faith and dogma, the human Jesus and the Cosmic Christ, and so on.

Teilhard realized that, considering evolution is happening everywhere, what especially needed to be reexamined was *the purpose of our human life on Earth.*

If God created a universe in continual evolution, and we are now fully aware of it, how can we *not* want to cooperate in that divine project?

Knowing evolution's direction and the laws guiding it, can we — especially we followers of Jesus — sit idly by?

Recognizing that we are riding the tip of the arrow of evolution in its forward and upward trajectory, how can we refuse to fully cooperate in this cosmic journey?

Aware that Christ Jesus, our life and our love, is waiting for us up ahead with open arms and a burning heart, how can we refuse anything he asks of us to accomplish on Earth, no matter how much sweat and tears it may demand?

Appendix

Teilhard on Evangelization

TEILHARD WROTE a short piece on the Gospels in 1919, while serving as a stretcher-bearer during World War I. He referred to this "Note" in a letter to his cousin as my "Note sur l'Apostolat."[1] He earlier refers to it as "Notes toward the Evangelization of New Times."[2] In a collection of his writings, *The Heart of Matter*, the title is revised to "Note on the Presentation of the Gospel in a New Age,"[3] as if it were meant to be an updated Gospel commentary. It is not.

The piece was never meant to be published. Teilhard sent it to a Jesuit friend for his comments and guidance. In a letter to his cousin, he also referred to it as a kind of "manifesto"[4] that he might show to his superiors, "if the occasion arises," to explain his perspective on how to present the good news to a human society fascinated with and absorbed in scientific progress. Teilhard, a priest, intended the "Note" as a comment to fellow priests. He is referring to priestly homilies that avoid mentioning what science has discovered about creation.

His major point is that "we have in our day...a *natural* religious movement of great force."[5] This movement is symbolized by the tremendous dedication and commitment that people have regarding human advancement in science, medicine, technology, communication, transportation, sociology, and world government. People possess a consciousness of the universe and humanity as a natural whole. They are actively participating in an exciting "reservoir of energy and mysteries."[6]

Teilhard felt that church leaders "appear to wish to impose on the men of today [committed to human progress] a ready-made Divinity from outside."[7] They offer what we would call a "prepackaged God." The packaging is prescientific and cosmologically static.

According to Teilhard, the gospel as it is currently preached from the pulpit seems to our contemporaries as "inevitably *inhuman* and *inferior,* both in its promise of individual happiness and in its precepts of renunciation." To them, the church's version of the gospel "leads to the formation of souls that *have an interest in* their own selfish advantages—*with no interest in* the common task" of humanity to transform the world.[8]

"'Christian' and 'Human' are tending no longer to coincide," writes Teilhard. "In that lies the great Schism that threatens the Church."[9]

Teilhard says we clergy (and Christians) need "to embrace the ideal they [people of today] reach out to…*to seek, with them,* the God whom we already possess who is as yet *amongst us* as though he were a stranger to us."[10]

"Who is the God whom our contemporaries see, and how can we succeed *in finding him, with them,* in Jesus?"[11]

"Although modern Man cannot yet give an exact name to the great Being who is being embodied *for him* and *through him* in the World, he already knows that he will never worship a divinity unless it possesses certain attributes by which he will be able to recognize it.

The God for whom our century is waiting must be:

1. As *vast* and as mysterious as the Cosmos;
2. As *immediate* and all-embracing as Life; and
3. As *linked* (in some way) *to our effort* as Mankind.

A God who made the World less mysterious, or smaller, or less important to us, than our heart and reason show it to be, that God—less beautiful than the God we await—will nevermore be He to whom the Earth kneels."[12]

To demonstrate that the gospel presents just such a God, Teilhard suggests, as a first step, that "we must preach and practice what I shall call 'the Gospel of human Effort.'"[13] The "we" refers primarily to clergy. Clergy are expected to practice personally what they preach. Clergy, above all, need to develop a fuller consciousness of the evolving cosmos.

"In a first introductory phase, I believe we [priests] must develop—in those who believe in Jesus Christ as much as in unbelievers—a *fuller consciousness of the Universe* that encompasses us, and of our capacity to influence its development by our action."[14]

Many (priests) who are totally absorbed by and committed to the narrow view of individual salvation, Teilhard points out, may need "special training."[15]

Notes

Preface/Acknowledgments

1. Pierre Teilhard de Chardin, *The Divine Milieu* (New York: Harper & Row, 1960), 117.

2. Pierre Teilhard de Chardin, *Christianity and Evolution*, trans. René Hague (New York: Harcourt Brace Jovanovich, 1971), 76–95.

3. Cf. John 10:10.

4. *Christianity and Evolution*, 91.

5. *Christianity and Evolution*, 92.

6. *Christianity and Evolution*, 93.

7. *Christianity and Evolution*, 95.

8. Teilhard made the connection between Christian theology and evolution from his earliest writings, dated 1916. See his *Writings in Time of War*, trans. René Hague (New York: Harper, 1968), e.g., 46–47, 114, 190–91, and the entire essay "Mastery of the World and the Kingdom of God," 75–91. See also *The Making of a Mind: Letters from a Soldier-Priest [1914–1919]*, trans. René Hague (New York: Harper & Row, 1961), 192, and *The Heart of Matter, trans. René Hague* (New York: Harcourt, 1978), 23–24. A collection of his essays in *Christianity and Evolution* relate to this topic. See especially the essay "How I Believe," 96–132.

9. Paulist Press has published a series of books on Teilhard's evolutionary approach to spirituality, love, suffering, and the moral life.

10. Among the books that I used by Neil Douglas-Klotz are *Prayers of the Cosmos: Reflections on the Original Meaning of Jesus' Words* (New York: HarperCollins, 1990), *The Hidden Gospel: Decoding the Spiritual Message of the Aramaic Jesus* (Wheaton, IL: Quest Books, 1999), and *Blessings of the Cosmos: Wisdom of the Heart from the Aramaic Words of Jesus* (Boulder, CO: Sounds True, 2006).

Part I: Hermeneutics, Evolution, and *Metanoia*

1. HERMENEUTICS

1. Hermeneutics is a discipline that develops the theory and methodology of interpretation, especially the interpretation of biblical texts, Wisdom literature, and philosophical writings.

2. Pierre Teilhard de Chardin, *Christianity and Evolution*, trans. René Hague (New York: Harcourt Brace Jovanovich, 1971), 92.

3. Teilhard understands this "spiritual dualism." "How can the man who believes in heaven and the Cross continue to believe seriously in the value of worldly occupations?" *The Divine Milieu* (New York: Harper & Row, 1960), 51.

4. Teilhard explores this challenge in many essays found in *Christianity and Evolution*.

5. This is the thesis of Teilhard's scientific masterpiece, *The Phenomenon of Man*, trans. Bernard Wall (New York: Harper & Row, 1959). For a more modern translation, see Sarah Appleton-Weber, *The Human Phenomenon* (Sussex, UK: Sussex Academic Press, 2003).

6. *Christianity and Evolution*, 23, 26–28.

7. *Christianity and Evolution*, 28.

8. *Christianity and Evolution*, 26–27.

9. *Christianity and Evolution*, 23.

10. Scripture scholars suggest that Jesus and the evangelists often used the expression *kingdom of heaven* in place of *kingdom of God* simply to avoid using the sacred word *God* too frequently.

11. Teilhard writes, "Whether we admit or not, we have today no choice: we have all become 'evolutionists'…we all inevitably think and act as if the World were in a continual formation and transformation." *The Heart of Matter*, trans. René Hague (New York: Harcourt, 1978), 84.

2. EVOLUTION

1. Similarly, any social system or any system of thought may be defined or identified by a combination of its appearance, form, structure, function, purpose, processes, and abilities.

2. In a 1947 essay, "The Formation of the Noosphere," Teilhard develops the growth to dominance of this sphere of mind and heart (*The Future of Man*, trans. Norman Denny [New York: Harper & Row, 1964], 161–91).

3. *The Future of Man*, 188. The mind and heart of humanity is "little by little being transformed into a common vision growing ever more intense…where everything is contained, and everything harmonized with the rest of the universe."

4. *The Future of Man*, 167–76.

5. *The Future of Man*, 171.

6. *The Future of Man*, 191.

7. *The Future of Man*, 173.

8. Other moral and social codes of conduct during this period beginning around 3000 BCE may be found among cultures of the Sumerians, Mesopotamians, Babylonians (Hammurabi), and Assyrians. In none of them is there a sense that poor persons ought to be respected.

9. Teilhard himself expresses the challenge this way: "Is the Christ of the Gospels, imagined and loved within the dimensions of a Mediterranean world, capable of still embracing and still forming the center of our prodigiously expanded universe?" *The Divine Milieu* (New York: Harper & Row, 1960), 46.

10. "Paradigm shift" was first introduced in Thomas Kuhn's book *The Structure of Scientific Revolutions* (Chicago: University of Chicago Press, 1962).

3. Metanoia

1. *The Divine Milieu* (New York: Harper & Row, 1960), 46. *The Phenomenon of Man*, trans. Bernard Wall (New York: Harper & Row, 1959), 31.

2. Biblical scholars include J. Glentworth Butler, A. Herbert George Marsh, James Hastings, and A. T. Robertson. For a more general view on this mistranslation of *metanoia*, see D. Tarrant's review of Aloys H. Dirksen, *The New Testament Concept of Metanoia* (Washington, DC: The Catholic University of America, 1932) in *Classical Review* 47, no. 4 (1933).

3. A. T. Robertson, *Word Pictures in the New Testament, vol. 1: Matthew, Mark* (Grand Rapids, MI: Baker Pub Group, 1982). See

Christian Classics Ethereal Library version at https://www.ccel.org/ccel/robertson_at/wp_matt.html.

4. *The Divine Milieu*, 46.

5. Joseph Cardinal Ratzinger, *Principles of Catholic Theology: Building Stones for a Fundamental Theology* (San Francisco: Ignatius Press, 1987). See especially the chapter called "Faith as Conversion—Metanoia."

6. *Metanoia* was also used colloquially in classic Greece to express an "afterthought," or "having second thoughts," or "realizing a truth too late," or "making an apology," thus its use as "repentance" or saying, "I'm sorry."

7. On the road to Damascus, St. Paul undergoes a *metanoia*, which causes him to totally change his understanding of Jesus Christ and his followers (see Acts 9:1–19).

8. He considered his writings as "a way of teaching how to see." *The Divine Milieu*, 46.

9. Teilhard also calls this process an "awakening to consciousness" or "an irreversible interiorization" (see *Future of Man*, trans. Norman Denny [New York: Harper & Row, 1964], 238).

10. *The Divine Milieu*, 47.

11. Jesus opened their minds. I can find no instance in the Gospels where Jesus "opened their hearts."

12. Robert N. Wilkin, "New Testament Repentance: Lexical Considerations," accessed May 1, 2019, https://bible.org/seriespage/new-testament-repentance-lexical-considerations.

13. *Metanoeite* is the present imperative tense of the verb *metanoéō*.

14. Edward J Anton, *Repentance: A Cosmic Shift of Mind and Heart* (Waltham, MA: Discipleship Publications, 2005), 32–33.

15. Teilhard's *The Divine Milieu* is devoted to teaching the *metanoia* process or how to develop "inner vision."

16. See also Acts 3:19.

17. Cited on the back cover of *Beautiful Mercy: Experiencing God's Unconditional Love So We Can Share It with Others* (Erlanger, KY: Dynamic Catholic Institute, 2015).

18. Teilhard discusses this collective transformation in the final pages of *The Divine Milieu*, 140–44.

19. In Luke, Jesus gives the power to heal and cast out demons to seventy-two disciples. It clearly worked (Luke 10:1–23).

20. I have used the NSRVCE (Catholic Edition) throughout. It is easily accessed at https://www.biblegateway.com/versions/New-Revised -Standard-Version-Catholic-Edition-NRSVCE-Bible/.

Part II: The Gospel of Matthew

1. Matt 1:22–23; 2:5–6; 2:15; 2:17–18; 2:23.

2. Matthew has Jesus saying to his disciples, "Go nowhere among the Gentiles, and enter no town of the Samaritans" (10:5). "I was sent only to the lost sheep of Israel" (15:24). Jesus acknowledges some of the Jewish customs, such as paying the temple tax (17:24–27), the central position of Moses (23:2), and observance of the Sabbath (24:20). Matthew also has Jesus castigating Israel's religious leaders, calling them "evil" (9:4; 12:34; 16:4), "brood of vipers" (12:34; 23:33), and saying, "Every plant that my heavenly Father has not planted will be uprooted" (15:13; 13:24–25).

3. "Christ the Evolver," in *Christianity and Evolution*, trans. René Hague (New York: Harcourt Brace Jovanovich, 1971), 138–50.

4. *Christianity and Evolution*, 91. Emphasis added.

5. See "Christ the Evolver."

4. Preparing for the Messiah

1. In part 2, all unidentified references, such as this one, are from Matthew's Gospel.

2. Joseph has four guidance dreams: to marry Mary (1:20–25), to flee to Egypt (2:13), to return to Israel (2:19–20), and to settle in Nazareth (2:22–23). The wise men were also warned in a dream to avoid Herod (2:12)

3. Cf. Vatican II document "Declaration on Religious Freedom" (*Dignitatis Humanae*), issued on December 7, 1965. In its second paragraph, it reads, "This Vatican Council declares that the human person has a right to religious freedom. This freedom means that all men are to be immune from coercion on the part of individuals or of social groups and of any human power, in such wise that no one is to be forced to act in a manner contrary to his own beliefs,

whether privately or publicly, whether alone or in association with others, within due limits."

4. Jesus uses the terms *kingdom of heaven* and *kingdom of God* interchangeably. This is because in Hebrew and Aramaic it is common to substitute the word *Heaven* for the word *God*, so as not to make too common usage of the divine name. For examples of this substitution, compare Matt 4:12–19 with Mark 1:14–17; Matt 5:3 with Luke 6:20; Matt 10:7 with Luke 9:2; Matt 13:31 with Mark 4:30; Matt 13:11 with Mark. 4:11; Matt 19:14 with Mark 10:14–15; and Matt 19:21–24 with Luke 18:22–25.

5. Compare Matt 4:17 to John 3:2.

5. The Mindsets of Jesus and of His Audience

1. This is the primary message of the Sermon on the Mount.

2. This is again the primary message of the Sermon on the Mount.

3. Where did he develop this powerful knowledge? He most likely developed it during his thirty years of prayer and reflection in Nazareth.

4. In contrast, some biblical scholars affirm that Mark wrote his Gospel precisely to prove that Jesus was divine.

5. The expression *the Son of man* occurs eighty-one times in the Greek text of the four canonical Gospels. Most of those times, Jesus is referring to himself.

6. People in the Nazareth community were reputed to be a very backward, religiously conservative people, according to Eli Lizorkin-Eyzenberg, PhD, an Israeli research professor of ancient cultures.

6. The Beatitudes

1. Richard Rohr, *Things Hidden: Scripture as Spirituality* (Cincinnati: St. Anthony Messenger Press, 2008), 44.

2. A similar psalm form opens Jesus's Sermon on the Plain as reported by Luke (6:17–49). Luke also adds four "Woes" to the "Blesseds."

3. Vincent Ryan Ruggiero, "What Does 'Blessed' Mean?" See https://mind-at-work.com/blessed-mean-2/ (accessed May 2, 2019). Vincent Ryan Ruggiero is Professor of Humanities Emeritus, Delhi College, New York.

4. Vincent Ryan Ruggiero, "What Does 'Blessed' Mean?"

5. We may apply the idea of "enlisting" or "calling" ordinary people to a statement common to all three Synoptic authors. "For I have come to call not the righteous but sinners" (Matt 9:13). "Sinners" is a common collective term used to describe the poor, homeless, sick, outcasts, prostitutes, tax collectors, and so on. These are the same "sinners" that Jesus is addressing in his Sermon on the Mount. He is "calling" (enlisting) them to help advance God's kingdom. St. Paul, in addressing the Corinthians, most of whom were poor, powerless, and persecuted, echoes the same active challenge (cf. 1 Cor 1:26–31).

6. *Toward the Future*, trans. René Hague (New York: Harcourt Brace Jovanovich, 1975) contains a number of articles describing Teilhard's vision of a future humanity where love is the dominant force in society. See, for example, "Two Principles" (155) and "The Evolution of Chastity" (86).

7. The Sermon on the Mount

1. Some of the richest Teilhardian material on love may be found in his collection *Human Energy*, trans. J. M. Cohen (New York: Harper & Row, 1969). In the essay "The Spirit of the Earth," he writes, "Love is the most universal, the most tremendous and the most mysterious of the cosmic forces," 32.

2. Although the ideal Jesus proposes is just a direct yes or no to any request, perhaps today, because of our complex society, we might allow our responses to include a "Maybe" or "Let me think on it."

3. It is certainly possible for people—or even angels—to see themselves as God's enemies. But an unconditional loving Creator cannot see them as "enemies," but only as his children.

4. The Hebrew term here is (phonetically) *tamim* or *tamam*. The Aramaic is very close: *t'mim* or *tamim*. The term would be used, for example, to describe a piece of fruit that has reached full maturity, when it is completely ripe or "perfect" for eating.

8. The Lord's Prayer

1. Typically, in a Greek text, the verb *is* is omitted. Literally, the Greek reads, "Our Father in the heavens."

2. For a fuller development of this contrast, see Neil Douglas-Klotz, *The Hidden Gospel: Decoding the Spiritual Message of the Aramaic Jesus* (Wheaton, IL: Quest Books, 1999), 27–31.

3. These ideas are more fully developed in John's letters. See 1 John 3:18–24; 4:17–21.

4. Matthew provides a version of the prayer as it was adopted and, perhaps enriched by believers in the Jerusalem community for use at liturgical gatherings. Luke's version (Luke 11:2–4) is more primitive. Throughout the centuries, liturgists have often embellished their ritual texts.

5. This is a summary of the interpretation given by Douglas-Klotz in *Prayers of the Cosmos: Reflections on the Original Meaning of Jesus' Words* (New York: HarperCollins, 1990), 12–41. Please note that the Aramaic spellings are merely phonetic.

6. St. Jerome's Latin: *Da nobis hodie…* ("Give to us today…"). Jerome is to be forgiven because Latin lacks the aorist tense altogether. He had nothing but the indicative imperative tense to use in these four petitions.

9. FAITH AS LOVE IN ACTION

1. *Catechism of the Catholic Church*, 142. See also Col 1:15; 1 Tim 1:17; Exod 33:11; John 15:14–15; Bar 3:38.

2. See Rom 1:5; 16:26.

10. FORGIVENESS AND FULLNESS OF LIFE

1. Mark's Gospel relates this miracle in much more detail and makes much the same point (see Mark 5:25–34).

2. In each of the four Gospels, Jesus is reported as raising someone from the dead: Matt 9:23–26; Mark 5:35–43; Luke 7:11–17; John 11:1–44.

11. DISCIPLESHIP

1. See Acts 22:3.

12. Explaining God's Project

1. See index for "parable" in John P. Meier, *A Marginal Jew*, vol. 2 (New York: Doubleday, 1994).

2. This parable's theme is like those of the lost sheep (Matt 18:12–14) and the lost coin (Luke 15:8–10).

Part III: The Gospel of Mark

1. The Acts of the Apostles mentions "John, who was also called Mark," "John Mark," or simply "John." See Acts 12:12; 12:25; 13:5; 13:13–14; 13:30; 15:37–40. Paul's letters also mention Mark. See Col 4:10; 2 Tim 4:11; Phil 1:24.

2. See, for example, Mark 1:43–45; 4:11; 8:29–30.

13. The Beloved Son

1. The Jewish view is that the phrase *the spirit of God* (or *breath of God*) in the sacred writings is merely a way of expressing the Creator's energy, grace, or blessing.

2. In *The Spiritual Exercises of St. Ignatius*, you may notice that the Holy Spirit is seldom focused upon. In the colloquies after each meditation, the person is encouraged to express personal spontaneous prayer, in turn, to the Father, Christ, and Mary. Prayer to the Spirit is not mentioned.

3. See *Christianity and Evolution*, trans. René Hague (New York: Harcourt Brace Jovanovich, 1971), 176–78; 225n.

14. Jesus and the Religious Leaders

1. From the Hebrew verb *sabat*, meaning "to stop, cease or keep from." Thus, the Sabbath became a day when one was free to stop or cease from prescribed or assigned work, labor, or business. According to Hebrew Scriptures, on the Sabbath, the seventh day, God ceased the divine work of creating the world and rested.

2. "Activities" and "passivities" and how to deal with them form the basic structure of Teilhard's spirituality as developed in his *The Divine Milieu* (New York: Harper & Row, 1960). Part 1 is called "The Divinization of Our Activities" and part 2 is called "The Divinization of Our Passivities."

15. PARABLES

1. Jesus is paraphrasing Isaiah 6:9. See also Mark 4:34.

2. This parable was treated at length in chapter 12 (cf. Matt 13:1–9).

3. See *Divine Milieu* (New York: Harper & Row, 1960), 72; *Phenomenon of Man*, trans. Bernard Wall (New York: Harper & Row, 1959), 285.

4. For many centuries, Earth was regarded as a place of *exile*. Only very recently, Pope Francis acknowledged Earth as our *home*. See his 2015 Encyclical Letter *Laudato Si'* (Praise Be to You): On Care for Our Common Home.

5. *Christianity and Evolution*, trans. René Hague (New York: Harcourt Brace Jovanovich, 1971), 176.

6. *Science and Christ*, trans. René Hague (New York: Harper & Row, 1968), 66–68, 96.

7. *Christianity and Evolution*, 174–75, 185.

16. HOLY WEEK

1. See John 10:10: "I came that they may have life, and have it abundantly."

2. See Col 1:19–23; 2:9–10; 3:3–4, 9–10; Eph 1:8–10; 2:15–16, 19–22; 3:16–19; Gal 3:13–14.

3. "He himself bore our sins in his body on the cross [stage one], so that, free from sins, we might live for righteousness [stage two]; by his wounds you have been healed [healed = made whole]" (1 Peter 2:24). And in John's Gospel: "I came so that they might have life, and have it abundantly" (John 10:10).

4. Pierre Teilhard de Chardin, "The Meaning and Constructive Value of Suffering," *Teilhard de Chardin: Pilgrim of the Future*, ed. Neville Braybrooke, trans. Noel Lindsay (New York: Seabury Press, 1964), 26. Emphasis added.

5. For ways to use the energy you expend in suffering positively, see Louis M. Savary and Patricia Berne, *Teilhard de Chardin—Seven Stages of Suffering: A Spiritual Path for Transformation* (New York: Paulist Press, 2015).

17. THE UPPER ROOM

1. See Eph 3. Teilhard often refers to this culminating cosmic moment of fulfillment as Point Omega. What is central to Teilhard's thinking is the *process of accomplishment* of this final consummation of all things in Christ as well as our essential role in God's project. Teilhard developed this *process of accomplishment* especially in two essays titled "The Heart of Matter" and "The Christic" in a collection of his essays on similar themes called *The Heart of Matter*, trans. René Hague (New York: Harcourt, 1978), 15–102.

2. In the Greek text, "given" is grammatically a present tense participle, i.e., "which is being given to you." Or more colloquially, "which I am now giving to you." It is as if to say, "What I am handing to you now is my body." It does not mean "which is being given *up* for you." The Greek uses the very simple verb *give* as in handing something to someone else. The text does not imply or infer "giving up" one's life or sacrificing something or losing something. The Greek preposition *uper* means "for" in the sense of "on your behalf" or "for your sake." It implies that they need the nourishment this bread provides right now and will need in the future.

3. In each of the three Synoptic Gospels, the Greek participle "poured out" is grammatically in the present tense, not the future. The pouring is happening in the moment. The Greek verb for "pour" or "pour out" is ἐκχεῶ (pronounced *ekzeo*). It is a very ordinary verb used to describe the action of pouring liquid out of one vessel into another vessel, as in pouring wine from a wineskin into a cup or goblet. The Greeks sometimes used the verb metaphorically, for example, "the words poured out of him," or in an exuberant expression of emotion to describe someone being "overjoyed" or someone who "bursts out laughing." Some translators, to tie the Last Supper to Jesus's passion and death, mistranslate the verb ἐκχεῶ as if it meant "to shed" blood, for example, on the cross. At the Last Supper, Jesus is not referring to shedding his blood on the cross, but pouring his blood into a cup for his disciples to drink—and for us in the future to drink. Some may claim that, on the cross, when the soldier pierced Jesus's side with a lance, blood and water

came out (John 19:34) claiming that it is the "blood" to which Jesus was referring at the Last Supper. However, after the piercing, John used, not ἐκχεῶ, but a very common verb, ἐξῆλθεν (pronounced *exêlthen*), which means "to come," "to come out," or "to exit."

18. PASSION AND DEATH

1. Teilhard takes up this issue in *The Divine Milieu* (New York: Harper & Row, 1960), 83–84. See also Louis M. Savary and Patricia Berne, *Teilhard de Chardin—Seven Stages of Suffering: A Spiritual Path for Transformation* (New York: Paulist Press, 2014).

19. THE SEVEN LAST WORDS

1. This assumes a direct nonstop flight to heaven and has no implications of purgatory.

2. *Christianity and Evolution*, trans. René Hague (New York: Harcourt Brace Jovanovich, 1971), 135, 146, 163.

3. *Christianity and Evolution*, 148.

4. Robert L. Faricy, *Teilhard de Chardin's Theology of the Christian in the World* (New York: Sheed & Ward, 1967), 173.

5. Faricy, *Teilhard de Chardin's Theology*, 173.

6. See Louis M. Savary, *Teilhard On Love: Evolving Human Relationships* (New York: Paulist Press, 2017).

7. Apparently, it was common for people then to reference a psalm by quoting its first line.

8. *Christianity and Evolution*, 33.

9. *Christianity and Evolution*, 33.

10. Teilhard develops these themes in a powerful essay called "My Universe," in *Science and Christ*, trans. René Hague (New York: Harper & Row, 1968), 37–85, esp. 78–85.

Part IV: The Gospel of Luke

1. The current English translation of Acts 11:18 is "Then God has given even to the Gentiles the repentance [*metanoia*] that leads to life." Or more colloquially, "the way of thinking (and behaving) that leads to life."

2. Luke 3:21; 5:16; 6:12, 28; 9:18, 28–29; 22:32, 41, 44–45; 10:21–22.

3. Luke 6:28; 18:1; 21:36; 22:40, 46.

4. Luke 11:5–8; 18:1–8, 9–14.

5. Spiritual family (9:57–62), the "cost" of discipleship (9:23–25; 14:26–27), basic requirements (9:47–48, 50; 17:7–10; 22:24–27), rejection and persecution (12:51–53; 21:12–18).

6. See Luke 9:51–56; 10:29–37; 17:11–19.

7. See Luke 2:32; 3:23–38; 4:24–27; 7:1–10; 24:47.

8. See Luke 3:12; 5:27–32; 7:34; 15:1–2; 18:9–14; 19:1–10.

9. See Luke 1:26–56; 2:36–38; 7:11–17, 36–50; 8:2, 42–48; 10:38–42; 21:1–4; 23:27–31; 23:55 — 24:11.

10. See Luke 1:53; 4:18; 6:20; 7:22; 14:13, 21; 16:20, 22; 19:8; 21:2–3.

11. See Luke 1:53; 6:24; 12:16–21; 16:1–9, 19–31; 19:1–10.

20. The Holy Spirit

1. During the Last Supper toward the end of John's Gospel, Jesus describes the Holy Spirit's role in detail (See John 14:15–25; 15:26–27; 16:7–15). Surprisingly, John makes little mention of the Holy Spirit in his earlier chapters.

2. God creates *by uniting* (*Science and Christ*, trans. René Hague [New York: Harper & Row, 1968], 45). Without naming the Holy Spirit, Teilhard describes the Spirit's "providential and indispensable inter-fertilization." *Christianity and Evolution*, trans. René Hague (New York: Harcourt Brace Jovanovich, 1971), 176.

3. *Christianity and Evolution*, 225n.

4. See Acts 1:8; 2:33, 38; 13:2, 52; 15:28; 16:6.

5. See Acts 4:8; 5:3; 6:3–5, 10; 7:55; 8:29; 10:19.

6. See Acts 8:15–17; 9:17; 10:44–48; 11:15–16.

22. The Spiritual Family

1. See also Mark 3:33–35.

2. See Luke 14:26–27, where Jesus makes essentially the same demand again.

3. See 1 Cor 12:12–27; Eph 5:30; Rom 12:1–8.

23. The Prodigal and the Samaritan

1. Again, mere "repentance" (sorrow for sin) is inadequate to describe the Greek word *metanoia* used here. The "joy in heaven" is far more than joy for someone who regrets that they did something bad. The joy in heaven is for a "lost sheep that has been found" and is reunited with the flock. It is for someone who has a conversion of mind and heart and sees his or her true meaning and purpose in God's eyes.

Part V: The Gospel of John

1. The Pauline letters, as well as John's Gospel, show an evolved Christian theology beyond that of the Synoptic Gospels.

2. The Greek word John uses here is *logos*. Although *logos* means "word," it can also mean "meaning," as in "What is the *logos* of this parable?"

24. From Beginning to End

1. This process of the coming together of countless subatomic particles into an organic whole or oneness is the true Creation story. Teilhard tells that story in scientific detail in his great book *The Phenomenon of Man*, trans. Bernard Wall (New York: Harper & Row, 1959). A more recent English translation (2003) is by Sarah Appleton-Weber, *The Human Phenomenon* (Sussex, UK: Sussex Academic Press, 2003).

2. See 1 Cor 2:13–16; Rom 12:2; Phil 2:5–11.

3. *The Phenomenon of Man*, 250–75.

4. See also John 1:14, 16; Luke 2:40; and Eph 1:23. Teilhard refers to Paul's *pleroma* several times in his *Divine Milieu* (New York: Harper & Row, 1960), 62, 122, 125, 143, 151.

5. This transition was fully in place with Pope Pius XII's encyclical *Mystici Corporis Christi* (The Mystical Body of Christ), 1943. For a more complete study of this issue, see Emile Mersch, SJ, *The Theology of the Mystical Body*, trans. Cyril Vollert, SJ (New York: Herder, 1952).

25. Born from Above

1. Nicodemus does get to look up at Jesus at his crucifixion and believe, for he and Joseph of Arimathea treat Jesus's body as sacred after he is taken down from the cross (see John 19:39).

27. The Holy Spirit and the Trinity

1. See, for example, John 14:15–28; 15:26–27; 16:4–15.

2. The three other evangelists introduced this *metanoia* with the baptism of John and Jesus's early preaching (see Matt 3:2; 4:17; Mark 1:4–8; Luke 3:3).

3. The Apostle Paul expressed this metamorphosis a few times in his letters. For example, "It is no longer I who live, but it is Christ who lives in me. And the life I now live in the flesh I live by faith in the Son of God" (Gal 2:20). And "For his sake I have suffered the loss of all things, and I regard them as rubbish, in order that I may gain Christ *and be found in him*" (Phil 3:8–9).

4. See Matt 10:16–20.

5. The author of John's Gospel has had over fifty years of interaction with the Holy Spirit, which is probably why he writes so coherently about the Spirit.

Part VI: Teilhard's *Metanoia*

28. The Hermeneutic Challenge

1. *Science and Christ*, trans. René Hague (New York: Harper & Row, 1968), 167–71. *Heart of Matter*, trans. René Hague (New York: Harcourt, 1978), 96.

2. *Christianity and Evolution*, trans. René Hague (New York: Harcourt Brace Jovanovich, 1971), 129.

3. *Human Energy*, trans. J. M. Cohen (New York: Harper & Row, 1969), 32–33.

4. *Science and Christ*, 45.

5. *Science and Christ*, 45. For a more complete treatment of this theme in Teilhard's writings, see Savary and Berne, *Teilhard de Chardin*

on Love: *Evolving Human Relationships* (New York: Paulist Press, 2017).

    6. *Science and Christ*, 179.
    7. *Science and Christ*, 124.
    8. *Human Energy*, 171–73.
    9. *Science and Christ*, 125.
    10. *Science and Christ*, 125.
    11. See also Matt 23:11–12 and Luke 22:26–27.

29. The Principles of Teilhard's Metanoia

    1. Pierre Teilhard de Chardin, *Christianity and Evolution* (New York: Harcourt Brace Jovanovich, 1971), 238–39. Pierre Teilhard de Chardin, *The Heart of Matter*, trans. René Hague (New York: Harcourt, 1978), 211–14.

    2. Pierre Teilhard de Chardin, *Activation of Energy*, trans. René Hague (New York: Harper & Row, 1970), 279; Pierre Teilhard de Chardin, *Science and Christ*, trans. René Hague (New York: Harper & Row, 1968), 17; *Christianity and Evolution*, 71–75, 177–79; Teilhard de Chardin, *The Divine Milieu* (New York: Harper Colophon Books, 1960), 61–62, 138–40; Pierre Teilhard de Chardin, *The Future of Man*, trans. Norman Denny (New York: Harper & Row, 1964), 22. *Heart of Matter*, 51.

    3. *Christianity and Evolution*, 182, 226, 239. The notion of love as energy is more fully developed in our book *Teilhard de Chardin On Love* (New York: Paulist Press, 2017).

    4. See John 3:16–17.

    5. Teilhard's scientific phenomenology of evolution is the principal theme in his most famous book *The Phenomenon of Man*, trans. Bernard Wall (New York: Harper & Row, 1959), or in a more recent translation *The Human Phenomenon*, trans. Sarah Appleton-Weber (Portland, OR: Sussex Academic Press, 2003). Teilhard wrote the original text of *Phenomenon* during his years in China, completing it in 1940. Evolution provides the underlying theme of almost every article or essay Teilhard wrote before and after that time.

    6. *Science and Christ*, 193.

    7. Teilhard discusses the evolutionary law he discovered in its original two-stage version (*Complexity-Consciousness*) in many places. For example, Pierre Teilhard de Chardin, *The Appearance of Man*,

trans. J. M. Cohen (New York: Harper & Row, 1965), 236–37. The reader deeply interested in this law may find of interest three essays in *Activation of Energy*: "The Atomism of Spirit," 21–58; "The Analysis of Life," 129–40; "On the Nature of the Phenomenon of Human Society," 165–68.

8. *Christianity and Evolution*, 49.

9. *Science and Christ*, 59–60.

10. *Christianity and Evolution*, 115; Teilhard de Chardin, *Human Energy*, trans. J. M. Cohen (New York: Harper & Row, 1969), 126; *Divine Milieu*, 70; *Science and Christ*, 167–73: "To cooperate in total cosmic evolution is the only deliberate act that can adequately express our devotion to an evolutive and universal Christ," 169.

11. *Christianity and Evolution*, 28, 31–34, 160, 179; *The Divine Milieu*, 62–64, 85; Pierre Teilhard de Chardin, *Hymn of the Universe* (New York: Harper & Row, 1965), 114–15.

12. *Divine Milieu*, 72.

13. *Science and Christ*, 175. Teilhard calls the scope of our talents and action "a field for our effort." See *Christianity and Evolution*, 226.

14. *Activation of Energy*, 279; *Science and Christ*, 17; *Christianity and Evolution*, 71–75, 177–79; *The Divine Milieu*, 61–62, 138–40; *The Future of Man*, 22; *Heart of Matter*, 214–22.

15. Teilhard develops this theme in a lengthy article published in *Revue des Questions Scientifiques* in 1947. An English translation titled "The Formation of the Noosphere" may be found in *The Future of Man*, 161–91.

16. *Christianity and Evolution*, 221–23. In this long paper, "How I Believe," Teilhard sets out some of his personal theological and ethical principles. *Christianity and Evolution*, 96–132.

17. *The Divine Milieu*, 45–47.

18. *Hymn of the Universe*, 114–15, 131–32; *Heart of Matter*, 216.

19. *The Future of Man* is a collection of essays exploring themes of the "not-yet" (the future) and the "invisible." *Human Energy*, 32.

20. *Science and Christ*, 77. This describes the metamorphosis that accompanies Teilhard's *metanoia*—what turns us from "caterpillars" into "butterflies."

21. *Heart of Matter*, 93, 215–16.

22. Just as the prodigal's father forgave his wayward son long before the son asked for forgiveness (see Luke 15:11–32).

23. Pope Francis expands on this notion of God's investment in us for building the kingdom of God on Earth in two encyclicals, Praise Be to You (*Laudato Si'*): On Care for Our Common Home (2015) and Rejoice and Be Glad (*Gaudete et Exsultate*): On the Call to Holiness in Today's World (2018).

24. In many essays throughout his life, Teilhard developed these three principles. In 1942, he summarized his thought on them in an essay "The New Spirit" (*The Future of Man*, 85–100).

25. *The Future of Man*, 95–96.

26. For Teilhard, "faith in the future" is a fundamental moral position. *The Future of Man*, 224.

27. *The Future of Man*, 95, 98–99, 188–91.

28. *The Future of Man*, 86–92, where Teilhard describes these increasingly inclusive states of consciousness.

30. The Evolution of Human Consciousness

1. *Phenomenon of Man*, trans. Bernard Wall (New York: Harper & Row, 1959), 184, 190.

2. Among the hominin line (our family tree), we know of the Neanderthals, the Denisovans, and *Homo naledi* that were before archaic *Homo sapiens*, and overlapped with us for a time. Although Teilhard would have been aware of the Neanderthals, the latter two species were discovered only in the twenty-first century.

3. *The Divine Milieu* (New York: Harper & Row, 1960), 117.

4. Teilhard describes how he began to enter his personal *metanoia*. *Heart of Matter*, trans. René Hague (New York: Harcourt, 1978), 52–55.

5. Pope Francis, Apostlic Exhortation *Evangelii Gaudium*, The Joy of the Gospel (2013), 14.

6. *Omnem novitatem attulit, semetipsum afferens.* Irenaeus, *Adversus Haereses*, IV, c. 34, n. 1: PG 7, pars prior, 1083.

7. The Joy of the Gospel, 15.

8. Rich Heffernan, "The Eternal Christ in the Cosmic Story," *National Catholic Reporter*, December 11, 2009. Heffernan is interviewing theologian and Franciscan priest Richard Rohr, who credits the "evacuation plan" metaphor to Brian McLaren.

9. Heffernan, "Eternal Christ in the Cosmic Story."

10. I attribute this insight to Brian Purfield in his article, "The Letter to the Colossians: Jesus and the Universe," June 23, 2009. See https://www.thinkingfaith.org/articles/20090623_1.htm.

11. In my book, *The New Spiritual Exercises in the Spirit of Teilhard: In the Spirit of Pierre Teilhard de Chardin* (Mahwah, NJ: Paulist Press, 2010), I consistently used the term *Christ Project*, since the Exercises are focused on Christ.

12. Don't get too distracted by the punishment of the "goats." This is not a parable about the fires of hell. Jesus is not out to scare us or strike fear into our hearts. Jesus is simply adopting the familiar literary device of "compare and contrast" used in many traditional children's stories, fables, and fairy tales. Its purpose is to highlight the importance of being good in contrast to being bad. Jesus uses the technique of compare and contrast between sheep and goats to emphasize the point that caring for one another is of utmost importance among his followers. He uses the same literary device in the parable of the virgins and their lamps. The foolish virgins are presented in the parable for contrast. The emphasis is on the importance of preparation and readiness in the kingdom of God. Without the goats and foolish virgins, these parables would lack their literary punch.

Appendix: Teilhard on Evangelization

1. Pierre Teilhard de Chardin, *Writings in Time of War* (New York: Harper & Row, 1968), 370.

2. *Writings in Time of War*, 272. The French reads, "Note pour servir a l'évangélisation des temps nouveaux."

3. Pierre Teilhard de Chardin, *The Heart of Matter*, trans. René Hague (New York: Harcourt, 1978), 209–24.

4. *The Heart of Matter*, 273.

5. *The Heart of Matter*, 210.

6. *The Heart of Matter*, 211.

7. *The Heart of Matter*, 210–11.

8. *The Heart of Matter*, 212.

9. *The Heart of Matter*.

10. *The Heart of Matter*, 211.

11. *The Heart of Matter.*
12. *The Heart of Matter,* 211–12. (Teilhard's italics.)
13. *The Heart of Matter,* 214.
14. *The Heart of Matter.*
15. *The Heart of Matter,* 214. The spirituality for this new vision is more fully developed in *The Divine Milieu.*

Select Bibliography

Books by Pierre Teilhard de Chardin

Activation of Energy. Translated by René Hague. New York: Harper & Row, 1970.

The Appearance of Man. Translated by J. M. Cohen. New York: Harper & Row, 1965.

Christianity and Evolution. Translated by René Hague. New York: Harcourt Brace Jovanovich, 1971.

The Divine Milieu. New York: Harper & Row, 1960.

The Future of Man. Translated by Norman Denny. New York: Harper & Row, 1964.

The Heart of Matter. Translated by René Hague. New York: Harcourt, 1978.

Human Energy. Translated by J. M. Cohen. New York: Harcourt Brace Jovanovich, 1969.

Hymn of the Universe. Translated by Gerald Vann. New York: Harper & Row, 1965.

The Making of a Mind: Letters from a Soldier-Priest [1914–1919]. Translated by René Hague. New York: Harper & Row, 1961.

The Phenomenon of Man. Translated by Bernard Wall. New York: Harper & Row, 1959. A more recent translation: *The Human Phenomenon.* Translated by Sarah Appleton-Weber. Sussex, UK: Sussex Academic Press, 2003.

Science and Christ. Translated by René Hague. New York: Harper & Row, 1965.

Teilhard de Chardin: Pilgrim of the Future. Edited by Neville Braybrooke. New York: Seabury Press, 1964.

Toward the Future. Translated by René Hague. New York: Harcourt Brace Jovanovich, 1975.

Writings in Time of War. Translated by René Hague. New York: Harper,
1968.

Other Titles

Faricy, Robert L. *Teilhard de Chardin's Theology of the Christian in the
World*. New York: Sheed & Ward, 1967.
Mooney, Christopher F. *Teilhard de Chardin and the Mystery of Christ*.
New York: Harper & Row, 1964.